AMORTIZE DEBT INTO PROSPERITY

A Book about Managing

Personal Finances and Eliminating Debt

By

Marc Griffin

All clip art courtesy Microsoft Corporation.

Cover designed by: Bart M. Griffin

Copyright © 2012 by Marc Griffin

All rights reserved.

ISBN-13: 978-1479360321

ISBNB-10: 1479360325

Dedication

This book is dedicated to my precious and lovely wife who encouraged me to pass on my personal financial knowledge to assist others in achieving their financial goals. I love you, Honey!

This book is also dedicated to my five talented, creative and active children, whom I love with all my heart, for all turning out so well and becoming very productive members of society.

And finally, I would like to thank all the people who had faith in me, took my financial advice, and were able to turn their finances around.

Table of Contents

INTRODUCTION 1

OVERVIEW 2

    SIDE BARS, RED FLAGS AND MONEY SENSE QUOTES 2

SECTION I 3

    FIVE MONEY SENSE PLANS 3

    INTRODUCTION TO SECTION I 3

        Plan 1 - Budget, Budget, and Budget Again! 3

        Plan 2 - Pay off Consumer Debt 12

        Plan 3 - Create and Maintain an Emergency Fund 20

        Plan 4 - Pay Down and then Pay Off your Mortgage 26

        Plan 5 - Net Worth and Retirement Go Hand-in-Hand! 41

    SECTION I IN REVIEW: 61

    SECTION II 62

        Question 1 - What exactly is an Amortization Schedule? 64

Question 2 - Why Should I Use Amortization Schedules? 71

Question 3 - What can an Amortization Schedule tell me about my loan that I don't already know? 76

Question 4 - How will the "Term" on a Loan affect my payment? 83

Question 5 - Can an Amortization Schedule help me convert my 30-Year Mortgage into A 15-Year Mortgage without refinancing? 87

Question 6 - Should I use Amortization Schedules to help me determine the Down Payment I should make on a house? 91

Question 7 - Should I use Amortization Schedules if I'm planning to refinance? 96

Question 8 - How can I use an Amortization Schedule for my Car Loan? 102

Question 9 - If I purchase a car for Zero Down and Zero Percent Interest would using an Amortization Schedule serve any purpose? 108

Question 10 - Can I use Amortization Schedules for planning "Debt Consolidation" strategies? 116

Question 11 - Can Amortization Schedules provide me with Financial Planning Strategies for Rental/Investment Property. 123

Question 12 - Can Amortization Schedules help eliminate my Credit Card debt? 135

Question 13 - Can an Amortization Schedule help me get rid of Private Mortgage Insurance (PMI)? 141

Question 14 - I'm not able to keep pace with the extra principal payments on my Amortization Schedule. What should I do? 145

SECTION III 153

AMORTIZATION SCHEDULES ILLUSTRATED 153

Quick Review from Question 2, Section II 153

Quick Review from Question 4, Section II 163

Quick Review from Question 6, Section II 175

Quick Review from Question 7, Section II 184

Quick Review from Question 8, Section II 192

Quick Review from Question 9, Section II 195

Quick Review from Question 10, Section II 197

CONCLUSION 212

ABOUT THE AUTHOR: 212

Disclaimers and General Notes

- The contents of this book are solely for the purpose of suggesting actions, methods, and strategies to pay-down, eliminate, or avoid debt, and improve personal fiscal management.

- The author of this book does not intend to replace or usurp the advice from Brokers, Certified Financial Planners, Lawyers, Tax Preparers, etc., but rather, offers fresh ideas and opinions in the area of personal financial management. If necessary, consult with a financial professional, tax specialist, or legal counsel before executing critical personal financial decisions.

- The author of this book is a financial advisor only and does not claim to be professionally certified or affiliated in any way with any company, business or organization in the field of finances or investments and will not be held responsible for any financial decisions made by the readers.

- All tables, spreadsheets and amortizations schedules in this book were created by the author without the use of computer programs.

- No statistical, research, or technical data/material illustrated in this book at the time of its gathering was sited due to the rapid change of such information. All such information is to be taken at face value and is only intended to be used as a measuring stick for the reader to compare such information as it might relate to his, her, or their own current financial position.

- This book contains a wide list of Websites to visit. It is by no means a complete list nor is there any guarantee that any of these sites will remain active, accurate, or will resolve any or all of your financial needs.

- All of the examples and names of people used in this book are fictional in nature and do not represent any real people living or dead.

AMORTIZE DEBT INTO PROSPERITY

INTRODUCTION

Amortize Debt into Prosperity is <u>not</u> a book about how to get rich. It is <u>not</u> a book about how to invest hard earned money in the stock market or any other venture public or private. But rather, it offers YOU, the reader, sound personal financial advice and provides the elementary fundamental building blocks needed to eliminate debt, and then generally remain debt free for the rest of your life. It also demonstrates in great detail how you and your family can secure financial freedom and achieve full ownership over everything in your possession that you've worked so hard to obtain.

Shortly after World War II, the American middle class ruled the economic world. It was a powerful force all through the 1950s. Children were still graduating from high school and college with a quality education, and innovations and creative passions abounded in the workplace and drove the world economy. There was money in the bank and families lived within their means and had little debt, but by the late 20th century the middle class was sadly in decline.

Today the American middle class is much poorer overall, relative to past generations, and is only a shadow of its former self. Millions of hard working Americans have lost trillions upon trillions of dollars of their personal wealth, most of it vanishing since 2008. And not all of it was lost in the stock market, but rather, as the result of a tremendous devaluation of real estate resulting from the housing-bubble implosion. Other material assets also lessened in value alongside home prices due to a consumer credit-lending-bubble bust as well, which exacerbated the economic crash even further in 2009. And we, as an economic class, have amassed tremendous consumer debt, but it was not totally of our own doing.

Remember Enron, WorldCom, Arthur Andersen, Lehman Brothers, and Bernard "Bernie" Madoff? Between toxic loans, fraud, and unethical lending practices within the loan and real estate industry and massive failures and corruption of giant American corporations, the American middle class was, and still is, on course for a major financial catastrophe.

Amortize Debt into Prosperity is aimed at returning the American middle class to its rightful place in the economic world. This book has been written and specifically designed as a blueprint for building a foolproof foundation that will enable all Americans, who wish, to have a stable financial future. No matter who you are, young people just starting out on your own, older folks who should be getting ready to retire, no matter who you are, if you're trying to become and/or stay debt free, this book was written with you in mind.

Now, more than any other time in our history, hardworking middle class Americans have their wealth scattered to the four winds of debt (mortgage, credit cards auto and equity loans) and all of it in the control of others. Let's return ownership back to its rightful owners: you and me. Amortize Debt into Prosperity has been divided into three stimulating sections for that purpose.

OVERVIEW

SECTION I — Begins with identifying five basic fundamental "Money Sense Plans" for organizing your personal finances. These plans will cover in detail Budgeting, Debt, Emergency Funds, Mortgages, and Retirement. Young adults will learn the difference between throwing money around foolishly on things they desire rather than on the things they actually need. Older adults will learn how to gain a much clearer insight into their financial position and successfully dig themselves out from under a mountain of debt. And everyone will learn how to organize their personal finances.

SECTION II — The core of this book begins with questions and answers about how to use Amortization Schedules to create options and "what if" strategies and scenarios to pay down and eliminate all debt (including your mortgage) enabling you to own everything you have outright. Today, as in the past, colleges teach courses in accounting and financing, but colleges offer no courses in the "school of hard knocks" area of personal finances, credit or interest. If we're lucky, most of us will learn from our financial mistakes and, in time, overcome them. If we don't learn, we run the risk of financial failure and no hope for a successful retirement in our golden years.

SECTION III — This section contains several of the Amortization Schedules discussed in Section II for further study and examination. I have included questions along with answers and a few sample schedules in this section to help increase your new-found expertise in using them to become debt free. Also, use them to practice your own "what if" strategies and scenarios. Unless you are out of debt and own outright every asset you have in your possession, there may be nothing tangible or concrete waiting for you in your future if our economic system eventually collapses.

SIDE BARS, RED FLAGS AND MONEY SENSE QUOTES appear throughout Sections I and II of this book. They are intended to offer additional perspectives on many of today's money issues, practices, and policies.

- **SIDE BARS** — were written to add additional substance related to material either just previously read or in general.

- **RED FLAGS** — were written as a warning and may pertain to material either just previously read or in general.

- **MONEY SENSE QUOTES** — were included purely for your edification and do not necessarily fulfill the principle values of this book; enjoy!

SECTION I

FIVE MONEY SENSE PLANS

INTRODUCTION TO SECTION I

This section contains the five fundamental money sense plans for personal financial health and well-being. Read them, study them, and then apply them to place yourself and your family on a path and in a position to achieve personal financial success and freedom. The sooner you have completed and incorporated these plans into *your own* successful money management system, the sooner you can read, study, and apply the Amortization Schedule concepts in Sections II and III to achieve all of your financial goals.

How to Build a Personal Financial Foundation

PLAN 1 - BUDGET, BUDGET, AND BUDGET AGAIN!

DEFINITION —
Budget: a). An Itemized summary of expenditures for a given period of time along with proposals for financing them. b) The total sum of money allocated for a particular purpose or period of time (The American Heritage College Dictionary).

Creating, then utilizing and maintaining a budget is absolutely essential to sound personal money management. Once you have mastered this concept, the next goal is to develop a system that will enable you to either store cash payments in physical envelopes, or in cyberspace using "virtual" envelopes where a check list system is used to track large sum expenditures or you may choose to use both of these methods. I will explain and blend, in detail, both concepts in this chapter.

Budgeting all of your household income each month is the first and most crucial step for managing and monitoring all personal finances. It's even more important than paying down debt or saving for retirement! Almost every book that's ever been published concerning personal finances stresses the value of budgeting more than any other point. It's the fundamental starting point to controlling:

- Living within your means.
- When bills get paid.
- Where personal money is spent.
- And, what is the best and most efficient way to save for retirement.

When talking to clients, many personal financial advisors might disguise the word "Budget" with the phrase "Income and Expenses", because many of their clients are turned off by the word "Budget". That word "budget" sort of implies a "big brother" or an overkill approach just to keep track of how all of their money is spent, so if that client, for whatever reason, fails to budget, they lose an opportunity to take control of their finances.

Don't be turned off by the thought of creating and using a budget, because without one you can easily waste 20, 30, or 40 percent of your income each and every month. Have you ever heard someone say, "I don't know where all my money goes every month"? They're right. Most people really don't know, because they have no budget. Budgeting is about monetary efficiency.

For example, how many haircuts do you get every year? How many espresso stands do you visit each week? How often do you dine out every month? There's nothing wrong with spending money on those things; it's only when you don't keep track of that spending that problems arise. How many income earners are in your household? Who pays what—when? Without a budget, it's almost impossible to track your expenses.

Here's how to create a budget. While generic budgets can be purchased at most office supply stores, I personally create my own on a spreadsheet. In doing so, I'm able to design and personalize a budget specifically for my own household needs.

Here's how to create a physical cash storage system for your budget. Use envelopes that you label and number to match each item in your budget. When you have cash for an item in your budget, place the appropriate cash amount in the envelope designated for that item and move to the next item.

On the next page is a *very brief* summary of a simplified budget you might create for your own household income and expenses. Begin right away by recording what your expenses are and when they need to be paid (e.g., House Payment/Rent, Utilities, Car Payments) and so on—the big items. Now list the little purchases you make that aren't always counted or considered as expenses.

NOTES:

A Money Sense Quote: If it cost a dollar to go around the world I wouldn't have enough to get out of sight. – Author unknown

		Budget Month: January—Year: 20XX					
#	Item	Projected	Week 1	Week 2	Week 3	Bank	Actual
1	House Payment	$1,149			1/1/20XX	Bank Paid	$1,149
2	Car Payment	357	357	357	1/15/20XX	Bank Paid	357
3	Groceries	450	275	100	Envelope		450
4	Gasoline	150	150	50	Envelope		150
5	Electric Bill	99	99	99		Bank	99
6	Water Bill	67	67	67	1/15/20XX	Bank	67
7	Property Taxes	241	241	238		Bank	241
8	Entertainment	75	48	25	Envelope		75
9	Hair Cut	20	20		Envelope		20
10	Allowance (His)	150	150	100			150
11	Allowance (Hers)	150	150	117			150
12	Misc. / Petty Cash	25	25	25	Envelope		25
13	Car Tabs	14	14	14	Envelope		14
14	Auto Insurance.	103	103	103		Bank	103
15	Medical / Dental	50	50	50	Envelope		50
16	Vitamins	20	16	16	Envelope		20
17	DVD Rentals	20			Envelope		20
	Total Expenses	$3,140	$1,755	$1,365			$3,140
	All Net Income Sources	3,510	1,755	1,755	$370		3,510
	Difference	$370	$0	$370	$370		$370

As you can see, I have listed all the items I need to budget for monthly and long term. Once I've set money aside, either to an envelope or to the bank, I shade the cell to indicate that item has been completely accounted for. Make your own design. When the month has been completed and everything has been paid, print a hard copy for your records. Update your budget to the next month and enter the new income and expense figures.

To succeed, track, as best you can, all of the money you spend in a week, then the next week, and then for the whole month. Don't stop there, after one year you should know that you got 7 haircuts at $30 each, counting tips. You purchased presents and cards for 8 birthdays, filled the car up with gas every week, had four oil changes, took three weekend trips and one vacation.

Then there are the 53 DVD rentals, that Super Bowl and Pizza bash, the Newspapers, Shoes, Clothes, Income Tax Preparation, Auto Insurance, Home Insurance, and Property Tax and so on. These items are not typical monthly expenses, but are items that reoccur once—twice—three times or more each year that tend to stump people who fail to use a budget to manage their money.

Take each item (e.g., Hair Cuts) and multiply the $30 cost of each by 7, which equals $210 a year. Divide that figure by 12 to get an average monthly cost ($17.50) round up to $20, give it an item number and include it on your permanent monthly budget along with the major items.

For example:

Budget Month: January—Year: 20XX							
#	Item	Projected	Week 1	Week 2	Week 3	Bank	Actual
9	Hair Cuts	20	20		Envelope		20

Then create and label an envelope—Hair Cuts—(for minor expenses only) and stuff $20 into it every month, even though you may not need your next hair cut for two more months. Put the envelope in a money box or home safe for safe keeping. Mark that item "Paid" on your budget sheet and move on to the next item and do the same.

Let's say the next minor item is your Car Tab Renewal and last year you paid $176.34 total for the Emission Test, Tabs, Taxes, and Fees, and you know the Emission Test won't be required this coming year. If that test typically costs $16. Subtract that amount from $176.34, then divide by 12 (months), round up, and stuff $14 into an envelope. This allows you to put away money on a monthly basis so you will be prepared when that expense is due. Do this for all the items on your budget sheet.

Budget Month: January—Year: 20XX							
#	Item	Projected	Week 1	Week 2	Week 3	Bank	Actual
13	Car Tabs	14	14		Envelope		14

Repeat this process until you have a monthly cost for each item. Major expenses, whether they occur every month or just a couple of times a year, should also appear on your budget sheet with their own item number.

Major <u>monthly</u> expenses should be deposited into a dedicated "budget only" checking account. As money is deposited, for each budgeted item, type in "Bank" for that item on the budget sheet itself.

Budget Month: January—Year: 20XX							
#	Item	Projected	Week 1	Week 2	Week 3	Bank	Actual
1	House Payment	$1,149				Bank	$1,149

When you actually pay the bill for each budgeted item, add "Paid" for that item on the budget sheet. You may also want to enter the check number and/or date paid.

Budget Month: January—Year: 20XX							
#	Item	Projected	Week 1	Week 2	Week 3	Bank	Actual
1	House Payment	$1,149			1/2/20XX	Bank Paid	$1,149

Major periodic expenses (e.g., Property Tax, Home Owner Insurance and so on) should be deposited and treated the same way!

Budget Month: January—Year: 20XX							
#	Item	Projected	Week 1	Week 2	Week 3	Bank	Actual
14	Auto Insurance	103	103	103		Bank	103

Now, after one year, you will have clear quantitative facts about every cent your household spends. At that point, you'll need to refine and update the entire budget. For example, those 53 DVD's rentals last year cost you $259.17—that works out to $22 a month. Now you might combine that item with the Entertainment item on your budget sheet.

For example, you put $75 away every month into an envelope for Entertainment.

Budget Month: January—Year: 20XX							
#	Item	Projected	Week 1	Week 2	Week 3	Bank	Actual
8	Entertainment	75	50	25	Envelope		75

And, you put $20 away every month into an envelope for DVDs.

Budget Month: January—Year: 20XX							
#	Item	Projected	Week 1	Week 2	Week 3	Bank	Actual
17	DVDs	20	10	10	Envelope		20

Now, that you know what you spend on each, you may want to combine each item into one under entertainment, and put away $95.

Budget Month: January—Year: 20XX							
#	Item	Projected	Week 1	Week 2	Week 3	Bank	Actual
8	Entertainment	95	50	45	Envelope		95

Maybe even combine Birthdays with Christmas and/or other combinations, but only to the extent that every penny dispersed can be accounted for on your budget. This should remain a continuous process year after year.

No one can ever successfully budget for everything all of the time. But, if you keep, use, and maintain a budget and make the slightest attempt at being proactive, you shouldn't be caught off guard with Weddings, Funerals, Medical/Dental costs, your children's Education, Emergencies, and so on.

One of the best features about a budget is that you're creating a means to visibly observe two critical aspects about your spending practices: 1. where all the fat is going every month and, 2. how to improve your spending practices so that your monthly budget is more lean and efficient. For example, the fat might be the amount of money you waste on eating lunch out every day. Here, to improve your budget so that it is more lean and efficient, might mean packing a lunch more often so you'll spend less.

Whatever the case, you'll have a permanent historical financial record to help reduce wasteful and unnecessary spending (fat), especially in times of crisis when you might need to "run lean" and stretch every dollar.

My colleague, who is an accountant, uses a checklist system in addition to budgeting as she pays her bills so absolutely nothing gets missed. And after refining her budget over the years, she now makes automatic bank transfers every month to several special savings accounts for groups of items, like taxes and insurance, or travel and entertainment that will be paid in the future. In this way, money is set aside for all expenditures at least 2 weeks (and up to several months) ahead of when the expense will be paid. This is just a variation of the envelope system. Use what works best for you.

Sample Checklist:

Due Date	Item	Amount	J	F	M	A	M	J	J	A	S	O	N	D
1	House Pmt.	$1,245.47	X	X	X	X	X	X						
4	Chevron	135.90	X											
7	VISA	27.29	X											
10	Phone	65.09	X											
15	Prop Tax	1,380.78				X								
17	House Ins.	564.00						X						
20	Auto Ins.	455.00				X								
21	Electric Bill	75.00		X		X		X						
24	Cable	55.76	X	X	X	X	X	X						
28	Internet	32.00	X	X	X	X	X	X						
31	Car Pmt.	234.12	X	X	X	X	X	X						

Again: Date, Save, Print out, and Store every hard copy budget sheet (and all checklists, if you choose to use them) for future reference. Now you will always know where all of your money goes and you'll have the money you need when things like property taxes come up. It's easier to set aside little bits every month than it is to come up with a large tax or insurance payment all at once!

The "My Money, Your Money, Whose Money Pays" Dilemma

For couples, budgets work best when all net income is applied to all monthly expenses regardless of the money each of you brings home every month. When it comes to personal money, your home should run like a business if it's to succeed financially. The "teamwork" spirit and "all for one and one for all" attitude should always prevail within the household. Just remember, personal finances are the leading cause of divorces in America today. If my money is always mine and yours is always yours, than whose money pays for what?

All earned income should go towards the whole, the entirety, the sum of the shared relationship and household. You're both doing your share striving towards the same goals. The worst case scenario should never go beyond one income contributor receiving more "allowance" than the other income contributor every month. The only reason for that scenario might be the one who brings the most money home every pay period keeps more, or the one who works more overtime consistently, or the only one who earns an income gets more mad money or allowance. But, from my observations, the most successful couples apply *all of their income* to a single monthly budget, regardless of who earns more, or how hard they work for it, or if they're the only bread winner. Work together and stay together. The only exception might be an inheritance, in which case you may <u>not</u> want to apply those dollars into the family budget or co-mingle them into a common bank account. You may intend for this money to be used for some purpose outside your immediate family and you may choose to leave it separate. Put inheritance funds into a separate dedicated account, in your name only, with primary and any secondary beneficiaries named in the event of your demise. Check the laws in your state with regards to sole ownership and survivorship of separate property.

Very important: a budget should be thought of as an entity, like an individual person or a corporation. Your budget should have total control over when, where, why, and how your money is to be dispensed. In other words, once you know the true yearly cost of all of the items you budget for monthly, don't rob from Peter to pay Paul if you fall short in any given month on any item (e.g., entertainment). For example, you know that on average the two of you spend $150 per month on entertainment (E.T.), but the first week of this month was your anniversary and all of the E.T. money went to that one occasion and now the E.T. money is gone for the remainder of the month. Here are your options:

- If you budget for "Miscellaneous" or "Petty Cash" use that money, if needed, to tide E.T. over for the remainder of the month, or
- If "Miscellaneous" or "Petty Cash" were never a part your original budget plan, then forego spending any more money for E.T. for the remainder of the month, or
- One or both of you use your monthly allowance for E.T., if needed, to get by for the rest of the month.

A poor option would be to use a credit or charge card to borrow from next month's budget because of this month's poor planning or special event.

To avoid this kind of short fall in the future, either add your anniversary to the total yearly cost of entertainment and divide by 12, or make your anniversary its own separate item with its own envelope that you contribute money to monthly. And keep in mind that the money put away in any given month is an average; therefore, there will be months when money in an envelope or bank account was not spent and was carried forward; and there will be months when you may fall short. So have contingency plans that allow your budget to control when, where, why, and how your money is to be dispersed without any deviations.

It would also be wise to maintain an emergency budget, "what if", sheet for your monthly income and expenses in the event that one or both of you loses an income due to a lay-off, medical event, or any other unplanned income reduction. There will be more discussion on this topic in plan 3.

Now, with your monthly budget in complete control of your personal finances, you can focus on paying off your consumer debt.

A Money Sense Quote: Budget: A mathematical confirmation of your suspicions. - A.A. Latimer

 Side Bar — Budget Sheets and the Envelope System

My very first monthly budget sheets were hand written and contained about six items. Item six was for $10s Spending/Mad money/Allowance—per month! I still have every budget sheet for every month for the last 28 years. I also produce a Grand Budget sheet that projects my expenses for 6 months out. I do this each and every month in an attempt to avoid any surprises. I have used the envelope method for collecting minor expenses for over 35 years.

There is no right or wrong way to do an envelope system. As mentioned, my colleague does her envelop system in a completely different way than I do. She uses a "virtual" envelope system whereby she debits funds out of her bank account (and keeps that information on a separate spreadsheet or ledger, illustrated earlier) and in other instances uses automatic monthly bank transfers for specific savings/items, (e.g. escrow, travel, or emergencies).

A Money Sense Quote: Empty pockets never held anyone back. Only empty heads and hearts can do that. - Norman Vincent Peale

RED FLAG — PLAN ALL FAMILY HOUSEHOLD FINANCIAL DECISIONS ON ONE PRIMARY INCOME.

DEFINITIONS —
Consumerism: The theory that a progressively greater consumption of goods is economically beneficial. (The American Heritage College Dictionary)

Materialism: The theory or attitude that physical well-being and worldly possessions constitute the greatest good and highest value in life. (The American Heritage College Dictionary)

Just a few generations ago a majority of traditional family household financial decisions were based on the earning power of a single wage earner. Generally speaking, the husband worked and the wife was a homemaker and/or a "stay-at-home mom." They typically owned a small 3 bedroom rambler, bath and a half, 1200 square foot home with a one car garage on a large lot, had two or more children, owned one car, and expected to retire on the husband's company pension and social security. Credit cards were for the "well-to-do" and if they purchased something expensive, they'd put it on a lay-away plan until it was paid off. Their only real debt was their home (financed on a 20, not 30, year fixed-rate loan) and an auto loan financed for no longer than three years. It was a pretty simple life style back then; they had money in the bank, and they lived within their means; and it worked out well for everyone.

Today the traditional family is considered atypical of past generations. Now most family household financial decisions are based on the earning power of two wage earners. Generally speaking, both husband and wife work, own a large 4 to 5 bedroom, 2 story, 3500, and up, square foot behemoth, with a 3 car garage, on a small lot just large enough to contain the foundation walls. They essentially financed it with little or nothing down utilizing new creative and exotic loan products, have less than one child, making a minimum of two car payments a month (financed for 72 months each), and are caught up in 30, 40, even 50 thousand dollars' worth of credit card debt and thinking about filing for bankruptcy. Materialism and consumerism dominate their egos well beyond the "keeping up with the Joneses" mind-set of previous generations, and as a result, they can expect to work well into their retirement years to pay it all off.

The marketplace has long since adjusted the inflation rate to accommodate the purchasing power of a two income family household. Auto dealerships now grant us small mortgage like loans to buy our cars. The credit card companies have long since spoiled us with easy access to credit and 2 percent minimum monthly payments. And advertisers and marketing departments have perfected the art of consumerism and sell us all the material gadgets and toys we desire but don't really need. People got caught up in the "50 decibels louder than regular TV programming" commercials and the "no money down" (where are they now) real estate infomercials that made one feel everyone else was getting rich but them. This "gold rush fever" to "buy, buy, buy" mantra didn't take place in a vacuum. We heard it loud and clear and responded to the advertisers' chants, claims and promises with open wallets. We have no one to blame but ourselves for getting caught up in the "buying hype" and irrational consumption of unneeded goods and services that lead to the biggest financial meltdown since the great depression.

It's fine to be a "two income" family. In fact, it's great to have access to double paychecks every pay period, as long as your family can pay all its monthly bills on the earnings of one person. Think about this: It is more likely than not that the recent generation of young folks moved out of mom and dad's house, went on their own and put off marriage until their mid to late 20s. If this is the case for the two of you then keep in mind that you both survived on your own separate incomes before you were married. So why wouldn't the two of you survive on one income after marriage? What basic changes require the need for additional money? Well, some of those basic changes might be: Paying off old debt, a need for more living space and bringing kids into the world. But those are the only reasons for relying on a second household income. So, before the two of you buy a house and have children, pay off all student loans, consumer debt, car loans, and any other remaining debt.

Now that you two *income earners* have married and paid off all existing debt, it's time to expand your living space and buy real estate of some sort (e.g., house, condominium, manufactured home, etc.). **Warning:** Buy as much property as you can afford to buy solely based on the qualifying *primary income power of one wage earner*. While this may seem impossible in today's economy, tenacity should prevail, so that even if it initially does take two incomes to qualify for the loan, the primary wage earner's income should increase enough over time that his/her income alone is able to pay all the bills and the mortgage payment as well. This is the best financial strategy one can employ to side-step most, if not all, potential financial catastrophes that take place in an average family household in the course of a lifetime.

Once a second income is no longer needed for the monthly budget, it becomes "icing on the cake," and should be used to pay down the mortgage and invest for retirement.

For those of you who have not yet employed a "one income" strategy – the remainder of this book is dedicated to that cause.

> *A Money Sense Quote:* After a visit to the beach, it's hard to believe that we live in a material world. *- Pam Shaw*

PLAN 2 - PAY OFF CONSUMER DEBT

DEFINITION —
Debt: a) Something owed, such as money. b) An obligation or liability to pay or render something to someone else. c) The condition of owing. (The American Heritage College Dictionary)

Debtor: A person who owes a sum of money or other obligations to another. (West's Business Law (Fourth Edition)

Ben Franklin said, "A penny saved is a penny earned". Consumers almost always save money when they buy items on sale unless the sale is rigged. They save money when they negotiate for the lowest price possible for goods and services. They can really save big when they shop around for the best deal on large ticket items (e.g., homes, cars, RV's, boats etc.). But as borrowers, most consumers don't do as well. The average household pays out thousands of dollars in interest on debt every year, and debt to credit card companies is responsible for most of that loss. Here are some things you may not know about Major Credit Card companies:

- Credit card holders currently carry over *Eight Hundred Billion* in unpaid balances.

- Credit Card companies have Five Hundred Billion more dollars available to lend consumers.

- There is an average of 8 credit cards per family spread out among 144 Million consumers. 55 Million of them pay off their balance every month, 35 Million consumers only make the minimum payment each month, and 90 Million consumers (revolvers) add new debt every month.

- There are 100 thousand credit card transactions per minute.

- More than 1 billion, or about 30 percent, of all credit and debit cards <u>already issued</u> have an embedded "Radio Frequency Identification Chip" (RFID). **Warning:** A <u>Credit Card scanner</u> can be purchased legally, by anyone, on-line or elsewhere and used in a fraudulent manner to read that RFID chip on your credit and/or debit cards. All of the key information on your cards can be easily accessed without your knowledge merely by being in close proximity to such a device. Special sleeves and/or wallets are available to protect your cards from this kind of fraud. For starters go online to a site such as *www.idstronghold.com*, or *www.Amazon.com* to find these sleeves or just wrap your cards in aluminum foil – it's cheaper and works just as well.

- If you have too many Major and Minor Credit Cards (about five and up) your FICO Credit Score will begin to lower, even if you don't use them very often and/or carry a balance on a regular basis.

- If any card balance exceeds 30 percent of the cards available credit line, your FICO Credit Score will begin to lower. Keep in mind that store credit cards are not considered major credit cards however, owning any of these cards will automatically lower your FICO Credit Score. The primary reason is because with one major purchase on your store card you can easily exceed 30 percent of the card's credit limit, which in most cases is very low on a store card.

- Credit Cards come in the Unsecured and Secured variety.

  - An unsecured credit card requires no collateral and is the preferred card. They're generally issued to students in college just starting out in the credit card world who are over the age of 21 and have proof of income, but without an established credit history (over 50 million people do not have a credit score) all the way up to established consumers with stellar credit scores. Credit lines start out low, but eventually increase upwards over time. Interest rates are relatively low to moderate depending on household income and other considerations.

- A secured credit card should be avoided. They're issued to consumers with a troubled credit history resulting in a poor credit score. It takes about one year to qualify for a secured credit card and the issuers require an up-front cash deposit or application fee. The credit line is low (about $500) and the interest rate is always at the upper limit. And as with store credit cards, it is very easy to spend and exceed 30 percent of the $500 credit limit.

- Credit Card companies aren't just satisfied with the interest they receive from consumers; they have created another profit stream by charging an assortment of fees ranging from over-the-limit fees, late fees, over-draft fees, returned check fees, inactivity fees, transactions over the phone fees, transactions over the internet fees, etc. Add to that; penalties and finance charges, and all the little trickerations set for you and as a consumer you don't stand a chance. You will fall prey to them and your credit score will suffer. Next they'll figure out how to add a surcharge to your monthly bill.

- Your credit score *will lower* if you cancel a major credit card. However, your credit score *will not lower* if a credit card company cancels a credit card sent to you (unsolicited) that you have not yet activated, with one caveat. That is that you have not exceeded 30 percent of the credit limit on the total of all your current cards. If you have, your credit score will lower, unless activating the new unsolicited credit card will put you below 30 percent of all available credit. I would recommend that if this is the case, you would be better off reducing your debt load rather than increasing your credit limit by activating any new credit cards.

Consumers borrow and spend money as though they want quality of life in their early years only and are willing to sacrifice dollars to interest rather than practice financial prudence for quality of life in their later years. In other words, most consumers want instant gratification rather than delayed gratification, but the average consumer can't have it both ways. Keep this in mind; the road to personal financial success is not a sprint, but rather a marathon.

For example, Sonny is single, earns 25 dollars an hour and owns very few assets. He's living high on the hog—like there's no tomorrow—and is swamped in debt to the gills. He pays out about $15,000 in pure interest for a mortgage loan, personal loans, credit card debt, a couple of car loans, and on and on each year. That $15,000 Sonny pays out every year equates to $7.21 an hour, times 2080 hours, a typical work year, which, in turn is roughly equivalent to 29 percent in reduced wages. Again, this is just interest, very little goes to principal.

If Sonny eliminates his debt and avoids paying out thousands of dollars in interest each year, it would be as though he really was earning 25 dollars an hour in wages because he would be paying dollar for dollar for all his goods and services without paying all that wasted interest. Paying out good hard-earned moola in interest does absolutely nothing good for anyone except lenders and credit card companies. Each time you're able to pay a dollar for a dollar's worth of goods or services while avoiding interest payments, you truly get "a bang for your buck." If, on the other hand you pay out 3, 4, or 5 dollars in interest for a dollar's worth of goods and services, the creditor(s) truly *receive* a much bigger bang for *your* buck.

It's so true, "a penny saved is a penny earned". Except for certain emergencies, if you can't pay cash for things other than your car, student loans or mortgage, then you don't need those things.

Paying off consumer debt also means paying off so called "Good Debt" such as Student Loans. There is no such thing, in my opinion, as good debt.

Let's explore another pay-off strategy. Robert is single, 25 years old and rents an apartment. He has a great job and brings home, after taxes and other deductions, about $5,000 a month. He hopes to pay off, within 3 years, an $80,000 student loan he acquired at a 5.5 percent interest rate. He financed it for 10 years and has eight years remaining. This loan has really put a damper on his future goals. Except for an $18,500 two year old - five year car loan, Robert has no other outstanding debt. He has $12,000 in the bank as an emergency cushion and contributes to a 401(k) plan at work. If Robert wants to succeed he must first create a budget. See Robert's current budget below.

#	Item	Projected	Week 1	Week 2	Week 3	Bank	Actual
	Budget Month: January—Year: 20XX						
1	Rent	1200.00					
2	Groceries	300.00					
3	Gas/Oil/Maint	175.00					
4	Electric Bill	85.00					
5	Cable/Ph./Internet	280.00					
6	Entertainment	800.00					
7	Hair Cut	20.00					
8	Car Tabs	38.00					
9	Auto Insurance.	105.00					
10	Medical/Dental	50.00					
11	Student Loan	868.21					
12	Roth IRA	200.00					
13	Car Payment	353.37					
14							
15							
16							
17							
	Total Expenses	$4,474.58					
	All Net Income Sources	5,000.00					
	Difference	$525.40					

As you can see, at the end of the month Robert still has a $525.40 surplus. But notice, from the previous page, how much he's spending on entertainment. This $800.00 a month he uses for discretionary spending is way out of sync with what he's trying to accomplish, and in addition, it's a tremendous waste of money every month.

Also notice, again from the previous page, the $200 he contributes to a Roth IRA each month. Since he already makes contributions to his 401(k) plan at work, that $200 needs to be redirected to serve a better strategic purpose.

Robert makes a new budget to better reflect his goal to pay off his student loan in three years. See below.

#	Item	Projected	Week 1	Week 2	Week 3	Bank	Actual
	Budget Month: January—Year: 20XX						
1	Rent	1200.00					
2	Groceries	300.00					
3	Gas/Oil/Maint	175.00					
4	Electric Bill	85.00					
5	Cable/Ph./Internet	280.00					
6	**Entertainment**	**200.00**					
7	Hair Cut	20.00					
8	Car Tabs	38.00					
9	Auto Insurance.	105.00					
10	Medical/Dental	50.00					
11	Student Loan	868.21					
12	**Emergency Fund**	**200.00**					
13	Car Payment	353.37					
14	**Ext. Principal Pmt.**	**1125.42**					
15							
16							
17							
Total Expenses		$5,000.00					
All Net Income Sources		5,000.00					
Difference		$0.00					

Robert found that he had room to make two dramatic changes to his budget that will enable him to pay off his student loan as soon as financially possible.

- First: He reduces his monthly outgo for entertainment from $800 to $200 a month, thereby saving himself $600 each month. And

- Secondly: He no longer contributes $200 to a Roth IRA since he is already making contributions to his 401(k) plan at work. He will instead add those extra dollars to his emergency fund. and

- Thirdly: He will generate an Amortization Schedule (with an extra payment feature built in) that will reflect the extra principal payments he intends to make.

There will be much more about how to use Amortization Schedules as a strategic tool to pay off all of your debt in Section II.

Robert has eight years remaining on his student loan. He will pay over $24,185.23 in pure interest on his loan if he does nothing. However, if he acts now –

- His new Amortization Schedule will include adding the $1,125 surplus from his new budget to his current payment obligation. If Robert is able to stick with this strategy he will pay off his loan in 37 months, five years ahead of schedule and

- He will avoid paying $18,120.23 more in pure interest and

- His car loan will be paid off at that point as well, leaving him with a $2,300 surplus at the end of every month and

- He will have added to his emergency fund another $7,200.

If an emergency or unplanned event does occur between now and when both loans are satisfied, he still has that emergency fund at his disposal. Congratulations to Robert, he did the right thing.

Good debt, bad debt, all debt – as long as someone else is profiting off of your financial activities, you must –

Pay your credit cards off as soon as possible, and don't use them again unless you can pay off your balance in full when you receive the bill in the mail—<u>every time</u>! But, it's not just credit card debt that creates a problem for us; it's other debt, too (e.g., personal loans, car loans, equity loans, consolidation loans and so on). Pay them all off to avoid financial deprivation! The following web sites can offer additional money management aid if you need it: try: *Mint.com*, *Wesabe.com*, or *Quicken.com* for extra tools for your war on debt.

Notes:

A Money Sense Quote: If a person gets his attitude toward money straight, it will help straighten out almost every other area in his life. - Billy Graham

 Side Bar — H.R. 627 credit cardholders "Bill of Rights"

The credit cardholders "Bill of Rights Act" of 2009 (H.R. 627) which amended the Truth in Lending Act, was signed by the president and is now the "law of the land" as of February 2010. Congress wanted, and got, rule changes to address "unfair billing practices" applied to credit cards, while at the same time adding more consumer protection rights.

However, this law *did not go far enough* to protect credit cardholders on either count. For example, **count one:** credit card issuers can still charge all the interest they want. They're also allowed to continue to charge outrageous fees.

And, the credit card's cousin the "Debit Card" received absolutely no attention in congress even though this is also an area plagued by many of the same abuses and billing practices. For example: many banks will <u>not</u> deny your purchase at the point of sale even though there is not enough money in your account to cover the 50 cent candy bar that you want to buy. The merchant and the bank will almost always allow the sale to take place. The bank will then charge you an over the limit or overdraft fee which generally ranges from $25 to $39 plus the 50 cents for the candy bar.

Another debit card *trick on you, treat for the banks* is that the banks tend to process your spending activities according to the highest amount of each transaction you made first, and then down to the next highest and so on until they reach the lowest transaction. As a result the bank empties out your account faster thereby increasing the chance of overdraft fees on many smaller purchases as opposed to charging one fee on one large purchase. If you exceed your account balance by purchasing 10 separate small inexpensive items, at say, $33 a pop overdraft fee, that's a cost to you of $330 in total fees, if, on the other hand, you do the same thing on just one large purchase it will cost you only $33 one time. The banks will process your transactions in a way that benefits only them.

Count two: As for consumer protection rights; until Congress creates a Consumer Protection Agency, to monitor and regulate the credit and debit card industry and all other pertinent financial institutions, consumers will still have no one in the federal government to turn to as lenders devise new insidious tactics and methods to gouge consumers at every turn.

Update: In late 2010 Congress created the Consumer Financial Protection Bureau (CFPB) consumer advocates have been clamoring for, but the new agency is bogged down in determining who it needs to protect. As of: the 2nd. Quarter 2012 the CFPB seems to be fence straddling between protecting consumers vs. protecting big financial institutions. The CFPB is supposed to be protecting consumers only – What gives? Apparently, real consumer protection may come very slowly as a result. Stay tuned!

In passing the credit cardholders "Bill of Rights Act" Congress merely removed table salt from a festering wound and replaced it with a supposedly less potent sea salt. Go to: *www.cbo.gov/doc.cfm?index=10099* on the Internet if you would like to examine this 52-page document in greater detail,

A Money Sense Quote: We live by the golden rule. Those who live by the gold make the rules. - Buzzie Bavasi

 RED FLAG — ACCESS TO CREDIT TODAY HAS BEEN MUCH TOO EASY.

DEFINITION —
Credit: Immediate purchasing power that is exchanged for a promise to repay it, with or without interest, at a later date. (The American Heritage College Dictionary)

Credit is like the proverbial rope: if given enough of it; many people will just hang themselves. There's so many of those people around right now, that it's not just their problem anymore. The American taxpayer is going to pay now because the federal government is bailing out individuals who over spent and over borrowed. It's been nothing but a *spendingpalooza* for decades; advanced primarily by easy credit, and now we all will pay the price.

Think about this: Back in antiquity, the history of money began with bartering. We actively traded goods and services for goods and services, or put more simply: traded *this* for *that*—even-steven, (one *this* and one *that* being equal) and everyone was happy. Imagine if we still used the bartering system in today's world—how would credit and interest work? Both might work something like this, I want *this*, and I'll give you three *thats* later for *this* now. You worked hard to get *this* in the first place, but it always seems as though you have to give *this* up for three or four *that's*, and you never catch up, and then, *that* which you got, was only worth *t* (the new depreciated value of that) when it was paid off, but you were 10 *thises* behind the eight ball when the smoke cleared.

Enough about this and that, you get the picture, it will be the hard working middle class consumers and taxpayers that will ultimately have to pay for uncontrolled easy access to credit.

A Money Sense Quote: Money does not pay for anything, never has, never will. It is an economic axiom as old as the hills that goods and services can be paid for only with goods and services.
- Albert Jay Nock, Memoirs of a superfluous Man, 1943

PLAN 3 - CREATE AND MAINTAIN AN EMERGENCY FUND

I highly recommend that a minimum of six months' worth of combined (two income earners) wages/salaries be saved for:

Job loss: All jobs are subject to economic and/or political conditions. There are now over six million people filing for unemployment claims each week and more than 14 million people out of work in America due to the economic downturn. I know first-hand what it's like to lose a job because of circumstances beyond our control.

I worked for a $100 million manufacturer of avionics and aerospace products for 15 years before the Iron Curtain came down in Eastern Europe and brought the Cold War to an end in 1989. I lost my job two and a half years later as a result. Later, I lost another job when I worked for a commercial airplane manufacturer and the events of 9/11 ultimately affected the airline industry. It took each company years to recover from those events.

My first major job lay-off: In 1991, my wife and I took a chance and refinanced our home so we could add an addition onto our house. We took out a new 30-year fixed mortgage loan. As luck would have it, I was laid off in mid-1992 with four kids to feed and care for, three of which were six years old and younger. I struggled with unemployment and temporary work for four years, while telling myself I would never let this happen to me again. I vowed that if I ever returned to steady employment again, I would pay off my house as fast as I possibly could. We had an emergency fund and no consumer debt at the time, and we were able to pull through a very difficult period.

My second major job lay-off: In 1996 I landed a steady, well-paying job, with an airplane manufacturer. By the end of that same year I had the chance to pay off our house, and I did—in full, and ohhhh lordy… what a great feeling of relief that was! By the time the events of September 11th, 2001 played out, we were better prepared for my eventual lay-off in December of that same year. Again, we had an emergency fund and no consumer debt, and better yet, no mortgage payments.

There is never a good time to get laid-off from work, especially when you're in debt and have bills to pay, but it happens to just about everyone at some point in their life. The trick, when it happens to you, is to be financially ready at all times for that event. Have an emergency fund that can last at least six months without relying on any other money source coming in.

However, before you begin saving your emergency fund, if you have any outstanding consumer debt, pay it off first, and then start your fund. It makes no sense to save money for an emergency at the same time you're paying interest on debt. Interest you pay on consumer debt is much higher than what you can earn on savings, so you would be going backwards.

Labor Strikes: Do you belong to a labor union?

In all my years in manufacturing, I had only been a union member once for a relatively short period of time. Never have I personally gone out on, nor had the opportunity to do so, but I have witnessed the results of the poor personal financial choices *many* union members made while on strike, and it goes something like this:

- They tend to have high consumer debt.
- They don't have an emergency fund.
- They have little or no money saved to outlast the strike.
- They tend to pay their bills with credit cards.
- They live on and meet all of their future needs with credit cards.
- They expect a large signing bonus, and then its immediate distribution.
- They don't seek or obtain temporary employment.
- They simply aren't prepared financially.

The bottom line, if you belong to a union, you should know its history with the company you work for. Have six months (12 months' worth if single) or longer saved up for a strike and never use a credit card while out on strike.

Medical Emergencies: Don't be caught off guard! Accidents and disease can happen at any time, job or no job, health insurance or no health insurance.

Even if you have a good job you could be the victim of an unexpected medical crisis, or an accident, and you could lose your job as a result.

Or

A major medical event could occur to you or some member of your family while you're unemployed. Medical crisis possibilities are endless. For example, there are more than:

- 36,000 deaths each year just from any run-of-the-mill influenza, and now we have the H1N1 flu, Bird flu and SARS to contend with that nations around the world are trying to keep at bay.
- 40,000 fatalities each year in automobile accidents.
- 200,000 deaths from medical accidents and mistakes in hospitals each year.
- 700,000 bankruptcies filed each year and most are due to health care issues.

The following events can be financially devastating, even with a job and an emergency fund.

Natural Disasters: Not intending to create paranoia or hasten impending doom, nature can strike any place and at any time without warning.

Flood, hurricane, tornado, earthquake, drought, land-slide, wild-fire, volcanic eruption or rising sea level are unpredictable. None of us know when or where they will happen, and we can only hope that none of those events will happen to us. But, they do happen to thousands of people every year, and unfortunately most people prone to these events are not covered by insurance. However, if you are covered, even insurance comes up short in many cases. While insurance companies promise to make you whole again after a covered event occurs, those same insurance companies may fight you at every turn on technicalities. Take for example Hurricane Katrina. Many big named insurance companies insured homeowners in that storm ravaged area, but refused to pay for all or part of the damages homeowners thought they were insured for. As a result, many people were wiped out financially because the lawyers for the insurance companies got them out of paying homeowners for damages on technicalities rather than doing what was right.

Having an emergency fund would allow you to obtain temporary shelter and hang on to your job in a natural disaster, and, if necessary, allow you the financial means for a court battle with the insurance company should you file a law suit against them for denying your claim.

The following events may not be covered by standard homeowner's insurance, for example:

- There are tens of thousands of people in America who live 80 miles or less from an active volcano. Many of their homes are on a mud flow plain and in danger of being destroyed should a major eruption occur. Is there even an insurance policy available for such an event?
- Global warming may increase the likelihood of wild-fires occurring in areas of the country that have not experienced them before.
- The western half of our country is known for earthquakes, but did you know the eastern half of our country is overdue for a major earthquake? Eastern quakes have the potential for greater devastation over a larger area than in the western half of the country.
- And, how close to sea level do you live, including in-land? The world's oceans are rising and your home may be vulnerable to floods, tidal waves, tsunamis, high tides, and/or damaging over-flow or spray from any of these conditions in the near future.

If you operate without a budget, have consumer debt, have no emergency fund and any of these conditions occur, you may lose everything.

Sometimes, having an emergency fund can create opportunity in an otherwise unfortunate situation.

Opportunity: Sometimes unfortunate circumstances can turn out well.

For example: Sharon and Greg have been married for 10 years and are going to file for divorce. Fortunately, they have no kids and share very little material wealth. However, they did purchase a house together 7 years ago for $100,000. The house was not affected by the housing market bust and now appraises for $153,870.00. They still owe a $92,242.15 balance on the mortgage loan. That's a $61,627.85 net gain over the 7-year period. Sharon and Greg live in a community property state which means they must split all property accumulated through joint effort evenly upon the dissolution of their marriage. Sharon wants to keep the house after the divorce but doesn't have $30,813.93 to pay Greg for his half of the net gain on the house. However, they will split all their personal property (i.e., two relatively new cars and a small amount of furniture and other household goods). They also have an *emergency fund* joint savings account in the bank totaling $20,000. But the account only earns 1.37 percent interest annually.

Sharon and Greg still share a very good relationship in spite of the pending divorce. So Greg would like to help Sharon keep the house. But she must pay him his share of the appreciated value somehow. His solution, if Sharon and all of the third parties agree, is to sell her his half of the house. The following is Greg's offer, listed in the property settlement agreement portion of their divorce papers. Greg will keep Sharon's half of the joint *emergency fund* savings account, which for him totals $10,000. Greg will also have Sharon sign a unilateral contract obligating her to pay him $20,813.93 at 1.37

percent interest over a 5-year period, which is equal to the interest he would have otherwise earned at his bank. This contract would settle *completely* his financial interest in the house. If all parties agree to the settlement, Greg will generate an Amortization Schedule reflecting the settlement values of the loan contract. This will allow Sharon to retain possession of the house without refinancing it, which in turn would have entailed closing costs and acquiring a new 30-year loan all over again.

In the event Sharon sells the house, within the contracted 5-year period with Greg, she will pay him, in full, *only* the remaining balance due on the Amortization Schedule. This means all additional increases, or loses, in the home's value since the contract was in force would belong to Sharon. Greg will retain Joint Tenancy in the house with rights of survivorship until Sharon satisfies the contract agreement.

This would have been a missed opportunity for Sharon and Greg had an *emergency fund* not been established early in their marriage.

> *A Money Sense Quote: The waste of money cures itself, for soon there is no more to waste.*
> *- M.W. Harrison*

Now that you have a budget in place, no debts, and have saved an emergency fund, it's time to pay down your mortgage.

 Side Bar — A special note about employer backed 401(k) retirement plans.

401(k) plans are offered to employees of private companies. If your employer offers a dollar for dollar match to your contributions, you should, without hesitation, contribute up to that match beyond any other financial considerations, even if you're in debt and have no emergency fund. Their match is free money to you and you can't afford to pass it up. All of your contributions as well as your company's match are made with pretax dollars. Both contributions remain un-taxable until you withdraw money from your 401(k) plan at retirement.

Fact: In early 2012, working 60 year olds who've made uninterrupted contributions to a 401(k) plan for a period of at least 30 years now enjoy an average account balance just slightly over $200,000. The average balance for those 65 and older is about $163,000.

Advisory only: If your company offers a 401(K) plan to their employees and offers within that plan its' own stock options, you may be wise to leave their stock <u>completely</u> out of your portfolio. Why? Because-

1. If you choose to own their stock, it may have been purchased purely out of loyalty to the company without any regard to its' potential for long term growth.

If the company files for bankruptcy, is found guilty of misconduct, is under investigation for corruption, or is mismanaged in any way, you may be left with worthless shares of company stock.

2. If upper management or an owner of a company knows, in advance, the company is going to close its' doors forever, they may continue to apply employee 401(k) contributions to their own stock (even though they know it's soon going to be worthless). This is similar to the way some companies that are going out of business will continue to take money from unsuspecting customers for goods and services they know they will never deliver.

3. We have all heard and read about the recent collapse of many major corporations, (as mentioned in my introduction). Many employees invested heavily; if not every penny they had, in those same large companies and over-night lost not only their jobs, but their entire life savings.

If your company offers a 401(k) plan, you would be wise to invest your contributions and their match in a well-diversified portfolio that excludes your company entirely.

A Money Sense Quote: In the old days a man who saved money was a miser, nowadays he's a wonder. - Author Unknown

RED FLAG — POOR SPENDING HABITS CAN BE CREATED JUST BY NURTURING NEGATIVE NOTIONS

Poor spending habits are often derived from the fact that many people deliberately nourishes negative notions simply to spend money foolishly, without repent. As a result, he or she knowingly lends support to an idea that will ultimately lead them to financial ruin.

For example, have you ever heard someone nourish this negative notion: "I spend all my money as soon as I get it because, who knows? I might die tomorrow and you can't take it with you!" A lot of well-educated, well-meaning and otherwise intelligent people live "paycheck to paycheck" because of this philosophical blunder or some variant thereof.

The problem with this unfortunate approach to spending is that individuals who adopt this notion really would have to die early in life, because if they didn't, and actually lived to old age they'd either become homeless and penniless, or be an ongoing burden to taxpayers and/or their own children for support.

The vast majority of folks who think in this fashion won't really die the next day, or the day after that, but might in fact, live out a long normal lifespan. So, all personal financial activity should be conducted as though one were going to live out, at least, an average lifespan.

So, for those of you who live each day deliberately nurturing your own poor spending habits with negative notions, as in this case, you will probably live out a long and non-prosperous life and have nothing left to leave to anyone. The fact that the person described above can't take it with them should not give them a reason to not take care of their affairs and family while they have time.

Here are some more very popular negative notions:

- "Money is the root of all evil." Evil is a human trait established long before the creation of money.
- "Money can't buy happiness." Incorrect, if used wisely… money can reduce stress thereby increasing a greater possibility for happiness.
- "It takes money to make money." Not true! It takes hard work and patience.

A Money Sense Quote: Made $60 million, spent 61…. - Evel Knievel

PLAN 4 - PAY DOWN AND THEN PAY OFF YOUR MORTGAGE

Maslow's "Hierarchy of Needs" model as it might relate to personal finances.

Abraham Maslow was a distinguished lifelong Psychologist, and was well known and respected in both academia and the business world. Maslow began work on human behavior at the University of Wisconsin-Madison in the mid-20th century and was acclaimed for his lifelong study and work in this field. In his clinical observations, Maslow determined that humans naturally seek to fulfill a variety of needs. His studies led him to develop the concept of the "hierarchy of needs" model, in which he arranged a sequence of five basic human needs into a five level pyramid according to their importance: The following are examples of Maslow's "hierarchy of needs" model as it might relate to personal finances.

- The first, or lowest, level of his pyramid is the most basic of human needs, physiological needs (e.g., water, food, clothes, and shelter). This need was first filled by our parents or guardians and sustained us throughout childhood. Later as we grew up and left home, we discovered very quickly that our physiological needs come before everything else. Satisfy these basic needs, and the chances are good that you will survive.
    - Unfortunately, Millions of Americans will live out their entire lives satisfying *only* these basic needs, and little else. They will, in fact, fail to reach the next level of needs. These people are, for the most part, the chronic poor. The

primary reasons for their failure to advance any higher on the pyramid may stem from self-destructive or uncontrolled behavior such as: drug abuse, alcoholism, persistent lethargy, mental illness, repeated criminal activity, and so on.

- Maslow next housed Safety needs on the second level in the pyramid. Safety needs, he discovered, are one's desire for: security and stability.

    o Tens of millions more Americans will live out their entire lives trying to fulfill these needs too. They will remain at this level of need with only flickering hopes and dreams of even temporarily, let alone permanently, reaching the next level of Maslow's pyramid. The primary reasons for their inability to move on is due to money issues that often stem from such things as: having less than a high school education, out of control debt due to their need for immediate gratification, gambling addiction(s), reckless spending habits, bankruptcy(s), or just a general ineptness at managing personal finances.

- The middle level of Maslow's pyramid is Social needs (e.g., love and affection, and a sense of belonging).

    o Most Americans will achieve these basic needs, but unfortunately, will spend the rest of their lifetime attempting to maintain a steady, consistent position on this level. The primary reasons for this are due to some of the following events such as: untimely layoffs, poor or inadequate job skills, medical catastrophe(s), an inability to accurately budget personal income, an acceptance of the living from "paycheck to paycheck" mentality, dysfunctional marriage(s), multiple divorces, poor planning strategies for retirement, and so on.

Maslow's hierarchy of needs implies that the first three needs must be satisfied before one can hope to achieve the final two needs on the upper levels of the pyramid.

- On the forth level of needs is Ego or Esteem. It's at this level that one is in a position to accomplish their financial goals and independence.

    o Maybe 25 percent of all Americans will ever reach and remain at this level in their lifetime. For this to occur, one must: maintain zero debt, be inclined to save and invest heavily, pay off one's mortgage, and have planned very well for retirement.

- And the last or highest level of Maslow's pyramid is Self-Realization or Actualization needs. There is no detailed explanation needed here because:

    o Only about one percent of all Americans will ever reach and then remain at this level. These are individuals who've succeeded because they've reached their full potential and status in life (e.g., Bills Gates, Warren Buffet, T. Boone Pickens, and more than 400 other billionaires in America today.)

If Maslow's needs theory contains any substance of truth, then it would stand to reason that a homebuyer who becomes a homeowner fulfills the first three of Maslow's <u>most basic</u> needs; physiological, safety and social needs. Imagine, if your mortgage is paid off, YOU, not your lender will keep your family warm, dry and safe, providing you and them with a permanent shelter and the ability to nurture love, affection, and a sense of belonging. There can be no greater peace of mind than to know you possess a little piece of the planet, a place that you can call your very own. When the economy sours, like it has recently and you lose your job, or run the risk of becoming unemployed, there can be no better place on earth that can provide a more stable foundation for you and your family's basic human needs than your own home.

Case Study: The Kelly and Mike Story

Kelly and Mike buy their first home. They're in their early thirties, happily married and have a 5 year old son. They live in a beautiful two-story Victorian home they purchased together a year ago. Mike works full-time as an Electrical Engineer for a large commercial airplane manufacturer. Kelly works teaching on-line classes at home part-time as a computer instructor for a small technical college. Both worry about Job Security!

Kelly and Mike each fear they could face a sudden layoff, at any time, as harsh economic times continue. Because of their fear they want to pay off their home as soon as possible because Mike's employer has a history of sudden layoffs due to cyclical economic conditions. And Kelly, too, is always subject to losing classes every academic quarter due to low enrollment or budget restraints. But it's Mike who really wants the security of owning their home outright. He knows first-hand what hard economic times can destroy.

As a young adult, before he met Kelly, Mike experienced personal financial disaster as the company he worked for went out of business without warning. Mike's employer had run his own business and offered no employee benefits. Mike didn't qualify for unemployment benefits when he lost his job. Without money coming in he was forced to move out of his apartment. Having nowhere to turn, Mike lived out of his car for a while. Eventually, he went to work for another company and went on to get a good education, meet and marry Kelly, begin and raise a family, and buy a home. But he vowed to pay their home mortgage loan off by any means possible, as soon as possible, and own their home outright so that no economic condition would ever cause the loss of their home and security!

Capitalism and the Free Market economic system in America is the best system in the world and beats any other system hands down! But, one of its flaws is that our system tends, at times, to be extremely cyclical. There always seem to be years of surging economic growth followed by years of staggering economic decline. Throw a little human nature into the mix (e.g., war, terrorism, stock and housing market crashes, greed, corruption, schemes, scams and politics) and then add to that a dwindling world-wide fossil fuel supply and it's a recipe for economic disaster. That's not even taking the national debt into account. The best way to prepare for major unexpected economic downturns and the potential job losses that ensue as a result is to pay off your mortgage in advance of any of these potential threats. If you own your own home outright and the economy "goes to hell in a hand-basket", you'll be in a better position to ride it out, whatever its cause or however long its duration.

Back to Maslow's "Hierarchy of Needs" model—in today's world of easy credit and over-zealous spending, people seem more interested in attempting to climb straight to the top of the pyramid first rather than passing through each level in a chronological fashion. Any attempt to blow through or hurdle over any level without any strategic purpose is a recipe for financial disaster. Start from the lowest level and methodically plan and strategize your way to the highest <u>sustainable</u> level you can obtain that will last for the rest of your life.

keep this in mind, history tells us that many lower and middle income earners who, *suddenly,* come into a large unexpected cash windfall (e.g., lottery or gambling winnings or an inheritance) more often than not *rise fast* and *fall hard* relative to Maslow's Pyramid. Why? Because it takes time to learn about money, gain experience putting it to work for the future and then acquire the proper assets and investments to secure the necessary stability required on each level. Without sound financial planning the odds are that not only will the lower levels get revisited sooner than later, but unfortunately, may become permanent.

You may ask, "Why should I pay down my mortgage rather than invest my extra cash in something with the potential of a much greater financial return"?

Not counting your emergency fund and retirement plan, where else could you invest your extra cash right now that is solid, stable, and safe in today's economic uncertainty, which would earn a guaranteed 6 percent interest rate of return for thirty years? A bank...? Not now! Currently your <u>piggy-bank</u> pays about the same interest on your savings as the <u>biggy-banks</u> are. The stock market...? Maybe. Think about this, if you had put a dollar in the stock market 12 years ago, it would only be worth about a buck 30 today. Or gold? It's hovering, depending on what day it is, anywhere from 50 to 70 percent above its 32 year high, and in September 2011, it was priced at $1,907, more than twice its highest value ever. Which means unless you bought gold say, a decade or so ago, you probably missed out on gold's most recent upward gains. How about Silver? It fetched about $48 an ounce 32 years ago; it's at less than $33 an ounce today.

- A note about gold: If the value of gold had kept pace with inflation over the last three decades, it would be priced at about $2,600 in today's market. Gold's growth has increased (annually) only about two to three percent in that time period. A good Certificate of Deposit would have earned roughly 6 percent interest (annually) in that same time period. And just like 32 years ago, when the economy does improve, gold prices may plummet just like they did back then.

The truth is the average hard working middle-class American is a novice in the world of finances and knows very little about investing their hard-earned dollars in the stock market, or anywhere else for that matter. Note: In March, 2009 the "Dow Jones" industrial average fell to 6,527 from an all-time high of 14,164 just a year and a half earlier. Many people with defined retirement plans were heavily exposed in that crash… and a great number of them panicked and jumped ship near or at the bottom. As a result, many of those novice investors stayed out of stocks and missed the ride back up thereby permanently devastating their retirement accounts.

Be risk-averse, with your hard earned dollars, by first putting all of your financial ducks in a row. Put extra, or disposable, income into your mortgage where it's safe. Remember, you don't own your home until it's paid off; the lender does. Once your financial foundation has been laid, by applying many of the personal financial strategies scattered throughout the three sections in this book, you may find yourself "house rich, but money poor". Yes, for a short period of time you will be strapped for cash, but you will still have your emergency fund and an active retirement plan. Keep this in mind: roughly 50 percent of all Americans only have about a one month financial cushion should they lose their job, but once *you're* debt free and you own your home free and clear, you will be in the perfect position to save and catch up with those same Americans in no time. At that point, you can <u>save and/or invest</u> your money however you choose and be house rich and <u>money rich!</u>

Wouldn't we pay more income tax if we paid off our home?

Yes, you would. If you both were renting a place to live in before the purchase of your home, you both, more than likely, filed a 1040A "<u>short form</u>" joint tax return. With this short form you were only able to claim your standard deduction and claim your dependent children, and with a few other exceptions, that was pretty much it.

Once the two of you signed for a mortgage loan, *that loan* enabled the two of you to file a 1040 "<u>long form</u>" with schedules A and B along with other forms creating the ability to write off mortgage interest, property tax, and other items which ultimately put the two of you into a lower tax bracket. But once you pay that home off, you're forced back into using the 1040A short form, the same one you used when you paid rent.

Before I go any further, I want to make the following points absolutely clear.

Gross Income: Is all wages, salaries, tips, interest, etc. one or both of you earn in a tax year.

Adjusted Gross Income (AGI): Is all <u>gross income</u> earned by one or the both of you in a tax year minus all deductions that can be <u>written off</u> on federal income taxes. It's your

AGI that determines how much income tax you will have to pay. The lower your AGI, the lower your taxes.

Write-offs (Itemized Deductions): This does not mean that if you're able to write off $1,000, you get that same $1,000 back, but rather a portion thereof. As a "rule of thumb", you'll receive back *roughly* ten cents for every dollar you're able to write off, depending on the tax bracket you fall into.

The following are the very simplistic tax consequences of paying off your home vs. not paying off your home. We will not, for this exercise, use personal exemptions, tax credits, or standard deductions that would ordinarily be applied to either tax return for the sake of eliminating redundancy.

If you choose to continue making house payments, your tax write-offs are as follows:

Long Form 1040 U.S. Individual Income Tax Return

Property Tax	$2,500
Mortgage Interest You Paid	14,000
Home Owners Insurance	800
State and Local Taxes / State Sales Tax	1,000
Miscellaneous Deductions (e.g., Auto Excise Tax)	100
Total dollar amount written off comes to:	$18,400

Note: The figures used above are typical dollar amounts for an average family (and home owners.)

If you both earned a combined income of say, $85,000, not counting exemptions, tax credits, or other deductions, your AGI would be reduced to $66,600. Your tax bracket would be in the 15 percent range and you would owe $9,990 in total taxes.

If you choose to pay off your home, and everything else is equal, your tax write-offs would be as follows:

Short Form 1040A U.S. Individual Income Tax Return

State and Local Taxes / State Sales Tax	$1,000
Total dollar amount written off comes to:	$1,000

You would no longer be able to write off your property tax, mortgage interest, insurance, or miscellaneous items, which totals $18,300.

If you both earned a combined income of $85,000, not counting exemptions, tax credits, or other deductions, your AGI would be reduced to only $84,000. Your tax bracket might jump up to the 25 percent range as a result, and if so, you would owe $21,000 in total taxes.

If you paid off your home, you would pay $11,010 more in additional taxes. Why on earth would you ever want to pay off your home if it's going to cost you thousands more in income taxes?

Here's why: say your mortgage payment is $1,743.11 for principal and interest only. Your house payments would total $20,917.32 each and every year for the term of your loan. Minus the $9,990 tax burden you would have to pay anyway had you not paid off your house, your total out of pocket savings would be $10,927.32. Now reduce that amount again by $3,400 for the other write-offs that you can no longer claim on your tax return and you're still ahead by $7,527.32. Again, none of these figures included exemptions, tax credits, or other deductions that would be used on either tax return.

This was a very simplified example, but in the final analysis, if you're not making thousands and thousands of dollars a year in house payments, that savings will far outpace any income tax burden you may have if you hadn't paid off your house.

What if we plan to be in our home for only a few years, or one of us changes jobs requiring that we relocate?

You may intend to eventually pull up stakes and put your house on the market for any number of reasons. But remember, you went through all the trouble to buy your home in the first place. Why not keep it? Before you sell your house, try renting it out—even if you move far away.

Here's why:

- Today's housing market is bleak at best, with declining prices and few buyers. Even if your property is priced right, the unemployment rate is at a 26 year high. With very few qualified buyers, your property may sit on the market for years.

- The only potential buyers may be professional speculators, the "We Buy Houses" types, just looking for bargains, and you'll never get out of them what you think your property is really worth.

- You may be "under water" right now on your mortgage, that is, you may owe more on your property than it's worth in today's market.

- If this is your situation, you'll either have to abandon the property, in which case you give up potential ownership and dominion with no intention of recovering it, or

    - default on your loan contract (foreclosure) or

    - settle for a "deed-in-lieu of foreclosure" in which case the lender sells the property after a negotiated agreement with you (the seller) or

- o sell the property yourself for a loss (short sale) with the lender's approval in which case you may still have to pay back the difference to your lender depending on the original contract you signed.

- Was the original loan a recourse or a non-recourse loan contract? And, if you sell the property for a loss, and you're not obliged to pay the difference back through an agreement you negotiated with the lender, there still may be taxes owed to the IRS by you on that difference you didn't pay back. And, in any case, your credit score may plummet by 200 points or more, and your credit will be damaged for up to 10 years.

    1. Recourse Loan: Is usually a Second Deed of Trust (e.g., Second Mortgage, Equity, Re-finance, or Investment Loan, etc.). Generally speaking, if the homeowner defaults on this type of loan and loses their house to foreclosure, deed-in-lieu of foreclosure, or short sale, the lender <u>is able</u> to come after the homeowner's personal assets for the difference between what the homeowner still owes the lender, and what the house eventually sells for on the open market. However, 10 states—Alaska, Arizona, California, Hawaii, Minnesota, Montana, North Dakota, Oklahoma, Oregon, and Washington—protect a buyer's assets with non-recourse protection from the lender—in most cases.

    2. Non-recourse Loan: Is usually a First Deed of Trust (e.g., the Original or New Purchase Loan). Generally speaking, if the homeowner defaults on this type of loan and loses their house to foreclosure, deed-in-lieu of foreclosure, or short sale, the lender is <u>unable</u> to come after the homeowner's personal assets for the difference between what the homeowner still owes to the lender, and what the house eventually sells for on the open market.

    3. Simultaneous Recourse and Non-recourse Loans: are when the homeowner is still paying on the original or new purchase loan, and then acquires a second mortgage, equity, re-finance, investment loan, etc. Generally speaking, if the homeowner defaults on both loans and loses their house to foreclosure, deed-in-lieu of foreclosure, or short sale, the lender is <u>unable</u> to come after the homeowner's personal assets for the difference between what the homeowner still owes to the lender on the non-recourse loan, however, the lender of the recourse loan <u>is able</u> to come after the homeowner's personal assets if they fail to satisfy the debt, including California, one of the 10 states with non-recourse loan protection laws.

    If you run the risk of losing your home to foreclosure, deed-in-lieu of foreclosure, or short sale, contact your lender or service provider to immediately try to arrange an agreement in which the lender or service provider agrees to accept a lesser sum than that owed by you in full satisfaction of the debt. This is known in contract law as a "creditors' compensation agreement."

- And last, but not least, there is always the trick of selling your house so you can purchase another one somewhere else, which is often a simultaneous proposition involving timing, luck, and getting a contingency clause OK'd by a seller on a purchase agreement, if and when you do find a home you want to buy. Some mortgage lenders offer a temporary "Bridge Loan" on the new home for little or no interest until the original home sells.

If you choose to rent out your house, you're only left with:

- Finding another place to live, and having plenty of time to do so without the added stress of timing or luck.

- Deciding what stays in the new rental and what goes (e.g., washer and dryer, furniture, other appliances, etc.).

- Hiring a property manager to take care of the property and fill vacancies. They can also handle the rental application forms, do reference checks and screen potential tenants, collect security deposits, etc.

- Consulting the Landlord Protection Agency at: <u>www.thelpa.com</u> for additional information.

Once you have committed to the idea of renting out your house, then it becomes a matter of collecting more in rent (positive cash flow) than is paid out for the mortgage, property tax, home owner's insurance, and property management fees; unless you've paid it off. Becoming a landlord and making mortgage payments on said rental property requires that you file the long form 1040 and schedule E, but no business license is needed. It also requires that you let go of your former home <u>emotionally</u>. See Section II, Question 13 for more specific details on this issue.

Should I still pay down my mortgage if my home's value declined by 30 percent, and I have 100 percent financing?

If this is your situation, you're sort of "stuck between a rock and a hard place", you could walk away from it (which is the wrong thing to do). Or you could try to get a loan modification through your lender, or you could hang on to it and try to recover the 30 percent loss utilizing some financial strategy.

Let's say you purchased your home with a plan to "flip it," that is, place it back on the market quickly for a substantially higher price than you paid for it (those days are gone.) But, if you purchased your house for permanent residency in a panic because you didn't want to be priced out of the market, you can still recover the 30 percent loss without selling, but rather, by paying the house off faster. This is assuming that you borrowed from a legitimate lender and your income is truly sufficient enough to cover your monthly budget and make the monthly payments.

For example, let's say you purchased a house for $550,000 and you borrowed that entire amount at say, 6.5 percent for 30 years, fixed. Your payment, principal and interest only, would be $3,476.37. If the loan went the full term, you would pay $701,494.71 in interest alone. With principal included, you would pay back a total of $1,251,494.71 for your house over the 30 years. Since the value of your home dropped by 30 percent, it's only worth $385,000 in today's market. That's a loss of $165,000. Just keep in mind: if you bought your house to keep for good, then whether the house goes up or down in value in the market place should not concern you. It should have no meaning; it's your home. However, if it's just the principle of the matter, that had you not panicked and just waited a little longer, you could have gotten the very same house for under $400,000, there's still a way to make it seem as though you originally did purchase your house for under $400,000.

Here's how: had you obtained the same loan, but at the new lower price of $385,000, that loan would cost you $876,046.27 over 30 years. That's $375,448.51 less than the deal you did get over the same 30 years. To ultimately pay only $876,046.27 or less for your house now, you must avoid paying that $375,448.51 difference.

This can be done several different ways, all requiring the utilization of an Amortization Schedule program to plan a payment strategy that will enable you to save hundreds of thousands over the life of your loan, provided your income has enough "staying power" to succeed.

One Amortization Schedule program might allow for a _fixed_ additional principal payment to be paid along with your regularly scheduled payment each month. In this case, you would have to pay an additional payment of $1,250 each and every month along with your scheduled payment to avoid paying that $375,448.51 difference between the two loans.

Disadvantage:
- A fixed rate principal payment of an extra $1,250 is a very hefty sum of money to come up with every month.

Advantages:
- With a fixed rate principal payment of an extra $1,250, you will avoid paying $375,448.51 interest.
- You will pay off your home in just over 15 years rather than 30.
- Your loan balance will be less than $385,000 in about six and a half years.

Another Amortization Schedule program might allow you to pay additional principal payments as you can afford them along with your regularly scheduled payment each month. In this case, you would likely pay the following month's principal payment every month along with your scheduled payment to avoid paying interest.

Disadvantage:

- To pay the following month's principal payment along with your regularly scheduled payment each month you will, at some point, exceed the $1,250 you would have continued to pay had you gone the fixed rate payment route.

Advantages:

- The extra principal payments would begin at just under $500 per month with the savings beginning at just under $3,000 per month.
- You will pay off your home in 15 years rather than 30 if you maintain that pay-off strategy.
- Your loan balance will be less than $385,000 in about eight years.

I have given you just a handful of sound and practical reasons to pay down your mortgage; it's up to you now.

Note: You will find more pay-off strategies utilizing Amortization Schedules for all sorts of debt relief cures in Sections II and III of this book.

Now that you have a budget in place, no debts, saved an emergency fund, and paid down your mortgage, you should focus all of your attention on retirement planning.

A Money Sense Quote: People are living longer than ever before, a phenomenon undoubtedly made necessary by the 30-year mortgage. - Doug Larson

 ***Side Bar — Where can one turn to get personal financial advice?***

Like any good engineer, doctor, or scientist, I keep up with the personal finances industry by reading, listening to the radio, and watching very famous and well known financial pundits on television giving advice about their profession. While I agree with them most of the time, I sometimes have a "difference of opinion" about what they advise people to do with their money, especially live on the radio call-in shows where someone calls with a complex question about their own personal finances, and the host of the show gives an "off the cuff", "shoot from the hip" response to the caller's question about what they should do.

For example, just the other day I was listening to one of my favorite radio call-in talk shows, about personal finances, when a lady called in with this question (I'm paraphrasing here): "Hi, my husband and I are both in our early 60's. Two years ago we purchased a home for $380,000 at a 6.0 percent interest rate for 30 years. We have $100,000 in the bank, which is our emergency fund, and have no other debt. Our home has since fallen in value and is now worth about $340,000. We can get a new 30 year fixed rate loan at 4.5 percent, but we would have to pay down $40,000 for the difference between the original value and what our house is worth now, and then make an additional 20 percent down payment on our house for the new loan. Should we do that if it leaves us with no emergency fund?"

The talk show host asked, "How much money do the two of you pull in annually?" She said together they make about $130,000 each year. He then asked, "Do you have any other money put away—like for retirement?" Her response, "We have $800,000 saved up in several retirement accounts." The host then said, "Well, if the two of you make $130,000 annually and have $800,000 saved up for retirement, it's a no brainer, yes by all means, use the $100,000 emergency fund and refinance your house. You'll probably knock your $3,300 monthly house payment down to $1,400 a month and with the money you both make, build your emergency fund back up in no time." She was very appreciative to the host for the advice, and said, "That's what we're going to do." The call ended and the host made a few additional comments about the call (i.e., "they would probably only make 0.3 percent interest on their $100,000 anyway") and then went to the next caller.

His advice was ok, but maybe not the only option, and that's the problem for people without a background in simple, let alone complex, financial issues who really need skilled professional financial advice. Who can they turn to with personal financial questions? There are books on the subject, and call-in talk shows on television and radio, but where else can one turn? Credit counselors specialize in bad debt, not financial advice. Certified Financial Planners (CFP), stock brokers, and other money managers all specialize in investing money for clients who have lots of it to invest, but they're not really compensated just to dispense personal financial advice. There are very few companies that actually specialize in administering personal financial advice. Why so few? Because there's no money in it for them! And the few companies that do offer help, well, they'll either charge a $100 to $300 fee for only an hour's worth of advice, or charge a commission, in which case there could be a potential conflict of interest should they stand to personally gain from their financial recommendations.

Whether the advice they dole out will work or is enough to turn someone around and headed in the right direction is anyone's guess. If you seek out one of these companies, you'll want a financial advisor who'll not be reckless, thoughtless and/or uncaring with your money. An advisor should accurately and precisely analyze your current financial position (e.g., income and expenses, consumer debt balances, current savings, mortgage, and retirement etc.) An advisor should then discuss your goals and objectives. Once all of that has been established, your advisor should be able to clearly show you where you might be going wrong and then present you with an array of options, including all risks, which will turn you around and <u>make sense</u> at the same time. And one of those options should include how you can easily make back, at least ten-fold, what you just paid them for their services. However, if all you need is help with some questions about the best way to execute a particular financial strategy, like the lady who called in to the talk show, an hour long session/discussion should be plenty of time for you and a financial advisor to come up with the best financial options to fit your needs. Just be sure to check out their claims with the Better Business Bureau, and your state's Attorney General's Office before making an appointment with them.

As for the lady who called in to the radio talk show, another option would be to retain the $100,000 in the bank for emergencies, pay the house off out of their retirement savings, and eliminate the house payment altogether.

Here are the reasons: These people are in their early 60s. If the bank owns their house for the next 30 years, and their house payment is $1,378.18 a month, after obtaining a new loan, they will eventually pay out $224,148.27 in interest alone. They will also be in their 90s when the house is paid off. One (or both) of them may want to retire soon. They would have to continue working longer if they wanted to replenish their $100,000 emergency fund while making a house payment. Meanwhile, their $800,000 is tied up in retirement accounts and at the mercy of a volatile stock market. Maybe that $800,000 was originally worth $1,600,000 before the market crashed in early 2009. What if it crashes again? If that were to happen and their house is already paid off, at least some of the retirement money would have gone to some good use. No one can determine the future, but there's no better rock solid foundation than owning your home outright if the economy does go from bad to worse.

The advantages of paying their house off early are:

* No more house payment. The $1,378.18 that would have been their new house payment doesn't come to realization.

* The $100,000 emergency fund is still intact. All or part of that fund can strategically purchase CDs at staggering and alternating terms that run no longer than 12 months each, and pay at least 2.0 percent interest.

DEFINITION —
Certificate of Deposit (CD): An instrument evidencing a promissory acknowledgment by a bank of a receipt of money with an engagement to repay it. (West's Business Law (Fourth Edition))

Staggering and alternating CD terms is simply purchasing a CD for say, a period of 12 months or less, and then purchasing another CD 2-3 months later for a similar term, and so on. So in time when higher interest rates become available on all CDs, due to an improving economic environment, you're able to take quick advantage as each of your CDs matures.

* Purchase $12,000 a year worth of Roth IRAs (with the house payments they no longer have to make) to replenish the money they took from their retirement account to pay off the house.

* One or both of them can quit working at a time of their own choosing knowing their home belongs to them no matter what happens to the economy.

Disadvantages of paying their house off early are:

* $340,000 less in their retirement account (used to pay off their house).

I think the "pay the house off" option is a no brainer! You decide.

> *A Money Sense Quote: A bank is a place where they lend you an umbrella in fair weather and ask for it back when it begins to rain. - Robert Frost*

🚩 RED FLAG — HAVE YOU EVER CO-SIGNED FOR SOMEONE OR ALLOWED SOMEONE TO ASSUME YOUR LOAN CONTRACT?

DEFINITIONS —
Cosign: a) To sign (a document) jointly. b) To endorse (another's signature) as for a loan. (The American Heritage College Dictionary)

Assumption: a) The act of taking to or upon oneself: assumption of an obligation. b) The act of taking possession or asserting claim. (The American Heritage College Dictionary)

Have you ever been asked to co-sign for someone on a loan? Maybe one of your teenage kids wanted to buy a car, but hadn't established credit yet, so you thought this would be a great way for them to get started. Or have you ever considered allowing a complete stranger to assume your mortgage loan because it was an option in your loan contract and an easier way to sell your house? It happens all the time. We want to help our kids get started in life by giving them a helping hand. Or, your mortgage contract allows a buyer to assume your loan when you're ready to sell your home. It's a good deal for you, right? After all, it's your kid that's responsible for the payment, not you! Or the house you sold on an assumable loan is no longer your problem. But, you'd be mistaken in both cases! Being a co-signer on a loan contract, or allowing your mortgage to be assumed, means you are still responsible to see to it that the debt is satisfied. In the event any payments are not paid on time by the primary debtor, the lender will automatically default back to you for payment-in-full and it would all go on your credit report.

For example, your 18 year old son wants to buy a car, but doesn't have enough to pay cash for it and needs a loan. But he has no credit history and needs you to co-sign for him in order to obtain a car loan. You want to help and agree to do it. You both sign a two year loan agreement with a lender and your son begins making payments. Five months go by, then the lender contacts you by mail stating that three payments have been missed and if you don't pay up, the car will be repossessed, sold at auction for less than is owed, and they will come after you for the difference. Not only can they do this, but your credit, as well as your son's credit, will be tainted. As for your son, even if he had made every payment on time, because you were the co-signer on his loan, you would get the full credit for satisfying the debt, not him. Co-signing for any loan, for any reason, is only an act of love and faith on your part. You carry all of the risks and responsibilities, and share little or none of the benefits. This kind of loan nightmare isn't the only one that can get you in hot water; loan contracts that allow for someone else to assume your loan can hurt your credit too.

For example, you have a house you want to sell, and your loan is assumable, which allows for a buyer to take over your payments when you choose to sell. Your loan has a low interest rate and there are only 21 years remaining when you place your home on the market with a real estate company. All that is needed now is for a buyer to step forward who is willing to pay you, in cash, the difference between what you want for the house and what is owed on the loan. A buyer finally comes along and makes you an offer you can't refuse. You accept their offer, which triggers all of the same credit checks and income requirements for them that you went through when you obtained your original loan. They pass muster, and the new buyer gets approved by the lender to assume the debt on the remainder of your loan. Four years pass—you've moved across country, started a new job, and purchased another home. Everything is going well when you hear from your former lender that the person who assumed your loan four years prior has defaulted on the loan and walked away from the property. Your former lender wants you to pay up. This can happen as well, because loan assumptions are written up with you as a sort of a co-signer, even though someone else was approved for that loan by your previous lender. So, even if someone else has bought your house and assumed your mortgage loan, you may still be responsible for their house payments for up to five years after you've sold them the home.

These two examples show the kind of traps (seldom verbalized as a warning by a lender) you can run into when co-signing on a loan or selling a home on an assumable loan. Maybe they're written somewhere in the "mice type" in the loan agreement everyone has to sign. Therefore, be aware that if someone—other than you—is responsible for satisfying a debt on a loan you co-signed for, or you sold a house on an assumable loan, YOU, not them stand to be the most damaged party if they fail to meet their obligation to pay on time or fail to satisfy the debt!

P.S. This is also true if you've co-signed for someone's credit card (e.g., a son or daughter.) You're responsible for that kind of debt as well!

A Money Sense Quote: Business is the art of extracting money from another man's pocket without resorting to violence. - Max Amsterdam

PLAN 5 - NET WORTH AND RETIREMENT GO HAND-IN-HAND!

DEFINITION -
Net worth: net worth is simply the difference between what you own and what you owe.

Young people in their late teens, just before striking out on their own, have virtually no net worth. That's primarily because what little they own in the world is offset by what little they owe.

For example, notice below Harry's total Net Worth just before he moved out of his parent's house.

Harry Owns	True Value	Harry Owes	Net Worth
Cash On Hand	$958.00	$0.00	$958.00
Clothes	2,000.00	150.00	1,850.00
Car Loan	3,500.00	3,850.00	-350.00
Consumer Debt	0.00	2,500.00	-2,500.00
Misc.	1,500.00	1,458.00	42.00
Total	$7,958.00	$7,958.00	$0.00

As you can see above, Harry owes as much as he owns which brings his total net worth to zero.

Harry is now in his early twenties. He's been out on his own for a few years, and he has begun to accumulate some additional debt (e.g., a student loan, a car payment, credit card debt, and so on). Most young adults in this age group will begin to owe much more than they own—this is called *negative net worth!*

Below is Harry's total net worth after just a few years on his own.

Harry Owns	True Value	Harry Owes	Net Worth
Cash On Hand	$752.00	$0.00	$752.00
Clothes	5,600.00	0.00	5,600.00
Car Loan	18,678.00	20,576.00	-1,898.00
Student Loan	0.00	19,000.00	-19,000.00
Credit Card Debt	0.00	4,489.00	-4,489.00
Personal Loan	0.00	478.00	-478.00
Total	$25,030.00	$44,543.00	-$19,513.00

Note: Harry is negative $19,513.00 in the "Net Worth" column, and this does not take into consideration all the interest he will have to pay, over time, on his loans.

Now Harry is in his late twenties, meets Sally and gets married, starts a real career, buys a house and wants to raise a family. Harry and Sally, like most people at this stage in their lives, will create even more debt for themselves. Harry and Sally continue acquiring more and more debt for as many as twenty more years or <u>even longer</u>. Their net worth may remain negative until they reach their mid to late forties. Even at this stage of their lives their net worth may only have just gone back to zero (i.e., like it was when they lived at home with their parents before striking out on their own).

Let's examine Harry and Sally's total Net Worth now that they're in their late forties.

Harry & Sally Own	True Value	Harry & Sally Owe	Net Worth
Cash on Hand	$15,269.00	$0.00	$15,269.00
Clothes	5,600.00	0.00	5,600.00
Collectables	1,678.00	0.00	1,678.00
Jewelry / Art	3,600.00	0.00	3,600.00
Harry's 401(k)	48,509.00	less 20% tax reserve	38,807.20
Sally's 403(b)	29,054.00	less 20% tax reserve	23,243.20
Car Loan #1	1,200.00	1,745.00	-545.00
Car Loan #2	1,500.00	2,689.00	-1,189.00
Mortgage Loan	0.00	65,024.40	-65,024.40
6 Credit Cards	0.00	17,761.00	-17,761.00
Personal Loan	0.00	3,678.00	-3,678.00
Total	$106,410.00	$106,410.00	$0.00

It took Harry and Sally about 20 years to get back to the break-even point financially. Let's examine some things about their current financial position.

- Harry and Sally's "Cash on Hand," (that is their checking and savings accounts) looks OK, but—well, we'll get back to that.

- Harry's 401(k) retirement plan account and Sally's 403(b) retirement plan account look good too, but keep in mind that if they pull money out of either account after reaching age 59½, they will lose 20 percent right off the top to the Internal Revenue Service, so we can only count 80 percent of their retirement accounts under the "Net Worth" column. *Additionally*, there is a 10 percent penalty if Harry or Sally were to pull money out of their own retirement account permanently before reaching age 59½.

- Harry and Sally's "Mortgage Loan," under the "True Value" column, indicates zero dollars. This is because their house is their primary residence so it's not considered "net worth." Home owners do not *live off* their primary residence in their retirement years unless they sell it. So, the remaining balance owed on Harry and Sally's home is negative dollars under the "Net Worth" column.

- Harry and Sally's remaining $23,173 balance in consumer debt, not counting their "Mortgage Loan," must be paid off as soon as possible. They're paying a high rate of interest on these outstanding loans, which might cost them thousands of dollars in interest well beyond their current balances.

- Back to Harry and Sally's "Cash on Hand." Even though they may need this money for an emergency, it's more important they get all of their debt paid off completely. If a true emergency arises, they can take money out of their home's equity to cover the expense. Once the emergency is resolved, then they can pay off their equity loan as soon as possible. When the equity loan is paid, then they should begin saving like there's no tomorrow.

Unfortunately, Harry and Sally will have only about twenty years to raise their net worth from zero to an amount that will sustain them throughout their retirement years, and their retirement years could last from age 62 to 102. *That's twenty years of saving to prepare for forty years of retirement.*

Fact: As of November 2011, the average couple at age 35 had a net worth of $3,662. At 65 and older, the average couple had a net worth of $170,494. In 2012, couples aged 65 and older should have a minimum net worth of $350,000 just to start thinking about retirement. How does your current net worth stack up?

Again, net worth does not include a primary residence, even though you may have already paid your home off years ago. Your home would be considered "Gross Worth", which is not tabulated for retirement income purposes.

A special point to ponder: It makes no difference how much you have in the way of material possessions (e.g., 10 houses, 4 BMWs, 50,000 acres of land, etc.) or how much money you have stuffed away in a Swiss bank account, or how much your retirement plan has accumulated over the years; it makes no difference if you're a doctor, lawyer, sport athlete, movie star, or a dog walker, or if you've made millions, struck gold, or won the super duper jumbo lottery, and no matter your age, because – if – at the end of the day you <u>still owe</u> more than you <u>own</u>, you are *in fact* financially penniless and worthless until you reverse this fundamental net worth equation. And if a four-year-old child wakes up in the morning and finds a quarter underneath her pillow from the tooth fairy, that child is in a more secure, stable and solvent financial position than you are.

Note: If you recall Evel Knievel's quote earlier, he implied that even with all the money he made up to that point in his lifetime he was still financially penniless and worthless and it was all simply because he had a negative net worth and still <u>owed</u> more than he <u>owned</u>.

Retirement: How much will you need to retire?

There is no magic formula, but for starters, retirement wealth comes from all accumulated employment, financial, household and personal assets in your "Net Worth" column plus certain entitlements from the federal government such as Social Security benefits and Medicare if you qualify.

Many financial experts claim that retirees need to bring in about 70 to 80 percent of their annual pre-retirement income. Some advisors may also claim there are "Retirement Formulas," such as the "4 percent drawdown rule." Not true! I'm going against the grain of conventional wisdom here but, we all have different needs, wants and desires. You may only initially need 20 or 30 percent of your annual pre-retirement income, or you may only need to drawdown on your retirement funds at a one or two percent pace adjusted for inflation. But, whatever amount you ultimately do need simply comes down to how long you and/or the two of you expect to live (your longevity) and how well you prepared your "Net Worth" column for the lifestyle you expect to enjoy in those retirement years.

A note about longevity: How long do members of your family typically live? The same question needs to be answered by your spouse. Knowing an approximate time frame will greatly influence all of the other decisions you ultimately make about your retirement options. However, keep in mind, people are living far longer today than ever before; so you certainly don't want to come up short in your planning and then have to resort to eating dog food because you're still healthy but broke. In my opinion, living to age 100 should always be the minimum base line for all of your retirement decisions, even if it means leaving unspent retirement dollars to your heirs should the two of you die well before age 100.

To properly calculate what you will need to retire, start with a budget. Creating and utilizing a budget is critical for accurately forecasting monthly and yearly costs associated with *your* specific retirement needs. Monthly expenses on a retirement budget should be somewhat lower than when you were working (i.e., no more mortgage payments or the cost of raising kids or even saving for retirement) but now more than ever, you must project your income and expenses well into the future.

DEFINITION —
Frugal: 1. Practicing or marked by economy, as in the expenditure of money or the use of material resources. 2. Costing little; inexpensive, thrifty. (The American Heritage College Dictionary)

Create a monthly budget just as you did when you worked, but be *frugal*, you'll want to economize at first to establish your basic needs while considering 30 to 40 years of inflation going forward. Calculate the yearly inflation rate at four percent. Next, you'll need to identify your income sources, how much monthly cash flow those sources will produce, and for how long.

Generally speaking, how much you'll need for retirement has little to do with matching household income received when you or both of you worked. For example, your monthly budget expenses before you retired may have resembled the following budget:

\#	Item	Projected	Week 1	Week 2	Week 3	Bank	Actual
	Budget Month: January—Year: 20XX						
1	House Payment	$1,567					$1,567
2	Car Payment	452					452
3	Groceries	650					650
4	Gas / Oil / Maint.	250					250
5	Electric Bill	109					109
6	Water Bill	67					67
7	Property Taxes	241					241
8	Entertainment	350					350
9	Hair Cut	20					20
10	Mad Money (His)	150					150
11	Mad Money (Hers)	150					150
12	Misc. / Petty Cash	25					25
13	Car Tabs	28					28
14	Auto Insurance	115					115
15	Medical / Dental	50					50
16	Vitamins	20					20
17	DVDs	20					20
18	Cell Phone	124					124
19	Clothing	35					35
20	Christmas	65					65
21	House Phone	65					65
22	Vacations/Trips	50					50
23	Cable TV	56					56
24	Master Card	35					35
25	Visa	26					26
26	Sears Card	10					10
Expenses		**$4,730**					**$4,730**
All Net Income Sources		**6,518**					**6,518**
Difference		**$1,788**					**$1,788**

There are many expenses in this budget that should go away, lessen, or change in some way at the point of retirement, starting with the "House Payment".

\#	Item	Projected	Week 1	Week 2	Week 3	Bank	Actual
1	House Payment	$1,567				Paid Off	$0.00

Your mortgage should be paid off before you retire. If you've purchased a house in, say, your late forties, you still have time to play catch-up.

Case in point — I have a very good friend we'll call Rob, who purchased his very first house when he was 40 years old. He acquired a 30-year mortgage which meant he would make his last scheduled payment at age 70, well beyond his retirement age!

I encouraged him to contact his lender and get the Amortization Schedule for his new loan. I then explained to him how to use that schedule to pay down his loan just by making additional principal payments along with his regular scheduled payments and save tens of thousands of dollars in the process.

Rob used his Amortization Schedule extremely well, so well, in fact, that in just 7 short years he has paid off 20 years of his 30-year mortgage. He is now 47 years old. I mentioned to him "it's as though you purchased your house when you were only 27 years old and had just made regular scheduled payments." He said that he had never really thought of it that way before. He seemed very exhilarated with what he had actually accomplished.

At this point Rob realized that if he had, in fact, paid only 7 years off, on his mortgage up until now, he would have to consider selling the house soon with no hope of ever making all his regular house payments much past age 60.

Now he doesn't have to worry about that and the best part is, if he just makes regular scheduled payments from here on out he will pay off his house by the time he's 57 years old, well ahead of retirement age!

So even if you've purchased a house late in life, remember Rob's example.

Next, some of the other expenses that should be gone before you retire are *all* consumer debt.

For example:

Budget Month: January—Year: 20XX							
#	Item	Projected	Week 1	Week 2	Week 3	Bank	Actual
2	Car Payment	$452				Paid Off	$0.00
24	Master Card	35				Paid Off	0.00
25	Visa	26				Paid Off	0.00
26	Sears Card	10				Paid Off	0.00
Expenses		**$523**					**0.00**

You should have no remaining debt, of any kind!

Note item #8 on the next page, Entertainment. This is a tough one for retirees, simply because retirees have more free time on their hands than working folks. Retirees tend to cook less and eat out more often than when they worked. This can be very costly and should be avoided, or at least minimized, to fit within the monthly budget while considering other cheaper entertainment options.

Budget Month: January—Year: 20XX						
#	Item	Projected	Week 1	Week 2	Week 3	Bank	Actual
8	Entertainment	$350					$200

Now, your new budget may resemble the following, with no more car payments or credit card bills:

Budget Month: January—Year: 20XX							
#	Item	Projected	Week 1	Week 2	Week 3	Bank	Actual
1	Long Term Health Care	$420					$420
2	Car Payment					Paid Off	
3	Groceries	350					350
4	Gas / Oil / Maint.	250					250
5	Electric Bill	109					109
6	Water Bill	47					47
7	Property Taxes	241					241
8	Entertainment	200					200
9	Hair Cut	20					20
10	Mad Money (His)	100					150
11	Mad Money (Hers)	100					150
12	Misc. / Petty Cash	25					25
13	Car Tabs	28					28
14	Auto Insurance	115					115
15	Medical / Dental	50					50
16	Vitamins	20					20
17	Prescriptions	25					25
18	Cell Phone	124					124
19	Clothing	25					25
20	Christmas	65					65
21	House Phone	65					65
22	Vacations/Trips	50					50
23	Cable TV	56					56
24	Master Card					Paid Off	
25	Visa					Paid Off	
26	Sears Card					Paid Off	
Expenses		**$2,485**					**$2,485**
All Net Income Sources		**3,567**					**3,567**
Difference		**$1,082**					**$1,082**

What's important now is to project your monthly expense requirements out 30 to 40 years with a four percent yearly inflation rate in mind. Let's say the budget above, with the $1,082 surplus each month, is yours. According to that budget you're currently paying $2,485 each month in expenses. Let's inflate that expense figure at four percent a year to determine when you'll begin to run a deficit. That is, more money going out each month than is coming in.

47

- Column 1: Represents the number of years you can maintain your current budget on a fixed net income of $3,567 a month, without making any changes to the budget.

- Column 2: Represents a 4 percent inflation rate by which your expenses will grow year after year, without making any changes to the budget.

- Column 3: Represents a diminishing income surplus base resulting in a loss of purchasing power of the total fixed $3,567 net income year after year, without making any changes to the budget.

As you can see below, you will run a deficit at year 11, without making any changes to the budget.

Each Year Retired	4% Budget Increases	Diminishing Income Surplus
62 Years Old	**$2,485.00**	**$1,082.00**
63	2,584.40	982.60
64	2,687.78	879.22
65	2,795.29	771.71
66	2,907.10	659.90
67	3,023.38	543.62
68	3,144.32	422.68
69	3,270.09	296.91
70	3,400.89	166.11
71	3,536.93	30.07
72	**3,678.41**	**Deficit**

Your monthly net income would only sustain your budget for 10 years before something would have to change. Knowing this in advance will afford you time to take some action.

For example, that $1,082 surplus each month adds to $12,984.40 for the first year of your retirement. That money, along with the surplus from the remaining nine years should be invested in an interest-producing portfolio, continued on the next page:

NOTES:

Each Year Retired	Diminishing Income Surplus	Yearly Surplus Savings
62 Years Old	$1,082.00	$12,984.40
63	982.60	11,791.12
64	879.22	10,550.64
65	771.71	9,260.52
66	659.90	7,918.80
67	543.62	6,523.44
68	422.68	5,072.16
69	296.91	3,562.92
70	166.11	1,993.32
71	30.07	360.84
Deficit Year	Total Savings Surplus	$70,018.16

If you invest your yearly surplus savings at 6 percent each and every year, you would save roughly $84,000 by year 11. Those dollars could then purchase, for example, a fixed annuity earning, say, 6 percent, for either 30, 20 or 10 years, producing additional funds which could then be added to your fixed income stream you're already receiving.

DEFINITION —
Annuity: The right to receive fixed periodic payments for a term of years or for life. (West's Business Law (Fourth Edition)
For example:

- A 30-year fixed annuity would produce a gross distribution of $503 a month which could be added to your $3,567 monthly income stream for a total of $4,070 per month. Inflation would catch up to your budget by year 13 or age 77.

- A 20-year fixed annuity would produce a gross distribution of $602 a month which could be added to your $3,567 monthly income stream for a total of $4,169 per month. Inflation would catch up to your budget by year 14 or age 75.

- A 10-year fixed annuity would produce a gross distribution of $932 a month which could be added to your $3,567 monthly income stream for a total of $4,519 per month. Inflation would catch up to your budget by year 16 or age 73.

- You may even want to consider a lifetime income annuity whereby you invest a lump sum of cash to receive a predetermined income for the rest of your life no matter how long you live.

- Annuities to avoid if you need to have a specified amount of cash coming in each month are:

    1. Equity-indexed annuities: Touting a "guaranteed" rate of return based on potentially ever changing index funds.

    2. Variable annuities: Usually come with notoriously high fees and "surrender charges" if you want or need your money back.

If you began your retirement at age 62, depending on the annuity you chose, you would now have some hard choices to make with regards to:

- Monthly Spending—You would be forced to cut spending for:
    - Entertainment (i.e., eating out less and less, fewer trips, shorter vacations and so on).
    - Energy (i.e., Utility costs and gasoline for the car).
    - Christmas, Birthdays and other holiday spending.
    - Groceries, you may be reduced to the basics.

or

- - Retire later at, say, age 65 and return to Work—you or even both of you may have to retire later and return to part-time or seasonal work to bring in more money just to maintain your monthly expenses.

or

- - Both—Cut spending, retire later, and return to work just to account for future inflation, or worse yet, future hyper-inflation!

So, to avoid this predicament, you should be proactive and calculate your retirement needs well in advance of their arrival. If not, one or both of you may run the risk of having to work well into your retirement years. To know how much you will need to *comfortably retire*, you must:

- Know what your basic needs will be, at what cost, and for how long. Almost every retiree's basic needs will be for:
    - Housing: If you own your home, figure in your property tax, insurance and the cost of home association fees, if any. Are you planning to rent or move into a vacation home?
    - Food: Maybe plant a garden to help out with cost? To combat future inflation, purchase items, (in quantity, bulk, or volume) that you'll always need, that have an endless/indefinite shelf life (e.g., toilet paper, soap, and napkins etc.).
    - Utilities (e.g., Phone, Water, Sewer, Garbage, Energy, Cable, Online, etc.).
    - Transportation (i.e., how many vehicles do you really need?) Remember, cars are liabilities that require continual maintenance, insurance and usually decrease in value over time. Also – One or both of you at some point in retirement may no longer want or be able to drive a vehicle for any number of reasons.

A brand new car off the showroom floor generally depreciates about 20 percent the minute you drive off of the lot. Cars generally depreciate by 50 percent in the first three years.

- o Health Care (i.e., Medicare only or with a supplemental health care insurance coverage such as Medigap or disability income insurance.) All long-term health, dental and eye care options should be examined, including *in-home and/or nursing-home care*. Once the best choice is made, fit it into your retirement equation. **Note:** Today's newly retired couples, even with a full array of health coverage, may still need over $200,000, dedicated dollars, just to cover medical costs for the remainder of their lives. **Caution:** Inflation continues each year to hit the health care industry at far greater annual monetary increases than even fossil fuels.

- Know what your secondary needs will be, at what cost, and for how long.

    Almost every retiree's secondary needs will be for:

    - o Entertainment (e.g., eating out, going to the movies, fishing, hiking, parties, barbeques, movie rentals, etc.)
    - o As mentioned above, car maintenance, repairs and licensing
    - o Christmas, Birthdays and Holiday events
    - o Vacations and Trips
    - o Personal care (e.g., Hair Cuts and Beauty Salons, etc.)
    - o Auto, Health, and Life Insurance
    - o Household Maintenance and repairs and periodic replacement of appliances
    - o Clothing and Shoes
    - o Technology gadgets (e.g., Computers, Cell Phones, etc.)
    - o Memberships (e.g., Costco, camp grounds, etc.)
    - o Spending (Mad) Money
    - o Miscellaneous (e.g., Driver's License renewals, auto tabs, etc.)

- Know what kind of lifestyle you hope to enjoy, at what cost, and for how long. Almost every retiree wants to enjoy a lifestyle that will allow them to:

    - o Travel (i.e., around the country or around the world, etc.)

- Buy an R.V. or Boat, etc. Keep in mind, RVs and Boats are liabilities with high annual maintenance, repair, storage, and fuel costs, and these luxury items usually decrease in value rapidly.

- Do volunteer work

- Enjoy hobbies (e.g., Painting, Writing, etc.)

- Maybe even become a philanthropist

Determine the initial and long term costs of all the items mentioned above that you may have an interest in, and of course include your own items not mentioned here. Then pick and choose to keep your monthly costs well below what you expect your monthly net retirement income to be. Remember, you and/or both of you may live 30 to 40 more years from the day you retire. If you expect your money to last that long you must account for a minimum four percent inflation rate over that period of time. For a more comprehensive understanding of all the retirement implications below, consult a financial professional in that area of expertise.

Where will your retirement income sources come from, and how much sustainable income will they produce?

For example, the following is only a small sampling of some of the possibilities:

Entitlements:

- Social Security—will you qualify and if so, at what age will you need to collect?

As of 2012, the average monthly benefit for retirees is $1,232. Important: for those of you born in 1945 or later, qualify for Social security - you may choose to continue working and forgo collecting benefits. Your benefit amount will continue to increase every month until age 70. However, if you were born in 1945 or later and choose to continue working and draw benefits, you may do so at a reduced benefit amount until age 66 plus completing the calendar year in which you tuned 66. As of 2012 you may earn up to $14,640 each year without any reduction in benefits.

For a free booklet on Retirement Benefits, call your local SSI office, or dial 1-800-772-1213 and ask for a free copy of Publication #05-10035.

- Medicare—doesn't produce retirement income but is basic healthcare insurance and you must be 65 years of age to qualify.
  Medicare has four parts:
  1. Hospital Insurance (Part A)
  2. Medical Insurance (Part B)
  3. Medicare Advantage (Part C)
  4. Prescription Drug Coverage (Part D)

For a free booklet on Medicare call your local SSI office, or dial 1-800-772-1213 and ask for a free copy of Publication #05-10043. To learn more about Social Security and Medicare and the publications they offer, visit: *www.socialsecurity.gov* on the internet.

- Medicaid—doesn't produce retirement income either but is basic healthcare insurance for people with low income and limited assets. Medicaid is run by your state's welfare system or human services agencies.

Important: You may qualify for both Medicare and Medicaid, contact your local medical assistance agency, social services or welfare office for details.

Real Property:

- Primary Residence (Gross Worth): Have it paid off if you plan to live in it. Even if you purchased your home late in life there is still time to prepare. If you're not making a mortgage payment, that's more money available for retirement!

- Investment/Rental Property: These items are Assets and usually retain or increase in value over time. **Special note:** Rental property produces rental income that can keep pace with inflation. Each rental property should be in its own separate Limited Liability Company (LLC) to protect all of your other assets from any litigation. You should also have a minimum three million dollar umbrella insurance policy.

Employee-sponsored retirement plans:

- 401(k) Retirement Plan: This is a retirement plan offered to employees of private companies. Your contributions to this plan are typically matched by your employer up to a certain pre-established monetary amount depending on the company you work for. You're subject to a 10 percent penalty if you withdraw money out of your plan before you reach age 59½. You can borrow from your 401(k) plan, but you must pay it back within a certain time period or risk penalty. If you're no longer an employee of the company, you can withdraw and roll your money over into another retirement plan with either the new company you become employed with or into a traditional I.R.A. Check with your company's retirement plan administrator for more details on roll-overs and required minimum distribution/withdrawal, from your plan.

- 403(b) Retirement Plan: This is a retirement plan offered to employees of hospitals and educational institutions. Your contributions to this plan are typically seven percent of your pay up to age 55 and then go to 10 percent. Your employer matches your contributions at a 100 percent match in both age brackets.

Individual Retirement Plans:

- Roth IRAs: Introduced in 1998, these IRAs earn tax free dollars after five years provided you have reached age 59½ before you make any withdraws. Principal contributions to your account can be withdrawn at any time for any reason with no tax or penalty. However, any gains withdrawn prior to maturity are subject to tax and penalties. Bonus: you can even have your own Roth account while enrolled in a retirement plan at work!

- Traditional Individual Retirement Accounts (IRAs). Virtually all the rules that apply to employee-sponsored retirement plans also apply to regular IRAs.

    For complete information about Roth IRAs, visit these sites on the internet:

    - American Association of Retired People:— www.aarp.org/money/work/articles/roth_iras.html

    - Congressional Budget Office:—www.cbo.gov/Online-TaxGuide/Page_2C1.htm

    - Fairmark:—www.fairmark.com/rothira/roth101.htm

    - Investopedia:—www.investopedia.com/terms/r/rothira.asp

Other retirement plans and accounts you may want to explore or investigate are:

- 457 Retirement Plans are available to government .employees.

- Simplified Employee Pensions (SEPs) are available for self-employed individuals.

- Employer Pensions, etc. Fewer and fewer companies offer pensions and many of those that still do are changing the rules. Also, if your company has or is about to file for chapter 7 or 11 bankruptcy, and you qualify for a company pension, you may be out of luck.

DEFINITIONS —
Bankruptcy: A legal procedure designed to protect an individual or business that cannot meet its financial obligations and protects the creditors involved. (The American Heritage College Dictionary)

Privately held Stocks, Bonds, Mutual Funds, etc.:

These items can be extremely volatile. The general rule of thumb is "the higher the return (interest earned) the greater the risk."

You may need to spend down, or liquidate assets to raise additional income as you both grow older:

If your home is paid off at retirement and you find yourself with social security as your only source of income, you may want to consider a —

- Reverse Mortgage: — More and more retirees are turning to reverse mortgages. Here's a simplified explanation on how they work: You can acquire a reverse mortgage loan for up to 80 percent of your home's value. In today's housing bust, that might not be much. But, you're not required to pay the loan back unless you sell your house or die. You have to be 62 years of age or older to qualify and you need no proof of income, and currently requires no proof of ownership of assets nor the need for a credit report, which may change in the future. You should be able to get a loan for around a four percent rate in today's market, but unless reverse mortgages are backed by the federal government, most private lenders have discontinued offering them. When you die, the home is sold and the lender gets paid back first, then the remaining money goes to the estate. Reverse mortgages are not right for everyone, but are attractive to many retirees who lost much of their money in the recent stock market downturn.

Caution: It is unethical, and even a disservice to the elderly, for a lender to cross-sell, as a prerequisite to obtaining a reverse mortgage loan, any other financial products or service contracts they may offer. Your loan should come with absolutely "no strings attached."

Some of the downsides to reverse mortgages are:

1. Heavy upfront origination fees, high insurance costs, and ongoing servicing charges.
2. There is no escrow account held in your name to pay property taxes and house insurance; those items become your responsibility. In the event your property-tax bill and/or house insurance premium becomes delinquent or goes into default, for what-ever reason, the Federal Housing Authority (FHA) will be forced into foreclosure proceedings on your property.
3. These loans are very complex to set up, time consuming, and counseling is required,
4. A reverse mortgage is <u>not</u> a government program or benefit, but is <u>always</u> a mortgage loan that requires repayment by you.
5. And, with few exceptions, you don't actually receive the full loan amount, but rather monthly payments are paid to you by the lender, <u>not for life</u>, but *only* until the loan amount is exhausted over its term period.

Visit: *www.reverse.org.* for more information on this topic.

- Sell your home: — Then down size to a Condominium, Manufactured Home, or you could even consider renting. The money from the sale of your home can be added to your "Net Worth" column for retirement purposes.
- Sell or auction off personal items: — Antiques, Coin/Stamp collections, Gold/Silver, Art, Classic Cars and many other items and collectables that are

valuable assets. These items may have retained their original value or quite likely increased in value over time.

Be sure to consult with a tax specialist on tax reduction strategies; it could save you money.

Do you know about "Saver's Credit"?

Saver's credit (also known as the retirement savings contributions credit) is a relatively new tax break offered by the Internal Revenue Service (IRS) to help low- and moderate-income workers save for retirement. If you're single, married filing jointly, head of household, or married filing separately you may qualify for this benefit. It's a tax credit to you on your income tax and may be matched by the federal government with *free money to you* up to $500 if single, and $1,000 if married. This is not a tax write off, but rather a tax credit!

The saver's credit enables workers, who qualify, to:

- Offset part of the first $1,000 if single, or $2,000 if married that was voluntarily contributed, by you, to most workplace retirement plans.
    - Increase your tax refund or maybe reduce the taxes owed, depending on the impact of other deductions and credits already applied.
    - Supplement other tax benefits available to you for retirement.

To qualify, you only need to be contributing money to an Individual Retirement Account (excluding Roth IRA's) or a workplace retirement plan such as a 401(k) plan, and be within certain income limits before the year taxes are filed. Other rules include:

- You must be 18 years old or older.
- You can't be claimed as a dependent on someone else's tax return.
- You can't be a full-time student for more than five months for the year you're filing a return.

The IRS form used for the saver's credit is <u>8880</u>. Read the instructions carefully. Contact your income tax preparer or go to: IRS.gov for assistance.

Now that you have prepared for a successful and comfortable retirement, prepare your estate planning with a living trust and will. Protect your legacy for your heirs! For additional information on trusts, visit: www.estateplanninglinks.com.

A Money Sense Quote: Put not your trust in money, but put your money in trust. - Oliver Wendell Holmes, The Autocrat of the breakfast-Table, 1857

Side Bar — Did your 401(k) Plan really lose money in the recent Stock Market crash?

Most 401(k) Retirement Plan accounts were hit hard in this recent economic downturn; many accounts were down as much as 50 percent. However, that big drop in your 401(k) plan may not be as bad as one might think. Let's assume you did make contributions to your company retirement plan, and your company matched dollar for dollar part or all of your contributions, and the account itself earned interest over time. Go through your records and add up your personal contributions. Let's say it comes to $45,000 to date. Now add up your company's match, and let's say that figure comes to $12,000 to date. The total of the two contributions is $57,000. Now let's say your account was worth $100,000 when the bottom dropped out of the market in 2009 and you lost 40 percent of your money over the last six months. Your 401(k) plan is now worth only $60,000. Well—just maybe—you haven't really lost any of the original contributions because you're still ahead by $3,000. You still retain all of your principal investment and the company's match, plus some interest, though it may not be much.

You would have to lose 55 percent or more of your money before you got into your own principal. Notice I said "or more", that's because you and your employer continued to add dollars to your account long after the market took a nose dive, thereby purchasing stocks and other funds at bargain-basement prices. This is known as "dollar-cost-averaging" (when you make your same monthly contribution to your 401(k)), you are able to purchase more shares when prices are low, while purchasing fewer when prices are high.) So don't panic and pull money out or discontinue contributions to your company plan. You may only hurt yourself if you do. This is true for 403 (b) plans too!

A Money Sense Quote: There is a very easy way to return from a casino with a small fortune: go there with a large one. - Jack Yelton

Red Flag — A mathematical consideration to be aware of if you're invested in the Stock Market

Before I begin I would like to relay two true accounts that have stayed with me for years.

The first account begins with a story I heard on the news about 15 years ago concerning the average American lifespan. I turned on the news one day and the news anchor was reporting a story about a recent medical study that had just been completed. The study concluded, according the reporter, that even though more Americans are exercising more often and eating a much healthier diet, the American lifespan has only increased, on average, by a few minutes. That was pretty much the entire story—aired on a well-respected news program.

The problem with the story was that it was apparently misunderstood by the news anchor and therefore misleading to the news audience. Anyone who watched the story probably thought to themselves, "If exercising regularly and eating healthy is only going to add a few minutes to my life, I may as well not concern myself with exercise at all, and eat whatever I want."

This was a reporter talking about numbers, but not understanding what those numbers were really saying. Fifteen years ago, our population was approaching 300 million people. If the American diet and exercise habits had been maintained at the same status quo as previous generations except for one person who chose to exercise more and eat healthy and as a result lived 10 years longer, how much time would that add to the average life span of 300 million people? The time probably couldn't be measured. That would still be true for ten, a hundred, or even a thousand people that began to develop a healthier life style. In fact, it would probably take tens of thousands of people living a healthier lifestyle before it could be measured with any accuracy. And, if it has truly increased by minutes, that probably meant that hundreds of thousands of people, or more, were living much longer than mere minutes, but in fact, may be living many years longer as a result of that healthier life style.

The second account happened about eleven years ago. I began listening to a well-known radio call-in talk show, whose host was quite peeved about the end result of two felony cases that had recently concluded in his state.

Case number one involved a woman who was taking her sick baby to the hospital when along the way she stopped at a beauty salon to have her hair done. When she was finished and about to leave, she noticed that her baby was not responding to her or anyone else. As it turned out, her baby had died, on the spot, from malnutrition. She was found guilty in a court of law for neglect and sentenced to five years in prison.

Case number two involved a man who killed a dog with a hatchet and was found guilty in a court of law for animal cruelty and also sentenced to five years in prison.

The host of the radio show was upset because he felt that the court system in the state in which he lived cared only as much about the dead baby as it did about a dead dog. He encouraged his listeners to call in to see if they could convince him otherwise. He wanted to know how in the world a woman could get only five years in prison for killing her baby while at the same time a man received the identical sentence for killing a dog.

Many listeners called in to the show to support his position. Few listeners called in with any argument to the contrary, but the few who did either didn't know how to state their opposition to his condemnation of the state's court system or understood correctly the math involved to convince the host he was incorrect in his judgment.

I had to think about it myself for a while. I thought and thought about it some more and then it hit me: the solution was to reverse his argument, or his math, by changing the criminal action in each case! Suppose, for a minute, that the man had killed the baby with the hatchet and the woman starved her dog to death. Would they each still receive the same sentence? Not at all! The man would have been, most likely, sentenced to a minimum of life in prison and the woman may have likely served less than a year in jail for neglecting her dog; and that's only if anyone found out that her dog had died from starvation in the first place.

Professional people, especially the media, can be tricked by numbers and math just like anyone else, but it's when those same professionals throw numbers and math around with little thought of their consequences that it confuses the rest of us. We think they're supposed to know the facts, and then clarify what the big picture is for us. However, if they inadvertently misstate the facts because they don't understand the math, we're the ones who get led down the wrong trail.

I used these two actual accounts to demonstrate the subtleties of mathematical calculations.

For example, let's pretend you purchased some stock two days ago, before the market closed, at a total cost of one dollar, then yesterday the bottom fell out of the market and your stock lost 50 percent of its value. Your stock would now be worth 50 cents. Now let's say the market rebounded and went back up by 50 percent today. Your stock would only be worth 75 cents. Here it is by the numbers: ($1.00 - 50% = .50¢). (.50 ¢ + 50% = .75¢).

Now let's suppose you purchased the same stock two days ago, before the market closed, at a total cost of one dollar. And, that stock was worth 100 points when you purchased it. Then yesterday the bottom fell out of the market and your stock lost 50 points. Your stock would now be worth 50 cents. The market rebounded and your stock goes back up by 50 points today. Your stock is again, back to 100 points, and it's now worth one dollar again. Here it is by the numbers: (100 pts. - 50 pts. = $1.00 - .50¢ = .50¢). A (50 pt. gain = 100 pts.) or (.50¢ + .50¢ = $1.00).

It's important to understand that many stocks in 2009 declined in value by about 50 percent from their all-time highs. So if this happened to you and your stock lost 50 percent of its value one day, and gained back 50 percent of its value the very next day, your shares of stock would have still been down by 25 percent. For example: Let's use the Dow Jones industrial average to make the point.

Day one, the Dow Jones equals 14,000 points.

Day two the Dow Jones loses 50 percent and now equals 7,000 points.

Day three the Dow Jones rebounds by 50 percent and climbs back to 10,500 points. The Dow Jones would still be down by 3,500 points (25 percent) from where it was on day one.

If you invest in the stock market, be aware of the mathematical difference between the rise and fall of points vs. the rise and fall in terms of percentages. The media often interchanges both terms as though they were equal. Either the media takes it for granted that the public, or investors, know what they mean without elaborating, or the media themselves are inadvertently using incorrect terms to explain the obvious. So make sure you listen carefully when you're relying on the numbers the so-called professionals are throwing around. - Just mathematical real world and financial 'food for thought'.

A Money Sense Quote: October: This is one of the peculiarly dangerous months to speculate in the stock market. The others are July, January, September, April, November, May, March, June, December, August and February. - Mark Twain, Puddn'head Wilson's Calendar for 1894

NOTES:

SECTION I IN REVIEW:

Section I began with identifying the five basic fundamental "Money Sense Plans" for organizing your personal finances:

- Plan 1 — was a discussion about the importance of creating, utilizing, and then maintaining a budget. Remember, if you fail to budget, you unwittingly budget to fail.

- Plan 2 — was a discussion about the value of paying off all consumer debt. Payments to ongoing debts are the building blocks to a mountain of debt. And, if you keep a balance, you'll soon lose your balance, fall down and hurt your wallet.

- Plan 3 — was a discussion about creating and maintaining an emergency fund. You must have quick easy access to money that can sustain you and your family for up to six months combined or 12 months single wage earner income in the event of job loss, medical emergencies, or maybe even unexpected opportunities.

- Plan 4 — was a discussion about paying down and then paying off your mortgage as soon as reasonably possible. That's so you and your family will have your own little piece of the planet in the event the economy collapses and possibly goes to hell in a hand basket.

- Plan 5 — was a discussion about how much money you and/or the both of you might need for retirement. The retirement options were based on projected longevity, net worth, existing retirement accounts, entitlements, health care, housing options, and much more, but should not be considered the final word on this ever-changing landscape. Chance and circumstances have the final say.

You should now have the know-how to be financially successful. Section II will provide you with the tools and strategy to help achieve that success.

SECTION II

Amortization Schedule Programs
Introduction to Section II

You will learn in this section how:

- Amortization Schedules offer a means for quantitative analysis and evaluation of interest paid on all outstanding loans and consumer debt.

- Utilizing Amortization Schedules provides all the strategic capabilities to pay off personal debt, auto, RV, boat loans, short/medium, or long-term loans; consolidation/equity and other mortgage loans, and even your credit card debt.

- To utilize Amortization Schedules before you borrow to create hypothetical loans for "What if" strategies and scenarios.

- Utilizing Amortization Schedules can cut tremendously *into the profits* commercial banks, mortgage brokers, credit unions, finance companies and thrift institutions *make on you*.

- Using these programs can potentially save you tens, hundreds, thousands, even hundreds of thousands of dollars in savings.

- Amortization Schedule programs provide good, sound, money management techniques that could even lead you to financial independence.

Read all the questions contained in this section, their detailed analysis, and the surprising answers to each. This section will teach you how to develop options, alternatives, and strategies using Amortization Schedules to explore pay-off tactics for loans and credit card debt, either real or hypothetical, to help you to pay down and eliminate all other debt, become financially secure, owe nothing, and own everything you have outright!

Let's keep the American "Middle Class" economically viable. Without us, our nation will no longer be what our forefathers had intended it to be: creative, ingenious, innovative, inventive, resourceful, tenacious, etc. Without the Middle Class, our good standing in the world, what's left of it, will wither away, and with it, our future as a free nation.

GENERAL NOTES

The following General Notes apply to all of the questions answered in Section II.

- ❖ Redundancy is written into many of the answers throughout this section for a more complete and thorough understanding of the awesome power created by utilizing Amortization Schedules as a personal financial tool.

- ❖ Countless references will be made about generating Amortization Schedules. This means to open the schedule that you crated on your computer monitor - using your own loan data/figures - for a visual observation and evaluation. You can print the page of the schedule that contains the pertinent information you require, or print the entire document itself for record keeping purposes.

- ❖ No matter how many full additional principal payments are made in advance on *any* loan, **regular** scheduled payments must be paid *in full* by the due date. Missing *any* **regularly** scheduled payments (on a mortgage loan in particular), could result in foreclosure! Again, a **regularly** scheduled payment *must* be made every month, and on time, no matter what!

- ❖ Every full *additional* principal payment paid out on *any* line of your Amortization Schedule over and above a regularly scheduled payment represents one *additional* month paid in full.

- ❖ Beware of any Prepayment Penalties or Rules that may apply to your mortgage loan. If any exist on your loan you could be charged a fee if you pay off your loan before it is due.

- ❖ Amortization Schedules only concern themselves with principal and interest paid on a loan. Private Mortgage Insurance, Property Taxes, House Insurance, etc. are all separate money issues and will not have a relationship with any schedules contained in this book.

- ❖ A lender, loan servicer, or creditor does not make a profit, or in fact, any money <u>at all</u> on any full *additional* principal payments applied to any loan. Lenders and creditors *only* make money when you pay interest on regular scheduled payments!

Read on and good luck!

QUESTION 1 - WHAT EXACTLY IS AN AMORTIZATION SCHEDULE?

DEFINITION —
The term "Amortization" or to "Amortize": Is used to describe the method used by lenders to equalize monthly payments over the life of a loan
The American Heritage College Dictionary

The "Amortization Schedule" breaks an entire loan down into all of its essential components (e.g., Month Number, Payment Due Date, Beginning Balance, Scheduled Payment, Principal, Interest, and Ending Balance). Let me explain this in greater detail.

Amortization Schedule computer programs have built-in formulas, require no mathematical expertise, and are very easy to use. Just fill in the blanks and hit "Enter". The computer does the rest. Computer generated Amortization Schedule programs have the user enter the following information.

Enter Loan Data Values

Loan Amount	Type Amount here, EX:	$100
Annual Interest Rate	Type Percent here, EX:	6.3%
Loan Period (generally in years)	Type in Months/Years, EX:	36
Start Date	Type Start/Due Date, EX:	1/1/XX

After filling in the blanks and hitting the "Enter" key, a breakdown of the entire loan is generated and will appear on your monitor. Don't let the seemingly endless rows, columns, and pages intimidate you. This book will help you understand very clearly and in great detail what all those rows and columns are telling you.

Make sure the loan calculator you choose has all the capabilities to produce an entire detailed spreadsheet of the loan you wish to observe or print out after the loan information has been entered. Some Loan Calculators located on many real estate websites will only provide the user with a monthly payment amount and possibly the total interest to be paid. The Amortization Schedule programs that you want to use for loan and payment strategies should show up on screen in their entirety and provide the following information:

Rows and Columns should appear for every:

Month Number	Payment Due Date	Beginning Balance	Scheduled Payment	Principal	Interest	Ending Balance
1	X/X/XX	$000.000	$000.000	$000.000	$000.000	$000.000

1. Month Number—the Month Number begins with 1 and ends with the last Month Number which equals the "Term" of the loan. After learning how to use

Amortization Schedules you will be able to significantly shorten your "Term" without refinancing, and save a lot of money in the process!

Month Number						
1						

2. **Payment Due Date**—is the date each and every scheduled payment is due *regardless* of extra principal payments made.

	Payment Due Date					
	X/X/XX					

3. **Beginning Balance**—is the new balance owed after the last scheduled payment has been made.

		Beginning Balance				
		$000.000				

4. **Scheduled Payment**—is the required monthly payment amount that will remain the same over the life of a loan. Only the proportion of principal to interest will change with each payment. That is, the principal portion will grow larger and larger with every scheduled payment and the interest portion will diminish proportionately with each scheduled payment. But the *total payment* will always remain constant. Any *additional* money included with a scheduled payment that is applied to principal should be clearly indicated as such on the return coupon or statement when you make your monthly payment.

It is important to note here again that *no matter how much extra* money is applied to the principal loan balance, the *entire* scheduled payment is always due in full and on time.

			Scheduled Payment			
			$000.000			

5. **Principal**—is the amount of money in each scheduled payment applied to a loan amount. This is money that goes directly into a home's equity by virtue of reducing the total amount owed on the loan. It *must* be paid back to the lender. If your investment is an asset, such as real estate, all money applied to principal should be recovered no matter *when or how much is paid in*, when that asset is sold. If, on the other hand, the loan is for a liability such as a car… you should

recover a *portion* of your principal investment when it is sold. The trick is to pay the principal down faster than the value of the liability drops. That's where Amortization Schedules really come in handy.

				Principal		
				$000.000		

6. Interest—is the amount of money paid in each scheduled payment that is lost forever! This money keeps lenders in business. You can avoid paying out a substantial amount of interest! For example, most of the interest is paid in the early part of any loan and is a very large portion of the scheduled payment. On a 30-year mortgage loan *a lender will make far more in interest from you than you will have paid in principal for the house.*

				Interest	
				$000.000	

7. Ending Balance—is the remaining amount of money owed on a loan after the last scheduled payment has been made.

					Ending Balance
					$000.000

Row and Column headings and other features found on web sites or on computer programs may differ somewhat from the Amortization Schedules used for this publication. But the basic concepts and strategies used for our purposes here will apply to them all.

Below is an example of an entire Amortization Schedule for a short 1-year bank loan as it might appear on a computer screen.

1 YEAR TERM

Loan Amount	$100.00
Annual Interest Rate	10%
Scheduled Monthly Payment	$8.79
Term/Period	1 Year
Total Interest Paid	$5.50

Now examine the entire Amortization Schedule on the next page to see how it all breaks down.

1 YEAR AMORTIZATION SCHEDULE FOR A $100 LOAN AT A 10% INTEREST RATE

Month Number	Payment Due Date	Beginning Balance	Scheduled Payment	Principal	Interest	Ending Balance
1	1/1/20XX	$100.00	$8.79	$7.96	$0.83	$92.04
2	2/1	92.04	8.79	8.02	0.77	84.02
3	3/1	84.02	8.79	8.09	0.70	75.93
4	4/1	75.93	8.79	8.16	0.63	67.77
5	5/1	67.77	8.79	8.23	0.56	59.54
6	6/1	59.54	8.79	8.30	0.50	51.24
7	7/1	51.24	8.79	8.36	0.43	42.88
8	8/1	42.88	8.79	8.43	0.36	34.45
9	9/1	34.45	8.79	8.50	0.29	25.94
10	10/1	25.94	8.79	8.58	0.22	17.37
11	11/1	17.37	8.79	8.65	0.14	8.72
12	12/1	8.72	8.79	8.72	0.07	00.0

Quick Review

An "Amortization Schedule" breaks an entire loan down into all of its essential components, as follows:

1. Month Number
2. Payment Due Date
3. Beginning Balance
4. Scheduled Payment
5. Principal
6. Interest
7. Ending Balance

Amortization Schedule computer programs have built-in formulas, require no mathematical expertise, and are very easy to use.

Footnote: See Side Bar, in Section II, at the end of Question 5 for some available Web sites, and Question 4 in Section II for more information about "Term."

A Money sense Quote: If all the economists were laid put end to end, they would point in all directions. - Arthur H. Motley

Side Bar — How are Amortization Schedules different from pre-printed Amortization Tables and Loan Payment Guides?

Amortization Tables, Loan Payment Guides, Comprehensive Mortgage Payment Tables, Proration Calendars, Monthly Payment Loan Progress Charts, etc. that have been pre-printed and found in books are very useful if only general information is needed. Tables, guides, calendars, and charts are primarily used only as a quick reference source and are not intended to provide specific month to month details that may be precise enough for your individual loan strategies either before and/or after you've signed or intend to sign a loan agreement. However, Amortization Schedules that can be generated from computer software or web sites, free of charge, can provide detailed specifics for your individual loan needs, either real or hypothetical. Read the remaining 13 questions for more details on this point.

A Money sense Quote: *How quickly nature falls into revolt*   *When gold becomes her object!*   *For this the foolish over-careful fathers*   *Have broke their sleep with thoughts, their brains with care,*   *Their bones with industry.*   *- William Shakespeare*

🚩 RED FLAG — "PAYDAY" LOANS, A CYCLE OF DEBT TRAP.

DEFINITION —
Collateral: Property of a debtor in which the secured party has a security interest, as security in case of non-payment by the debtor.- (West's Business Law (Fourth Edition))

When I was young and in the military service, I really struggled with 30-day pay periods. I didn't know anything about using budgets at the time and therefore couldn't seem to make my money last for an entire month, even though I didn't pay for food or shelter. I remember buying a watch shortly after one pay day and pawning it, as collateral, before the month was up because I needed money so desperately. There were many times I hocked that old watch at the end of the month, only to buy it back from the pawn shop at the beginning of the next month, again and again. I'll bet that $50 watch (back in the mid-60s) cost me over $150 before I separated from the service.

Young people from every generation struggle with "how to make money last" between paydays when first starting out on their own in life. Aside from not budgeting, at all, young folks fail to anticipate all of their monthly needs accurately. However, they do an excellent job of anticipating the things they want.

Well, one doesn't need to be in the service to struggle with making money last through the appropriate pay periods, nor does one need a pawn shop to come to the rescue in time of monetary need. Payday loan stores are here!

Remember the discussion earlier about Congress passing the credit cardholders "Bill of Rights Act?" They had a chance then to incorporate payday loan stores into that bill as well but failed to do so. So we still have this monkey on our backs and only the protection of each individual state to protect our rights.

What is a payday loan store?

They're sort of like a pawn shop inasmuch as they provide short-term money, with a "high-grade octane" interest rate cost, secured by your post-dated check, analogous to the pawn shop holding my watch as collateral. There are now twice as many Payday loan stores in America as there are Starbucks coffee shops.

Facts:

There are no federal regulations in place to protect you from payday loan stores. Only states that allow payday loans to operate within their borders regulate these stores to varying degrees.

Payday lenders charge a fee for their services, but that fee is actually a synonym or decoy word for interest.

Payday loan stores are not allowed to do business at all in Washington D.C. or 15 U.S. states.

In most states, you cannot refinance, renew, or extend your current payday loan with a new loan from that same payday lender.

Some payday lenders operate on the internet and off shore only. You will have no protection at all if you choose do business with them.

There is a 36 percent annual percentage rate cap to military personnel for any payday loan, and as a result many payday lenders no longer do business with the armed forces. And it is illegal for military personnel to do business with lenders who charge above a certain fee for their services.

Here's how payday store loans basically operate:

With your valid I.D. and proof of employment, you would write the payday lender a check, as collateral, for the amount of money (on the posted chart mounted on a wall in their store) you want to borrow, including the fee. They then typically pay you in cash or issue you a debit card that enables you the ability to make electronic withdrawals for the borrowed amount; however, if they pay you by check, they cannot charge you a fee to cash their own check. The loan period (term) usually runs between two weeks up to 45 days. The store then deposits your post-dated check for the appropriate term of the loan contract or you can claim your check with the proper cash balance, at which time the loan is satisfied.

Now let's say you borrowed $100 for two weeks and the fee for that amount is $15. On the surface that seems pretty reasonable, and it is, if that's how it plays out, and it's the only time you do it. But what often happens is that at the end of two weeks you will likely need to borrow another $100 to keep going. Now think about this: you still only have their $100, but because you now borrowed it twice it will cost you $30 ($15 for the first two weeks and $15 for two more weeks) and it has only been four weeks since you started the cycle. If you were to continue this cycle of behavior for a year you would pay $360 in fees alone which amounts to 449.927 percent in total annualized interest for the lender. That's 24 times their fee for the $100 cash loan you began with. It's your repeat, long-term borrowing habits on short-term loans they're counting on. Once they have you coming back over and over again, a payday lender can, in one year, make 450 percent interest on your assorted and multiple borrowing transactions.

Here is the same $100 loan amortized out over a one year period:

LOAN DATA

Loan Amount	$100.00
Absolute Interest Rate Paid	449.927%
Scheduled Monthly Payment	$38.33
Term/Period	1 Year
Total Interest Paid	$360.00

1-YEAR AMORTIZATION SCHEDULE

Month Number	Payment Due Date	Beginning Balance	Scheduled Payment	Principal	Interest	Ending Balance
1	1/1/20XX	$100.00	$38.33	$0.84	$37.49	$99.16
2	2/1	99.16	38.33	1.15	37.18	98.01
3	3/1	98.01	38.33	1.59	36.75	96.42
4	4/1	96.42	38.33	2.18	36.15	94.24
5	5/1	94.24	38.33	3.00	35.33	91.23
6	6/1	91.23	38.33	4.13	34.21	87.11
7	7/1	87.11	38.33	5.67	32.66	81.43
8	8/1	81.43	38.33	7.80	30.53	73.63
9	9/1	73.63	38.33	10.73	27.61	62.91
10	10/1	62.91	38.33	14.75	23.59	48.16
11	11/1	48.16	38.33	20.28	18.06	99.16
12	12/1	27.88	38.33	27.88	10.45	0.00

Another negative might be when, and if, your check(s) begin to bounce for insufficient funds or you're charged a fee for an overdraft on the debit card you were issued. Either of these simple mistakes would create additional expenditures in the form of heavy fees and penalties charged to you. At least when I pawned my watch, if I were not able to buy it back the following pay period, I would only be out the watch and the money I put into it up to that point, but the long-term borrow and buy-back cycle would be over. Learn to make your money last by creating and then utilizing a budget, and always avoid payday loan stores and the endless cycle of debt they could potentially create.

All states that allow payday loan stores to operate within their borders do so with enacted laws that govern their actions and protect your rights, to varying degrees. Contact your state's Attorney General's office for more information on payday lender/stores with regards to your rights and their responsibilities.

A Money Sense Quote: If you make money your god, it will plague you like the devil. - Henry Fielding

QUESTION 2 - WHY SHOULD I USE AMORTIZATION SCHEDULES?

Amortization Schedule computer programs are one of the best personal financial tools ever created for quantitative analysis of personal debt. No matter if you're overwhelmed by debt or just want to be smart with your personal finances, schedules are easy to use and understand. Use them wisely, and you'll be able to pay off *all of your debt* and stay relatively debt free leading into your retirement years.

Look at it this way: you (and your spouse) are only going to earn so much money in a lifetime of work. You will lose many of those hard earned dollars to taxes, and most people do everything they can to legally minimize their tax burden.

You'll remember the old saying? "There are only two things certain in life: death and taxes." Well, interest on debt should be added to that certainty. What can you do to minimize it? You can generate and utilize Amortization Schedules on loans (of any type) to plan strategies that will allow you to avoid paying so much interest!

For example, Luke and Maria just purchased a condominium. They acquired a $150,000 loan at 7.0 percent interest over 30 years. The total amount they will pay for their condo over those 30 years is exactly $359,263.35. See below.

Original Loan Amount	$150,000.00
Accrued Interest Paid	$209,263.35
360 Payments Made	$359,263.35

Luke and Maria asked for an Amortization Schedule for their loan from their lender, and they examined it thoroughly.

The very first thing they noticed is that the schedule is front-loaded with interest. That is to say, most of the interest on their house payments will be paid in the earliest years.

Take Notes:

- They would pay more than half the interest on this loan ($104,631.67) in the first 11 years.

- It would take them until Month Number 243 (20 years) before the principal portion of their house payment would finally be greater than their interest portion.

- It would take them almost 22 years to pay off half the balance on this loan.

- They would pay 139.51 percent in absolute interest on this 7.0 percent loan over the 30-year term period.

- If they sold the $150,000.00 condo in 30 years they would have to sell it for $359,263.35 to break even.

Luke and Maria put their Amortization Schedule to work, and in doing so, will avoid paying large amounts of money in interest. Note their steps by examining the brief Amortization Schedule, which begins in the month of September. Examine their schedule summary below.

Here is the first 6 months of Luke and Maria's schedule.

Month Number	Payment Due Date	Beginning Balance	Scheduled Payment	Principal	Interest	Ending Balance
1	9/1/20XX	$150,000.00	$997.95	$122.95	$875.00	$149,877.05
2	10/1	149,877.05	997.95	123.67	874.28	149,753.38
3	11/1	149,753.38	997.95	124.39	873.56	149,628.98
4	12/1	149,628.98	997.95	125.12	872.84	149,503.87
5	1/1/20XX	149,503.87	997.95	125.85	871.37	149,378.02
6	2/1	149,378.02	997.95	126.58	870.63	149,251.44

Step 1. Luke and Maria begin at Month Number 1 and dissect the entire row. See below:

Their first scheduled payment will consist of $122.95 under the Principal Column. This amount goes towards the payoff of their loan and is subtracted from the Beginning Balance.

Month Number	Due Date	Beginning Balance	Scheduled Payment	Principal	Interest	Ending Balance
1	9/1/20XX	$150,000.00	$997.95	$122.95	$875.00	$149,877.05

Now examine below in the Interest column. The interest amount is $875.00. This is pure absolute interest paid to the lender. Luke and Maria will never recover this money.

Month Number	Due Date	Beginning Balance	Scheduled Payment	Principal	Interest	Ending Balance
1	9/1/20XX	$150,000.00	$997.95	$122.95	$875.00	$149,877.05

Note in the next set the total sum of the Principal and Interest column is equal to $997.95 under the Scheduled Payment column. This amount will remain constant throughout the life of their loan. Only the principal and interest will change.

Month Number	Due Date	Beginning Balance	Scheduled Payment	Principal	Interest	Ending Balance
1	9/1/20XX	$150,000.00	$997.95	$122.95	$875.00	$149,877.05

After the scheduled payment has been made, they look to the Ending Balance column and note the 150 thousand dollar loan amount has only been reduced by $122.95 to $149,877.05. See Below.

Month Number	Due Date	Beginning Balance	Scheduled Payment	Principal	Interest	Ending Balance
1	9/1/20XX	150,000.00	997.95	122.95	875.00	$149,877.05

Step 2. Now Luke and Maria take the first step towards reducing the amount of pure absolute interest they will pay over the life of the loan. They drop to month number 2, which would ordinarily be the next payment due date, and include (with their first $997.95 payment) the $123.67 under the Principal column in row 2. See Below.

Month Number	Due Date	Beginning Balance	Scheduled Payment	Principal	Interest	Ending Balance
2	10/1/20XX	149,877.05	997.95	$123.67	874.28	149,753.38

That $123.67 will be added along with their $997.95 from Month Number 1 for a grand total of $1,121.62. They will indicate on their payment coupon that the additional money sent is to be applied as an extra principal payment.

Because Luke and Maria included the principal portion from Month Number 2 with their first payment (Month Number 1) they will *not* have to pay $874.28 absolute interest for payment number 2. See below.

Month Number	Due Date	Beginning Balance	Scheduled Payment	Principal	Interest	Ending Balance
2	10/1/20XX	149,877.05	997.95	123.68	874.28	149,753.38

Quick Review

- Luke and Maria's scheduled payment amount equals $997.95.
- Their additional principal paid from Month Number 2 equals $123.67.
- The total amount paid in their first payment equals $1,121.62.
- The total absolute interest saved from Month Number 2 equals $874.28.

Step 3. Next month Luke and Maria will repeat steps 1 and 2 for Month Numbers 3 and 4 and again for Month Numbers 5 and 6 and so on for as long as they can make full additional principal payments.

Step 4. They will check off and date, on their Amortization Schedule, each Scheduled Payment made in black for record keeping.

For example, Month Number 1 would be checked off in black and dated.

Month Number	Due Date	Beginning Balance	Scheduled Payment	Principal	Interest	Ending Balance
1	9/1/20XX	$150,000.00	$997.95	$122.95	$875.00	$149,877.05

Step 5. They will check off and Date, on their Amortization Schedule, each Principal Payment made in red or light color for record keeping.

For example, Month Number 2 would be checked off in red and dated.

Month Number	Due Date	Beginning Balance	Scheduled Payment	Principal	Interest	Ending Balance
1	9/1/20XX	$150,000.00	$997.95	$122.95	$875.00	$149,877.05
2	10/1/20XX	149,877.05	997.95	123.67	874.28	149,753.38

Step 6. Luke and Maria add up the interest saved as additional principal payments are made.

- Luke and Maria make their scheduled payment of $997.95 for Month Number 1 and their Principal payment of $123.67 for Month Number 2: Their total interest saved in Month Number 2 equals $874.28.

Month Number	Due Date	Beginning Balance	Scheduled. Payment	Principal	Interest	Ending Balance
1	9/1/20XX	$150,000.00	$997.95	$122.95	$875.00	$149,877.05
2	10/1/XX	149,877.05	997.95	123.67	874.28	149,753.38

- For their second payment, Luke and Maria make their scheduled payment of $997.95 for Month Number 3 and their Principal payment of $125.12 for Month

Number 4: Their total interest saved in Month Number 2 and 4 equals $1,747.12.

Month Number	Payment Due Date	Beginning Balance	Scheduled Payment	Principal	Interest	Ending Balance
1	9/1/20XX	$150,000.00	$997.95	$122.95	$875.00	$149,877.05
2	10/1	149,877.05	997.95	123.67	874.28	149,753.38
3	11/1	149,753.38	997.95	124.39	873.56	149,628.98
4	12/1	149,628.98	997.95	125.12	872.84	149,503.38

- For their third payment, they make their scheduled payment of $997.95 for Month Number 5 and their Principal payment of $126.58 for Month Number 6: Their total interest saved in Month Number 2, 4, and 6 equals $2,617.75.

Month Number	Payment Due Date	Beginning Balance	Scheduled Payment	Principal	Interest	Ending Balance
1	9/1/20XX	$150,000.00	$997.95	$122.95	$875.00	149,877.05
2	10/1	149,877.05	997.95	123.67	874.28	149,753.38
3	11/1	149,753.38	997.95	124.39	873.56	149,628.98
4	12/1	149,628.98	997.95	125.12	872.84	149,503.87
5	1/1/20XX	149,503.87	997.95	125.85	871.37	149,378.02
6	2/1	149,378.02	997.95	126.58	870.63	149,251.44

By paying Month Numbers 1, 3 and 5 as scheduled payments and Month Numbers 2, 4, and 6 as additional principal payments they discovered the Term was reduced by 6 months in the first 3 months. Again, each *additional* principal payment reduces the "Term" by one full month on top of the scheduled payment. Put another way, each time an additional principal payment is made it's as though the *entire* payment was made for that month.

Any money a borrower pays to principal will go directly into their investment/equity. It's like they're paying themselves. As long as their home hasn't depreciated in value they will recover every penny. Of course this depends on when the home is sold and the state of the local economy and real estate market at the time of sale.

Again, if Luke and Maria make every scheduled payment on time and in full over 30 years without making any additional principal payments they will pay 139.51 percent absolute Interest on their 7 percent loan.

Exercise: Examine Luke and Maria's entire Amortization Schedule in Section III.

A Money Sense Quote: Money will buy you a pretty good dog, but it won't buy the wag of his tail. - Henry Wheeler Shaw

Side Bar — Can my Loan Officer or Lender provide me with an Amortization Schedule for my Mortgage Loan?

Yes! If a borrower is not able to generate their own Amortization Schedule for a mortgage loan, for whatever reason, the lender can provide them with a schedule for their loan. Some lenders may charge a small fee for this service, but it is well worth the money.

Also, computer programs to run Amortization Schedules for mortgage loans (as well as most other types of loans) may be found on the following web sites:

http://realestate.yahoo.com/calculators/amortization.html

http://www.myamortization.com/

http://www.hsh.com/calc-amort.html

www.dinkytown.net

> *A Money Sense Quote: This Planet has or rather had a problem, which was this: most of the people living on it were unhappy for pretty much of the time. Many solutions were suggested for this problem, but most of these were largely concerned with the movement of small green pieces of paper, which is odd because on the whole it wasn't the small green pieces of paper that were unhappy. - Douglas Adams*

QUESTION 3 - WHAT CAN AN AMORTIZATION SCHEDULE TELL ME ABOUT MY LOAN THAT I DON'T ALREADY KNOW?

Plenty! Like most people--what you *do* know about your loan is probably very little. You may know:

- how much you borrowed, and
- what the payment is, and
- how long the term is that you'll have to make payments, and
- maybe the interest rate—but that's probably it, nothing more.

What an Amortization Schedule will tell you is:

- How much of each monthly payment applies to the principal amount of your loan.
- How much applies to interest in that same payment.
- At what point half the interest will be paid on your loan.
- At what point half the balance is paid, and much more!

Schedules simply provide valuable insight into your loan(s) that you won't get any other way.

Let's examine a hypothetical loan for $10,000 at 8.5 percent over a 3-year period in the Amortization Schedule below.

Amortization Schedule

Loan Data

Loan Amount	$10,000.00
Interest Rate	8.5%
Scheduled Monthly Payment	$315.68
Term / Loan Period	36 Months
Total Interest Paid	$1,364.31

Note below the entire 36 month schedule.

36-Month Amortization Schedule

Month Number	Payment Due Date	Beginning Balance	Scheduled Payment	Principal	Interest	Ending Balance
1	1/1/20XX	$10,000.00	$315.68	$244.84	$70.83	$9,755.16
2	2/1	9,755.16	$315.68	246.58	69.10	9,508.58
3	3/1	9,508.58	$315.68	248.32	67.35	9,260.26
4	4/1	9,260.26	$315.68	250.08	65.59	9,010.18
5	5/1	9,010.18	$315.68	251.85	63.82	8,758.32
6	6/1	8,758.32	$315.68	253.64	62.04	8,504.69
7	7/1	8,504.69	$315.68	255.43	60.24	8,249.25
8	8/1	8,249.25	$315.68	257.24	58.43	7,992.01
9	9/1	7,992.01	$315.68	259.07	56.61	7,732.94
10	10/1	7,732.94	$315.68	260.90	54.78	7,472.94
11	11/1	7,472.94	$315.68	262.75	52.93	7,209.30
12	12/1	7,209.30	$315.68	264.61	51.07	6,944.69
13	1/1/20XX	6,944.69	$315.68	266.48	49.19	6,678.20
14	2/1	6,678.20	$315.68	268.37	47.30	6,409.83
15	3/1	6,409.83	$315.68	270.27	45.40	6,139.37
16	4/1	6,139.37	$315.68	272.19	43.49	5,867.37
17	5/1	5,867.37	$315.68	274.11	41.56	5,593.26
18	6/1	5,593.26	$315.68	276.06	39.62	5,317.20
19	7/1	5,317.20	$315.68	278.01	37.66	5,039.19
20	8/1	5,039.19	$315.68	279.98	35.69	4,759.21
21	9/1	4,759.21	$315.68	281.96	33.71	4,477.24
22	10/1	4,477.24	$315.68	283.96	31.71	4,193.28
23	11/1	4,193.28	$315.68	285.97	29.70	3,907.31
24	12/1	3,907.31	$315.68	288.00	27.68	3,619.31

Month Number	Payment Due Date	Beginning Balance	Scheduled Payment	Principal	Interest	Ending Balance
25	1/1/20XX	3,619.31	$315.68	290.04	25.64	3,329.27
26	2/1	3,329.27	$315.68	292.09	23.58	3,037.18
27	3/1	3,037.18	$315.68	294.18	21.51	2,743.02
28	4/1	2,743.02	$315.68	296.25	19.43	2,446.77
29	5/1	2,446.77	$315.68	298.34	17.33	2,148.43
30	6/1	2,148.43	$315.68	300.46	15.22	1,847.97
31	7/1	1,847.97	$315.68	302.59	13.09	1,545.38
32	8/1	1,545.38	$315.68	304.73	10.95	1,240.65
33	9/1	1,240.65	$315.68	306.69	8.79	933.77
34	10/1	933.77	$315.68	309.06	6.61	624.71
35	11/1	624.71	$315.68	311.25	4.42	313.46
36	12/1	313.46	$315.68	313.46	2.22	0.00

There are some key elements in this schedule you would not know without it.

Let's say this is your loan and you make your first (month number 1) scheduled payment on 1/1/20XX.

Here is Month Number 1 from the Amortization Schedule above.

Month Number	Payment Due Date	Beginning Balance	Scheduled Payment	Principal	Interest	Ending Balance
1	1/1/20XX	$10,000.00	$315.68	$244.84	$70.83	$9,755.16

We can learn the following about the scheduled payment for Month Number 1:

- Your payment is $315.68 (the same as the remaining 35 payments).
- Out of that first $315.68 payment, you will pay $70.83 in interest.
- Only $244.84 will go towards paying off the actual loan.

Using your Amortization Schedule above once more, let's separate out and examine Month Number 11.

Here is Month Number 11 almost 1 year later.

Month Number	Payment Due Date	Beginning Balance	Scheduled Payment	Principal	Interest	Ending Balance
11	11/1/20XX	$7,472.04	$315.68	$262.75	$52.93	$7,209.30

Note the following:

- If you add up the interest as payments are made, notice by Month Number 11 you'll have paid $681.72 in interest, which is half the $1,364.31 total interest to be paid.

- The remaining $682.59 or remaining half of the interest will be paid over the next 25 months.

As with most loans the interest you pay is front-loaded. In this case half the interest was paid in slightly less than 1 year on your 3 year loan.

Using an Amortization Schedule clearly allows you to see when *half* of the $10,000 balance will be paid off. Without a schedule you might assume that this loan would be half paid by month 18, the halfway point. Your schedule shows this will occur around Month Number 20.

It will take 20 months to pay off half the original loan amount.

Month Number	Payment Due Date	Beginning Balance	Scheduled Payment	Principal	Interest	Ending Balance
20	11/1/20XX	$5,039.19	$315.68	$279.98	$35.69	$4,759.21

So, without an actual Amortization Schedule you would have only basic knowledge about your loan. With it you have all the necessary information needed to pay off your loan in the most efficient and cost effective way possible.

If you made every payment, for this loan, on time and for the full term you would pay 11.36 percent absolute interest on your 8.5 percent loan.

A Money Sense Quote: Intaxication: Euphoria at getting a refund from the IRS, which lasts until you realize it was your money to start with. - From a Washington Post word contest

Side Bar — Do Amortization Schedules work with Adjustable Rate Mortgage (ARM) Loans?

Yes! They work much the same way for ARMs as they work for Conventional Mortgage Loans with one exception, the interest rate on an ARM is periodically adjusted up or down depending on what specific financial index a particular ARM loan is tied to, such as a 1-year, 3-year, 5-year Adjustable Rate Mortgage loan and so on. The interest rate on ARMs tend to increase over time but usually do have a cap or limit that controls how much the interest rate can eventually increase over a period of time and/or the life of the loan.

> *A Money Sense Quote:* To suppose as we all suppose, that we could be rich and not behave as the rich behave, is like supposing that we could drink all day and stay sober. - Logan Pearsall Smith

 RED FLAG — ARMS AND PAYMENT CAPS.

Some ARMs may come with a payment cap rather than an interest rate cap. If this is the case with your ARM, you may be ultimately adding unpaid interest to your loan balance, causing the principal owed to increase rather than decrease every month. If your ARM has a payment cap, not an interest rate cap, it would be difficult to generate an Amortization Schedule to continuously reflect the unpaid interest added to your loan balance each time this occurs.

ARMs are attractive and ultimately chosen by many mortgage borrowers because of their (initially) low interest rates offered relative to any conventional mortgage rates usually offered at the time of choosing. The artificially low teaser rates often start several percentage points lower than a conventional mortgage loan but over time can exceed the conventional mortgage rate offered at the time you may have elected to take out an ARM loan. And worse, the interest rate paid on an ARM may easily exceed the current conventional mortgage rates by several percentage points forcing you to consider converting to a conventional mortgage loan. It's generally at this point that a mortgage borrower with an ARM may discover they might be paying a much higher rate of interest for their loan than their conventional loan counterpart, thus creating potentially expensive refinancing what-if options.

For example, let's say that 3 years ago you elected to take out a 3-year ARM loan for 30 years (the low rate stays fixed for 3 years, after which the rate becomes adjustable) at a 4.0 percent interest rate when the best you could get on a conventional mortgage loan at the time was a 6.5 percent interest rate. And, let's say, at that time you generated your own 30-year loan Amortization Schedule for that loan. And in those 3 years you did use your schedule to pay 1 additional principal payment with each of your scheduled payments. As a result, you reduced your loan "Term" by 6 years, and avoided paying the interest on those extra principal payments. Now it's 3 years later and you received, in the mail, your 60-day notice from your lender that your interest rate is going to increase to 6 percent. Using your schedule to pay down your principal, you avoided paying the interest for 3 years on the additional principal payments, and have given yourself some unique planning options.

Option 1. You can stay with the existing loan and generate a new 27-year Amortization Schedule that reflects the current balance of the loan at the new 6 percent annual interest rate. In doing so, you'll continue making payments, but at your new higher scheduled payment amount. You may also decide at this point, to continue making additional principal payments with every scheduled payment thereby avoiding paying even more interest in the process. Note: Your lender will also make a new 27-year Amortization Schedule reflecting the new interest rate. The potential problems with this option might be:

Even though you have paid 1 additional principal payment with every scheduled payment and reduced your "Term" by 6 years on the old schedule, the new interest rate (higher or lower) requires that a new schedule be generated to reflect the new rate. That is precisely what your lender has done! Since you have made only 3 years' worth of coupon or statement payments, regardless of any extra or additional principal payments made, your lender only counts 3 years paid—period! So, your new Amortization Schedule must start at the new lower loan balance and new higher interest rate over a new 27-year period. This is the only substantial difference between an ARM and a conventional mortgage loan. Every time you significantly reduce the "Term" on your existing ARM schedule, at some point down the road the rate will change and the real "Term" is really only reduced by the actual scheduled payments made to that point. Whereas with a conventional mortgage loan nothing changes over time, but the loan balance itself. So, all additional principal payments that accompany your scheduled payment do actually reduce the "Term" each time they're paid.

Option 2. Depending on what the new interest rate is on your existing ARM, you may want to consider refinancing your loan to a 24-year term conventional mortgage loan at the current available interest rates if they're lower than your current ARM rate. With a 24-year loan you won't lose the 6 years you have already reduced the "Term" by on your old ARM schedule. The new loan might be for a substantially lower amount of money because of the extra principal payments you already applied to the original loan. You may even want to generate your own 24-year hypothetical conventional mortgage loan at the estimated new loan balance with closing costs included to better evaluate this option. The potential problems with this option might be:

Another round of closing costs, which could offset all of those extra principal payments you made on your ARM loan.

It may take 4 to 6 weeks before you can close on the loan, which may require 1 to 2 more scheduled payments be made on your existing ARM loan. The interest paid on those payments is lost forever!

If your new scheduled payment is in fact lower, it may still take several years to recoup the closing costs.

Option 3. Again depending on what the new interest rate on your ARM is, you may want to consider refinancing a new 30-year conventional mortgage loan at the current available interest rates. If the interest rate is lower than your current ARM rate, the new loan might be for a substantially lower dollar amount because of the extra principal payments applied to the original loan. You may even want to generate your own 30-year hypothetical conventional mortgage loan at the estimated new loan balance plus closing costs to better evaluate this option. The potential problems with this option might be:

All of the same problems that exist with option 2 plus you're also giving up the 6 years already paid off on your ARM loan, which could mean every scheduled and additional principal payment you made for the last 3 years could be lost forever.

Quick Review:

The only real difference between an ARM loan and a Conventional Mortgage Loan is:

- The Interest Rate on an Adjustable Rate Mortgage Loan changes over time.

- It's not easy to reduce the Term on an ARM beyond the normal rate of scheduled payments because when the interest rate changes the lender's Amortization Schedule will only reflect the scheduled payments already made.

- And, in the final analysis you could have put your Amortization Schedule to work right in the beginning of your ARM loan by paying as many extra principal payments as possible before your interest rate changed to give yourself even more options at the rate change point.

Generate hypothetical schedules to compare and study all of your options.

Amortization Schedules do work for Adjustable Rate Mortgage Loans!

NOTES:

A Money Sense Quote: That money talks I'll not deny, I heard it once: It said, "Goodbye."
- Richard Armour

QUESTION 4 - HOW WILL THE "TERM" ON A LOAN AFFECT MY PAYMENT?

DEFINITION —
Term: A fixed period of time. (The American Heritage College Dictionary)

The "Term" is the period of time that is legally agreed on by all parties to repay a loan. It not only determines the amount of each payment, but also how much total interest will be paid on a particular loan during that Term. In fact, the Term that is assigned in a loan contract will have as much bearing, if not more, on the total interest paid as the "Interest Rate" itself. Luckily, I found this out before it was too late.

When I was in my 20s, and even early 30s, I thought that if I borrowed … uh, $3,000, at say, a 10 percent interest rate, regardless of the Term, I would *repay* the original $3,000 I borrowed plus another $300 (10 percent) in interest. I just assumed the Term *only* determined the amount of my monthly payment and nothing more (i.e., the longer my Term the lower my monthly payment.) That is partly true, a longer Term would lower my payment, but the true absolute percentage paid on my loan would depend as much on the Term as it would the interest rate itself. So, I generated five Amortization Schedules, all at different Terms on this same $3,000 loan and discovered some surprising facts.

Let's examine the following table. Of the five schedules generated note the actual total absolute percentage I would pay *over and above* my original $3,000 loan scenario of 10 percent. (Again, *only the Term is different*).

Here are five different Terms on a $3,000 Loan at 10%.

Loan Term	Monthly Payment	Total Interest Paid	Real Interest Percentage Paid	Total Amount Paid Back
12 Months	$263.75	$164.97	5.5%	$3,164.97
24 Months	$138.43	$322.42	10.75%	$3,322.42
36 Months	$96.80	$484.86	16.16%	$3,484.86
48 Months	$76.09	$652.21	21.74%	$3,652.21
30 Years	$26.33	$6,477.77	215.93%	$9,478.80

As you can see, the Term affects the total amount paid back regardless of the 10 percent fixed Interest Rate.

The 12 month term in my scenario is a great deal. My true percentage pay back is 5.5 percent. I would only pay $164.97 above the three thousand dollars I borrowed.

Even the 24 month term puts me at just under 11 percent for the 10 percent loan.

As I extend the loan beyond 24 months, the 10 percent interest rate loan becomes less of a great deal. However, the monthly payment does come down as the term lengthens.

Let's re-examine the Term in a slightly different light. I'll take my $3,000 loan and *maintain it at a constant Term*, say, for a 3-year term only, but I will try using variable interest rates. Notice what happens to my payment and actual percentage paid over and above my $3,000 loan. Examine below this table showing my *3-year Term loan,* but at variable interest rates.

Here is a $3,000 Loan at variable Interest Rates for a 3-Year Term.

Variable Rates	Monthly Payment	Total Interest Paid	Real Interest Percentage Paid	Total Amount Paid Back
3.0%	$87.24	$140.77	4.69%	$3,140.77
5.0%	$89.91	$236.86	7.90%	$3,236.86
12.0%	$99.64	$587.15	19.57%	$3,587.15
19.0%	$109.97	$958.97	31.97%	$3,958.97
21.0%	$113.03	$1,068.91	35.63%	$4,068.91

As you can see, whether my loan is at a 10 percent interest rate (as in the first table) or for a single Term, but at variable interest rates (as in the last table), the actual percentage paid is determined as much by the Term as by the various interest rates.

This is why a used-car salesperson may ask, "How much do you want to pay each month"? They will control not just the interest rate you ultimately get, but the term, as well, to get that payment you want.

Sales people don't always care how much money a borrower will actually pay in interest. Their primary concern is to get them in that car "TODAY" and receive their commission! Don't be fooled into thinking that the "Interest Rate" alone will determine the total dollars you will ultimately pay in interest.

Generate your own hypothetical Amortization Schedules at various "Terms" before you borrow money. In doing this you can determine your own term and payment before you make a loan agreement.

NOTES:

Quick Review

The "Term" on a loan will affect your payment as much, if not more, than the interest rate will.

- Don't focus on interest rates alone when considering a loan. The "Interest Rate" does not determine *by itself* the total dollars paid back on a loan.

- The "Term" *also* has a tremendous influence on the total amount of interest paid on a loan.

- Always generate your own hypothetical Amortization Schedules at various "Terms" before you borrow money from a lender.

Examine more: How the "Term" on a loan affects the total interest you'll pay, in Section III, page?

A Money Sense Quote: The real measure of your wealth is how much you would be worth if you lost all your money. - Author Unknown

Side Bar — "Rule of thumb"—An 11.63 percent interest rate roughly equals a one percent monthly payment, Principal and Interest (P&I), on a 30 year fixed rate mortgage.
Here's how it works:

If you borrow say, $3,500, $35,000, or $350,000 at 11.63 percent interest rate on a 30 year fixed rate loan, your monthly payment (P&I together) will equal one percent (1%) of the loan amount every month until the loan is satisfied. For example:

$3,500 would equal a P&I payment of $35.01 every month for 30 years.

$35,000 would equal a P&I payment of $350.08 every month for 30 years.

$350,000 would equal a P&I payment of $3,500.78 every month for 30 years.

This payment is principal and interest only and does not include property tax, home insurance, PMI (private mortgage insurance) or anything else that might be paid with the payment.

This "rule of Thumb" doesn't care what you paid for the property or how much you put down on the property, but rather, only the actual money that was borrowed for the loan.

This "rule of Thumb" also doesn't mean that if your payment is always equal to one percent of the loan amount that the loan is satisfied after only 100 payments.

This "rule of Thumb" is only meant to assist anyone who might be in the market for a 30 year fixed mortgage loan and needs as a quick way to calculate a monthly payment when considering a particular loan amount(s) at varying interest rates for 30 years.

If you borrow, $3,500, $35,000, or $350,000 at 4.39 percent interest rate on a 30 year fixed rate loan, your monthly payment (P&I together) will equal one half percent (0.5%) of the loan amount every month until the loan is satisfied. For example:

$3,500 would equal a P&I of $17.51 every month for 30 years.

$35,000 would equal a P&I payment of $175.06 every month for 30 years.

$350,000 would equal a P&I payment of $1,750.60 every month for 30 years.

The 11.63 and the 4.39 percent interest rates at a 30-year fixed rate will always remain as a constant 1% and 0.5% monthly payment respectively regardless of the amount of the loan.

These parameters can always be used as a rough calculation tool to assist you in determining how much a new 30-year fixed rate loan will cost you every month. So don't worry so much about what you have to pay for a property, but rather what you borrow.

 RED **F**LAG – "B**RING US YOUR AUTO LOAN AND GET** $100!"

Recently my wife and I purchased a new car. We paid zero down at 1.9 percent interest and got a 36 month term. Our payment is about $793 a month and the total interest to be paid back over the life of the loan is only $835 (this is very low).

We just received an unsolicited offer in the mail, <u>in our name</u>; from a lender who "wants our car loan" so bad that they will give us $100 to get it. They say our new payment will be as low as $351 per month, and we can save $445 each and every month. We have even been prequalified for this new loan.

If we accepted their offer our payment would be about $351 per month as promised, but the loan would have to be extended from 36 to 84 months for that dollar value to work. We would also have a new 4.24 percent interest rate up from the current 1.9 percent interest rate we now enjoy. The new longer term and higher interest rate loan would cost us more than $4,000 interest over the entire loan period, and we would wipe out the five months of payments and interest already paid.

On the surface these offers can be very enticing, especially when lower payments and free cash incentives are made.   Even in our case their $100 offer would need to be more like $4,000 free cash for us to even consider jumping ship with our current lender.

This offer would obviously be a win for the new lender. However, many offers can be much less obvious than my example and may require running an Amortization Schedule program to better examine any and all unsolicited offers made to you.

Caution: An unsolicited preapproved/prequalified offer made to you, even if the lender is legitimate and credible, is almost always a better deal for the lender than it is for you; otherwise they wouldn't make the offer in the first place.

A Money Sense Quote: Inflation hasn't ruined everything. A dime can still be used as a screwdriver. - Quoted in P.S. I Love You, compiled by H. Jackson Brown

QUESTION 5 - CAN AN AMORTIZATION SCHEDULE HELP ME CONVERT MY 30-YEAR MORTGAGE INTO A 15-YEAR MORTGAGE WITHOUT REFINANCING?

You Bet! An Amortization Schedule generated for your mortgage loan can be used to help you determine whatever Term (length) you choose. You can easily choose a 25, 20, 15, 10, 5-year Term or anything between. There's no re-financing involved and no need to contact your lender. In fact, I recommend a 30-year mortgage loan over anything shorter. Here's why: remember the earlier question about how the Term of a loan determines, to a great degree, what the scheduled payment will be? We found that the longer the Term on a loan, the lower the scheduled payment will be! So, if you choose a <u>shorter</u> loan period because the interest rate is lower or you just want to pay the loan off faster, you could put yourself in a precarious financial position with higher monthly payments.

If you have a short-term loan and you're suddenly faced with a financial hardship such as a layoff, medical emergency, or there is some other major unexpected financial disruption in the interim, you will have *no choice* but to make that higher scheduled house payment. On the other hand, if you have a longer, 30-year term loan, your scheduled house payments will be lower and more manageable if something does go wrong for *any* reason.

So let's say you choose a more conservative 30-year mortgage loan to keep your house payments lower. You can still *shorten* your Term without re-financing or contacting your lender. Here's what you can do with your existing 30-year mortgage loan while your finances are in good shape:

To turn that 30-year mortgage loan into a 15-year mortgage refer to your Amortization Schedule and:

- Make 1 additional principal payment along with every scheduled payment you make.
- If you're able to maintain that pace until the last regular payment is made on your schedule you will have paid your mortgage off in 15 years.
- You will have saved thousands of dollars in interest you will <u>never</u> have to pay.

- If you step it up and make 2 additional payments with each scheduled payment, and maintain that pace, you will pay the mortgage off in 10 years and save even more interest!

In fact, you can design limitless pay off strategies. That's especially true in the beginning of a 30-year loan when the principal portion of each regular payment is low and the interest portion is high.

For example, let's say Dan just acquired a $215,000 mortgage loan at 8.5 percent interest rate over a 30-year period. The first year of his Amortization Schedule would resemble the schedule on the next page.

DAN'S LOAN DATA

Loan Amount	$215,000.00
Interest Rate	8.5%
Scheduled Monthly Payment	$1,653.16
Term/ Loan Period	30 Years
Total Interest Paid	$380,139.04

THE FIRST YEAR OF DAN'S AMORTIZATION SCHEDULE

Month Number	Payment Due Date	Beginning Balance	Scheduled Payment	Principal	Interest	Ending Balance
1	1/1/XX	$215,000.00	$1,653.16	$130.25	$1,522.92	$214,869.75
2	2/1	214,869.75	1,653.16	131.17	1,521.99	214,738.58
3	3/1	214,738.58	1,653.16	132.10	1,521.06	214,606.48
4	4/1	214,606.48	1,653.16	133.03	1,520.13	214,473.45
5	5/1	214,473.45	1,653.16	133.98	1,519.19	214,204.55
6	6/1	214,204.55	1,653.16	134.93	1,518.24	214,068.66
7	7/1	214,068.66	1,653.16	135.88	1,517.28	213,931.01
8	8/1	213,931.01	1,653.16	136.84	1,516.32	213,655.22
9	9/1	213,655.22	1,653.16	137.81	1,515.35	213,515.44
10	10/1	213,515.44	1,653.16	138.79	1,514.37	213,374.68
11	11/1	213,374.68	1,653.16	139.77	1,513.39	213,232.92
12	12/1	213,232.92	1,653.16	140.76	1,512.39	213,090.16

Notice how *little* principal is actually applied to the ending balance and how *much* interest is paid each time Dan makes a single scheduled payment. The lender will make most of their money (in the form of interest) up front on his loan. If Dan makes 2, 3, 4 or more principal payments in the beginning of his loan, while they are small, he will stand to reduce his term at a much faster pace than at the end of his schedule. For each principal payment he makes in the beginning of the loan, the greater will be the amount of interest he saves. Let's make Dan's first scheduled payment:

DAN'S FIRST SCHEDULED PAYMENT

Month Number	Payment Due Date	Beginning Balance	Scheduled Payment	Principal	Interest	Ending Balance
~~1~~	~~1/1/XX~~	~~$215,000.00~~	~~$1,653.16~~	~~$130.25~~	~~$1,522.92~~	~~$241,869.75~~

Now, because the principal payments are so low, Dan makes four additional principal payments along with the first scheduled payment.

DAN PAYS THE ADDITIONAL PRINCIPAL PAYMENTS FOR MONTH NUMBERS 2-5

Month Number	Payment Due Date	Beginning Balance	Scheduled Payment	Principal	Interest	Ending Balance
1	1/1/XX	$215,000.00	$1,653.16	$130.25	$1,522.92	$241,869.75
2	2/1/XX	241,869.75	1,653.16	131.17	1,521.99	214,738.58
3	3/1/XX	214,738.58	1,653.16	132.10	1,521.07	214,606.48
4	4/1/XX	214,606.48	1,653.16	133.03	1.520.13	214.473.45
5	5/1/XX	214.473.45	1,653.16	133.98	1,519.19	214,204.55
			Totals	$530.28	$6,082.38	

Here is what he accomplished with that payment strategy:

- Dan pays, for months numbered 2 through 5, an additional $530.28 in principal along with his first scheduled payment of $1,653.16, for month number 1, for a total payment of $2,885.34.
- In Month Number 1, Dan paid in interest alone $1,522.92 with his first scheduled payment.
- But, because he made 4 additional principal payments (for month numbers 2, 3, 4, and 5) along with his scheduled payment, he reduced the 360 month Term of his loan by 5 months rather than 1.
- And, Dan saved *$6,082.38* in absolute interest he will <u>never ever</u> have to pay.

NOW LET'S EXAMINE THE LAST YEAR OF DAN'S AMORTIZATION SCHEDULE.

Month Number	Payment Due Date	Beginning Balance	Scheduled Payment	Principal	Interest	Ending Balance
349	9/1/XX	$18,954.00	$1,653.16	$1,518.91	$134.26	$17,435.10
350	10/1	17,435.10	1,653.16	1,529.67	123.50	15,905.43
351	11/1	15,905.43	1,653.16	1,540.50	112.66	14,364.93
352	12/1	14,364.93	1,653.16	1,551.41	101.75	12,813.52
353	1/1	12,813.52	1,653.16	1,562.40	90.76	11,251.12
354	2/1	11,251.12	1,653.16	1,573.47	79.70	9,677.65
355	3/1	9,677.65	1,653.16	1,584.61	68.55	8,093.03
356	4/1	8,093.03	1,653.16	1,595.84	57.33	6,497.20
357	5/1	6,497.20	1,653.16	1,607.14	46.02	4,890.05
358	6/1	4,890.05	1,653.16	1,618.53	34.64	3,271.53
359	7/1	3,271.53	1,653.16	1,629.99	23.17	1,641.54
360	8/1	1,641.54	1,653.16	1,641.54	11.63	0.00

Notice, as Dan nears the end of his mortgage loan, the principal and interest have done a flip-flop. The lender made almost all of its money in interest a long time ago and now Dan is left with virtually nothing but principal to pay. Any extra principal payments made at this point will save him very little interest.

For example, when Dan makes scheduled payment number 349 and sends in the additional principal on month number 350 for $1,529.67 he would in fact reduce his term by 1 additional month, but Dan would only save $123.50 in interest. Imagine how many months his term would have been reduced had he applied that very same payment amount to the principal in the beginning months.

There is no wrong way to use an Amortization Schedule. The important thing to remember is that schedules provide so much valuable information and insight that the payment options and choices available are virtually endless.

Quick Review

Again, to turn that 30-year mortgage loan into a 15-year mortgage, refer to your Amortization Schedule and:

- Make 1 additional principal payment along with every scheduled payment you make.
- If you're able to maintain that pace until the last regular payment is made on your schedule you will have paid your mortgage off in 15 years.
- You will have saved thousands of dollars in interest you will <u>never</u> have to pay.
- If you step it up and make 2 additional payments with each scheduled payment, and maintain that pace, you will pay the mortgage off in 10 years and save even more interest!

Good luck!

A Money Sense Quote: They who are of the opinion that money will do everything, may very well be suspected to do everything for money. - George Savile, Complete Works, 1912

Side Bar — A confluence of positive events has merged into one, creating tremendous bargains in the housing market right now!

DEFINITION —
Foreclosure: A proceeding in equity whereby a mortgagee either takes title to or forces the sale of the mortgagor's property in satisfaction of the debt. West's Business Law (Fourth Edition)

Right of Redemption: The right to free property from the encumbrances of a foreclosure or judicial sale, or to recover the title passing thereby, by paying what is due, with all costs and interest. Includes both equity and the statutory periods of redemption. (West's Business Law (Fourth Edition))

Now is an incredible time to buy low. There are an abundance of homes and condominiums currently available on the real estate market today, many of which can be acquired via short sale, home auctions, or while still in foreclosure.

Along with a high volume of properties available are diminished prices, still down more than 50 percent in some housing markets. And interest rates are lower than they've been in generations (remember the 18 percent mortgage rates back in the early 80s?) Imagine…, a confluence of positive events has merged into one.

First, there's an ample supply of homes, and

Second, there's virtually no demand for them, and

Third, interest rates are at historic lows.

However, be wary if you decide to cash-in on a foreclosure or short sale. That home you make an offer on may have renters, or unwanted and non-paying occupants, or even a derelict or two living in it. At the same time, the owner may still possess a "right of redemption" in which he/she retains the right for a certain period of time (usually six months in most states) to make up all past-due payments, thereby terminating the foreclosure process. Also, if you're willing to wait out the right of redemption period, many of these homes will have suffered damages by then due to neglect, vandalism, or material theft (e.g., plumbing, wiring, fixtures, appliances, etc.) and may require extra attention be given during the inspection process. Make every effort to find a real estate agent who specializes in foreclosures and homes sold on short sale. Once an offer is made, it could still take up to a year to close.

> *A Money Sense Quote: It is natural that affluence should be followed by influence.* - Augustus William Hare and Julius Charles Hare, Guesses ay truth, by Two Brothers, 1827

QUESTION 6 - SHOULD I USE AMORTIZATION SCHEDULES TO HELP ME DETERMINE THE DOWN PAYMENT I SHOULD MAKE ON A HOUSE?

Yes! Using schedules before committing to a mortgage loan can help any borrower determine the best down payment strategy.

For example, Terry and Elaine have just made an offer on a house. They have enough money to make a 20 percent down payment to avoid paying private mortgage insurance (PMI). But, because they have an excellent credit rating, enjoy good incomes, and have no major debt, they qualify for 100 percent of the financing on the house they want to buy.

This choice presents a bit of a dilemma for them because they want to maximize their down payment dollars in the most efficient way possible. This means exploring two possible scenarios.

- Scenario 1 pays the 20 percent up front and finances the remaining 80 percent needed.
- Scenario 2 has them finance 100 percent of the loan and then apply the 20 percent, set aside for their down payment, along with their first scheduled house payment

Terry and Elaine generate two Amortization Schedules for a more thoroughly detailed evaluation. Schedule 1 is for the 80 percent loan and schedule 2 is for the 100 percent loan. They will need to finance either $100,000 or $80,000 at 6.5 percent interest rate over a 30-year term. Let's examine both schedule summaries (1 and 2).

LOAN DATA SUMMARY 1

20 PERCENT DOWN AND 80 PERCENT FINANCED	
Scheduled Monthly Payment	$505.65
Total Interest to be Paid	$102,035.59
Actual Number of Payments	360
No Private Mortgage Insurance Required	0.00

LOAN DATA SUMMARY 2

0 PERCENT DOWN AND 100 PERCENT FINANCED	
Scheduled Monthly Payment	$632.07
Total Interest to be Paid	$127,544.49
Actual Number of Payments	360
Private Mortgage Insurance Required	Yes! $$$

On the surface it seems as though Terry and Elaine will be much better off with a 20 percent down payment--*until* we examine the 0 down payment Amortization Schedule in more detail. Let's look at the 100 percent financed Schedule summary below.

AMORTIZATION SCHEDULE SUMMARY

Month Number	Payment Due Date	Beginning Balance	Scheduled Payment	Principal	Interest	Ending Balance
1	1/1/20XX	$100,000.00	$632.07	$90.40	$541.67	$99,909.60

If they send in the $20,000 in the form of an additional principal payment with scheduled payment 1, they will:

- Cut their remaining balance to slightly less than $80,000.00.

- Reduce their term by about 146 months with about 214 months remaining. Their second mortgage payment will begin at month number 147, see below.

Month Number	Payment Due Date	Beginning Balance	Scheduled Payment	Principal	Interest	Ending Balance
147	3/1/XX	79,963.74	632.07	198.93	433.14	79,764.81

- Pay just a little more than $72,000 total interest over the remaining loan period.

- Avoid paying approximately $55,000.00 in interest for month numbers 2 through 146.

- Have their PMI canceled because they would have a 20 percent equity stake in the house.

Let's revise the numbers in summary 2 with the supposition that Terry and Elaine decide to borrow 100 percent of the loan and make a $20,000 principal payment along with their first scheduled payment.

LOAN DATA SUMMARY 2 REVISED

0 PERCENT DOWN AND 100 PERCENT FINANCED	
Scheduled Monthly Payment	$632.07
Total Interest to be Paid (Approx.)	$72,000
Number of Payments (Approx.)	214
Private Mortgage Insurance Required	For 1 month maybe?

Needless to say, Terry and Elaine chose to finance 100 percent of the loan and make a $20,000 principal payment along with their first scheduled payment.

A Money Sense Quote: When you let money speak for you, it drowns out anything else you meant to say. - Mignon McLaughlin, The Second Neurotic's Notebook, 1966

 Side Bar — A 30 Year Refrigerator vs. a Two Year Refrigerator.

Almost all newly constructed homes for sale on the market today lack some basic amenities (e.g., refrigerators, window screens, dead bolt locks, window coverings, garage door openers, etc.). If you have these items installed, be careful <u>not</u> to include the cost of them in with the loan amount you intend to borrow as these items can be very costly in the long run unless you pay cash.

For example, Will and Stacey just made an offer on a brand new home. Their offer was accepted by the seller, which, in this case is the builder. They were told the deal would close in about 6 weeks. Will and Stacey were a little concerned about moving into a new house that had no refrigerator. So they asked their agent about having the builder install a refrigerator at his cost. Will and Stacey expect to add the extra cost onto the accepted offer of their mortgage loan. The builder obliged by installing a refrigerator at his cost, which came to $1,050.00.

Will and Stacey did in fact add the extra cost of the refrigerator to the total loan amount. As a result they will ultimately pay $1,339.22 in interest alone for their new refrigerator over the 30-year loan period. See below.

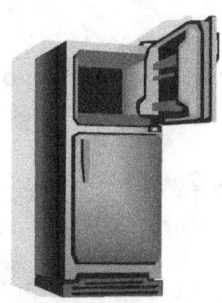

THE 30-YEAR REFRIGERATOR

Builder's Cost	The interest to be paid out over a 30 year period at a 6.5% rate	Absolute interest to be paid over a 30 Year Period	Total cost of the Refrigerator with interest
$1,050.00	$1,339.22	122.78%	$2,389.22

If Will and Stacey had gotten a separate loan for their new refrigerator for, say, a 2-year period, even at the same 6.5 percent interest rate, the total cost would have been substantially lower. See below.

THE 2-YEAR REFRIGERATOR

Acquired Separate Loan Amount for the Builder's Cost	The Interest to be paid over a 2 Year period at a 6.5% Rate	Absolute interest to be paid over a 2 Year Period	Total cost of the Refrigerator with interest
$1,050.00	$72.57	6.91%	$1,122.57

See their 2-year schedule on the next page.

THE ENTIRE 2-YEAR AMORTIZATION SCHEDULE

Month Number	Payment Due Date	Beginning Balance	Scheduled Payment	Principal	Interest	Ending Balance
1	1/1/20XX	$1,050.00	$46.77	$41.09	$5.69	$1,008.91
2	2/1	1,008.91	46.77	41.31	5.46	967.61
3	3/1	967.61	46.77	41.53	5.24	926.07
4	4/1	926.07	46.77	41.76	5.02	884.32
5	5/1	884.32	46.77	41.98	4.79	842.33
6	6/1	842.33	46.77	42.21	4.56	800.12
7	7/1	800.12	46.77	42.44	4.33	757.68
8	8/1	757.68	46.77	42.67	4.10	715.01
9	9/1	715.01	46.77	42.90	3.87	672.11
10	10/1	672.11	46.77	43.13	3.64	628.98
11	11/1	628.98	46.77	43.37	3.41	585.61
12	12/1	585.61	46.77	43.60	3.17	542.01
13	1/1/20XX	542.01	46.77	43.84	2.94	498.17
14	2/1	498.17	46.77	44.08	2.70	454.10
15	3/1	454.10	46.77	44.31	2.46	409.78
16	4/1	409.78	46.77	44.55	2.22	365.23
17	5/1	365.23	46.77	44.80	1.98	320.43
18	6/1	320.43	46.77	45.04	1.74	275.40
19	7/1	275.40	46.77	45.28	1.49	230.11
20	8/1	230.11	46.77	45.53	1.25	184.59
21	9/1	184.59	46.77	45.77	1.00	138.81
22	10/1	138.81	46.77	46.02	0.75	92.79
23	11/1	92.79	46.77	46.27	0.50	46.52
24	12/1	46.52	46.77	46.52	0.25	0.00

Had they taken out a separate 2-year loan, the interest saved would have been $1,216.65, and, they would have paid the refrigerator off in two years rather than 30. Will and Stacey will probably need to replace their new refrigerator in 10 to 15 years. When they do, they will still be paying on the first refrigerator for about 15 to 20 more years.

While there is nothing wrong with a buyer having the additional cost of amenities added to a home's total purchase price, it is very important to get separate short term financing for items of this nature outside the mortgage loan process whenever possible. Remember… refrigerators, window screens, dead bolt locks, window coverings, garage door openers, etc. all add to the total interest paid on a long term (30-year) fixed rate loan.

A Money Sense Quote: Put not your trust in money, but put your money in trust. - Oliver Wendall Holmes, The Autocrat of the Breakfast Club, 1857

 **Red Flag — Service Contracts.**

Definition —
Contract: 1. A set of promises constituting an agreement between parties, giving each a legal duty to the other and also the right to seek legal remedy for breach of the promises/duties owed to each other. The elements of an enforceable contract are competent parties, a proper or legal purpose, consideration (an exchange of promises), and mutuality of agreement and obligation. (West's Business Law (Fourth Edition))

If there's a need for something, there's probably a service available somewhere that will provide for that need. And, with many services comes a contract (e.g., lawn care services, security alarm services, TV broadcast services, etc.) whereupon a set of promises are agreed to between parties. You know why you hired the service to begin with, and as long as they do what they promised, you're happy. However, a problem can arise when a customer wants to end the relationship with the company when the term expires.

Why can a problem arise? Because many service contracts are written in such a manner that the customer is clearly given the impression the service automatically terminates when the contract expires. But in fact, with many of these service companies, the original contract was written to automatically renew (roll-over) giving the customer anywhere from 10 to 30 days to cancel the renewal. Moreover, many service companies require that a letter be written by the customer and then sent by registered mail requesting the cancellation or termination of the service.

Don't be fooled by their trickery. Ask the sales representative, in the initial interview, to go beyond the sales veneer, and show you how the contract terminates, and then make sure you understand it clearly before you sign the contract.

A Money Sense Quote: A rich man is nothing but a poor man with money. - W.C. Fields

Question 7 - Should I use Amortization Schedules if I'm planning to refinance?

After the recent sub-prime mortgage meltdown, the credit market may be rather difficult to access for a loan of any kind, especially for refinancing a mortgage. In order to do so you must:

- Have a good stable and sustainable income source and the ability to document it, <u>and</u> maintain it.

- Have a better than average FICO (credit) score, preferably mid to upper 700s. Note: Obtaining your credit score will cost you, but to check your credit report for <u>free</u>, call 1-877-322-8228, or visit: <u>www.annualcreditreport.com</u> to get started. Get copies of your credit report from all three main agencies at the following websites:

1. Experian - *<u>www.experian.com</u>*

2. Equifax - *<u>www.equilfax.com</u>*

3. Trans Union - *<u>www.tuc.com</u>*

- Have your home Appraised.
- Have 20 percent equity (or more) on the new value of your home, which may be much less than just a short time ago.
- Avoid Private Mortgage Insurance (PMI).
- Check for prepayment penalties that may exist on your current loan.
- Plan to live in the home long enough to make the refinancing economically sensible.

If those things are resolved, then *yes, you should use Amortization Schedules if you're planning to refinance!*

Begin by generating and evaluating the Amortization Schedule for your current loan. Then run several hypothetical loan Amortization Schedules and compare them to your current loan to be sure you're doing the right thing. Run all of the numbers and the "what-if" scenarios. You should be able to see that you can recoup your costs within two years.

Running an Amortization Schedule program will enable you to plan the best strategy for your situation—like refinancing an adjustable-rate mortgage (ARM) or combining two mortgages into one. Use realistic interest rates for which you believe you will qualify. Then adjust the term to control your monthly payments.

Amortization Schedules also provide borrowers with the ability to look at other loan options available beyond refinancing an entire new loan. Again, use hypothetical loan schedules to help choose which loan option is best for you before signing on the dotted line.

You may discover that you're better off with a consolidation loan, second mortgage, or just a simple home equity loan. Try every possibility to find what will work best for your situation.

If you do decide that refinancing is for you, then expect to:

- Find a (Federally or State Regulated) new lender (e.g., Bank, Credit Union, Mortgage Company etc.).

- Commit to the time-consuming process of taking out a new loan to pay off the old one.
- Go through all the same hoops and expenses (Closing Costs and Fees) you went through with the original loan.

Let's examine how Doug and Lisa use refinancing to overcome two original loan packages for their mortgage that did not serve them well over the years.

They purchased a home ten years ago for $195,000. They had no money for a down payment and even added an additional $5,000 to the loan for closing costs. They each had good credit, little debt, and earned average incomes. Their (unregulated) lender approved them for 100 percent financing, including all closing costs. Doug and Lisa would need to obtain PMI to protect the lender, (not them) from default.

Doug and Lisa were advised by a loan officer that they might be better off getting a "piggy-back" loan for a down payment rather than paying for PMI. They agreed and now have two mortgage payments.

Their primary loan, with closing costs, was for $156,000 at 7.14 percent interest rate for 30 years. Their down payment (piggy-back) loan, including fees, was for $44,528.90 at 8.5 percent interest rate, also for 30 years. See the Loan Data below on each separate loan and then note the combined totals.

PRIMARY LOAN

Loan Amount	$156,000.00
Interest Rate	7.14%
Scheduled Monthly Payment	$1,052.58
Term / Loan period	30-years
Total Interest Paid	$222,929.05

PIGGY-BACK LOAN

Loan Amount	$44,528.90
Interest Rate	8.5%
Scheduled Monthly Payment	$342.39
Term / Loan Period	30-years
Total Interest Paid	$78,679.94

COMBINED TOTALS:
- Amount Borrowed—$200,528.90
- Combined Monthly Payments—$1,394.67
- Remaining Combined Balance—$173,758.65
- Years Remaining on each loan—20

Doug and Lisa know that even though their home has lost value in recent years, (about 28 percent due to the mortgage crisis), it will still appraise for about $225,000. This amount will allow them to get a loan for about $180,000 with 20 percent equity still remaining in the house, and no PMI required.

Doug and Lisa get to work designing several hypothetical Amortization Schedules and come up with the one that works best for them.

Doug and Lisa decide to get a 20-year fixed rate loan so they don't lose the time already paid on their first loan. They feel they can get an interest rate between 5.0 and 5.2 percent. They will pay all the closing costs out-of-pocket up front, and finance about $173,758.65. Their new payment will be about $1,146 a month, or roughly $248 a month less than they were paying for the two old loans, and they will recover their out-of-pocket expenses in less than two years.

Doug and Lisa could have gone straight to a lender and been at their mercy, but instead chose to use an Amortization Schedule program to better analyze what was right for them. They can now go to a lender armed with all the basic quantitative information they need to get the best deal in town.

After Doug and Lisa recover their closing costs (in less than two years) they will use the extra money they no longer pay each month along with their Amortization Schedule, to pay-down their mortgage as fast as they can.

Quick Review

Use Amortization Schedules if you're planning to refinance, but first:

- Have a good stable income source and the ability to document it, <u>and</u> maintain it.
- Have a better than average FICO score, preferably mid to upper 700s. Again, obtaining your credit score will cost you, but to check your credit report for <u>free</u>, call 1-877-322-8228, or visit: *www.annualcreditreport.com* to get started.
- Have your home Appraised.
- Have 20 percent equity (or more) on the new value of your home, which may be much less than just a short time ago.
- Avoid Private Mortgage Insurance PMI.
- Check for prepayment penalties that may exist on your current loan.
- Plan to live in the home long enough to make the refinancing economically sensible.

If those things are resolved then *yes, you should use Amortization Schedules if you're planning to refinance!*

Examine: Doug and Lisa's hypothetical Amortization Schedule they used to help them plan a strategy to refinance their house, in Section III.

> *A Money Sense Quote: He is rich or poor according to what he is, not according to what he has. - Henry Ward BeeJudy*

 Side Bar — Appraisals, the rules have changed.

DEFINITION —
Appraisal: An estimate of the value of property determined by a suitably qualified individual who has no interest in the property. (West's Business Law (Fourth Edition))

When a homebuyer chooses a lender, or one has been chosen for them due to circumstances, and in either case has tentatively accepted the lender, that lender will require that an appraisal be completed to properly estimate the true market worth/value of that property. The buyer of the property pays a one-time fee for that appraisal. An independent appraiser, completely unaffiliated with the lender, but in the lender's behalf, then calculates a variety of absolute facts (e.g., square footage, number of bedrooms, bathrooms, garage capacity, on sewers, lot size, location, etc.) about that property. From those facts, and other facts on similar types of properties the appraiser makes comparisons, or "comps" as they're called in the industry, that have recently sold in the same area. The appraiser then forms an expert opinion on the true market worth/value of the property and reports that estimated worth/value to the lender. The buyer then, before the housing market crashed in 2008, paid the one-time fee out of earnest money deposited by them when an offer was made and accepted by the owner of the property.

However, recent rule changes affect how often a buyer pays for appraisal fees. The old rule, before the real estate crash, allowed for the buyer to accept and then reject a lender's offer for a loan countless times while relying on the estimated worth/value of a property with one appraisal, thus paying that one-time fee for the appraisal at closing once an acceptable lender was confirmed by the buyer, again, regardless of the number of lenders accepted and then rejected by the buyer originally. Today the rules are slightly different: the buyer pays a fee for every appraisal each lender accepts. In the event the lender is rejected by the homebuyer (for any reason before closing) that rejection voids the previous appraisal requiring that a new appraisal be completed. To avoid paying hundreds of dollars for appraisals each time you reject a lender, be careful to choose your lender wisely—the first time.

Here's what you want to examine before you accept a final mortgage lender:

You want a lender that can give you the lowest interest rate available that you qualify for, including the annual percentage rate (APR), and—

A lender that offers the fewest points charged to you and paid up front to them to lower the interest rate on the loan. Each point charged to you equals 1 percent of the loan amount. Well-qualified buyers should not have to pay any points to obtain the lowest interest rate, and—

A lender that charges the lowest fees to you that are paid to them up front, and that are over and above "closing costs" normally associated with the settlement that makes the contract final, and—

A lender that will offer you a lock-in period allowing you an opportunity to lock-in a lower interest rate, should the rates drop suddenly during the approval process. Many lenders offer a 30 day lock-in period. Once you've locked-in, the remainder of the loan process begins, and—

A lender that will guarantee a short processing time. How long will it take them to gather the necessary documents to approve your loan application? The processing time should take no more than 10 working days. And last but not least—

A lender that <u>will not charge</u> you a pre-payment penalty for paying additional principal payments towards your loan or paying off your entire loan before it's due. Even if all else is right with the lender you choose, this is one penalty you should never accept from any lender—period!

Note: Mortgage Interest is tax-deductible, and if you have to pay points, they're also tax-deductible (but may need to be amortized over the life of the loan. Only the interest on a, $100,000, or less loan is tax-deductible on rental or vacation homes. Check with a tax professional.)

If you're looking to purchase a home in today's real estate market, determine the right lender (including VA/FHA lenders) first, and then you'll only pay for one appraisal.

🚩 Red Flag — Stock up now on goods you need—to guard against future inflation.

Definition —
Inflation: A persistent increase in the level of consumer prices or a decline in the purchasing power of money, caused by an increase in available currency and credit beyond the proportion of available goods and services. (The American Heritage College Dictionary)

As we approach the coming years there's one thing that's certain: we're all going to face high inflation, maybe even hyper-inflation, at a pace that may rival that of the double-digit inflation rate of the late 1970s. Inflation was so bad back then that the cost of most goods and services was on pace to double in cost to consumers every six years or less. A hamburger, for example, that once cost 30 cent, cost 60 cents in less than six years. A typical house that cost $40,000, cost $80,000 six years later. Now, as our national debt continues to accelerate at an alarming rate and the dollar continues to weaken at home and abroad, high inflation at some point in the near future will certainly strike again.

In order protect yourself from this certainty, to some small degree, you may want to stock up now, at today's prices and low inflation rate on goods you will need in the future that will not deteriorate, dissolve, evaporate, spoil, blow up/explode or become rancid etc., while at the same time, retaining an infinite shelf life.

For example, if you're fortunate enough to have an abundance of storage capacity, you may want to buy, on sale, and in bulk items such as:

Paper products (e.g., toilet paper, napkins, paper towels, and so on.)

"Pure Soap" Bars. Non-soap bath bars may contain perfumes and chemical additives that may degrade or change composition over time.

Light Bulbs, Trash Bags, Razor Blades, Office Supplies, or any item that you know you will need and use, and can store indefinitely.

"Food for thought": let's use toilet paper (TP) as a further example. Let's suppose you buy all of your TP at some giant discount warehouse store for, say, $19 for a 36-count package and you decide to stock up and store. And let's say you've now reached maximum capacity for storage. Now treat the TP like it's locked up in a seven year CD savings account collecting 10 to 12 percent interest until the high inflation rate kicks in. Now, say, five years later we experience double digit inflation once again and TP is doubling in price every six years. By then a 36-count package might be on pace to eventually cost $40, $50, or $60 per trip. I know it's a stretch to think this way, but that strategy can pay great dividends if thought out well enough and then exercised.

P.S. Food items and water are <u>not</u> good candidates for long term storage just to stave off inflation. They must be items that you'll need, use, and will last indefinitely.

A Money Sense Quote: My old father used to say: If you make a bad bargain, hug it all the tighter. - Abraham Lincoln

QUESTION 8 - HOW CAN I USE AN AMORTIZATION SCHEDULE FOR MY CAR LOAN?

Since Amortization Schedules work on almost any kind of loan, they especially come in handy when buying a new or used car. Schedules can help save borrowers thousands of dollars even after signing a loan that wasn't in their best interest.

For example, John is buying his dream car! John, mid-twenties and single, has just found "*that Perfect Car*" at a dealership. Out of nowhere a salesperson appears, "Hi there… my name is Fred, what's your name?" "Hi, I'm John," he replies as they shake hands. Fred says, "We just got this beauty in today and it won't last long; do you want to take it out for a spin?" "Yes!" John replies again. Fred gets the keys and joins John for a little spin 'round town. They're back in 45 minutes and John is hooked on the car but is hesitant to make an offer.

Fred knows John is operating on pure emotion and *will* act on impulse with just the right amount of finesse. Fred says, "I can get you into this car today." John's excited at the prospect of leaving the lot with the car TODAY! He cautiously utters in a timid, barely discernible, sort of quizzical voice, "Maybe, but uh, uh… how much is it?" Fred fires back, "well John, what kind of monthly payment can you afford?" "Oh… I don't know," John says. Fred is maneuvering John into position now. John stalls a little longer but feels *obligated* to quickly convey his sincere desire to purchase the car. After all – he just drove it all over town. So, in desperation he calculates a figure he thinks he can afford and proclaims aloud, "around $400 a month—maybe?" Fred quips, "*If* I can get you into this car for around $400 a month can we make you a deal?" "Sure can!" John says. But first uuuh, uh… what's the asking price again?" Fred says, "I'll go check with my boss. But, keep in mind we wanna get you into *this beauty* TODAY and for under $400 a month!" "That should be our primary focus… wouldn't you like that John – 400 a month?" "Yes sir," John says. Fred mentions, "The dealership is even willing to handle the financing!" John says, "OK I'll take it if you can get me financing." An hour goes by and the paperwork is approved and ready to go. John is eager to sign all the forms and drive off with his new car.

John is taken inside and introduced to the Finance Manager (Bob) to complete the transaction. John, thinking Bob has no vested interest in his purchase, lets his guard down and signs all the forms without thorough examination. He also fails to note which documents he signed and *will never* see again. John didn't quite reach the "under $400 a month" payment he had hoped for but did get the car he wanted, and at a reduced price. And Fred – What a guy! He assisted John every step of the way….

Bob and the dealership had John sign for a $15,000 loan at a 9 percent interest rate for 5 years (60 Months). John's monthly payment will be $405.80, close to what he had asked for. He will pay $9,348.02 in interest which amounts to 62.32 percent total absolute interest on his 9 percent loan.

But it's not too late to help John save hundreds or even thousands of dollars on his bad deal. Let's examine the loan numbers and portions of john's Amortization Schedule below more thoroughly to see what he can do.

Financed Amount	Interest Rate	Scheduled Payment	Loan Period	Interest Paid	Actual % Paid
$15,000.00	9%	$405.80	60 Months	$9,348.02	62.32%

John can begin saving money on his very first payment.

Step 1. He makes the first scheduled payment of $405.80 as required.

Month Number	Payment Due Date	Beginning Balance	Scheduled Payment	Principal	Interest	Month Number
~~1~~	~~1/1/XX~~	~~$15,000.00~~	~~$405.80~~	~~$143.30~~	~~$$262.50~~	~~$14,856.70~~

Step 2. He then looks at Month Number 2 and includes, with his scheduled payment, the $145.81 under the "principal" column.

Month Number	Payment Due Date	Beginning Balance	Scheduled Payment	Principal	Interest	Month Number
2	2/1/XX	14,856.70	405.80	145.81	259.99	14,710.89

That makes for a whopping $551.61 total for his first payment but he will avoid paying $259.99 interest for Month Number 2. He also reduces his term by two months rather than one.

Step 3. John checks off and dates his scheduled payment in black for record keeping.

Step 4. He checks off and dates in red his additional principal payment for record keeping.

Step 5. John will repeat the same strategy for Month Numbers 3 and 4 and again for Month Numbers 5 and 6 and so on for as long as he can make additional principal payments.

If John continues to make one <u>regularly</u> scheduled payment and one <u>principal</u> payment for, say, 12 months, he will save over $2,700 interest, and will have reduced his term by 24 months--12 *regular* months paid-off and 12 *principal* months paid-off.

- In fact, with each regularly scheduled payment, John can make as many extra principal payments as he chooses. Each time he makes an *extra principal payment* he reduces the term by one full month.

- By utilizing his schedule John can easily calculate the money he is saving, right to the penny, *every month*!

Quick Review

USE AN AMORTIZATION SCHEDULE FOR ALL CAR LOANS.
- Since Amortization Schedules work on almost any kind of loan, they especially come in handy when buying a new or used car.

- Schedules can help save borrowers thousands of dollars even after signing a loan that wasn't in their best interest.

Exercise: Examine John's entire Amortization Schedule in Section III.

A Money Sense Quote: We have profoundly forgotten everywhere that Cash-payment is not the sole relation of human beings. - Thomas Carlyle, Past and Present

Side Bar — Are you going to purchase a car soon? If so, I would like to offer some minor tips on dos and don'ts:

DEFINITION —
Puffing: A salesperson's often exaggerated claims concerning the quality of the goods offered for sale. Such claims involve opinions rather than facts and are not considered to be legally binding promises or warranties. (West's Business Law (Fourth Edition))

Don't fall for "puffing". It's a legal term, and if you choose to litigate on the grounds that you were made verbal promises that turned out less than truthful, you'll lose in court. So, if you're purchasing a used car, do know its history (i.e., especially flood damage or major accidents). Do know its "Blue Book" value, do take it for a test drive, and by all means, do have it checked out by a trusted, qualified auto mechanic.

Don't fall in love or be blown away with one car. Visit more than one dealership or used car lot to shop around. Check the classified ads and web sites for used vehicles.

Don't trade-in your car for another. Sell it outright and use that money for a down payment. Your trade-in will only confuse the issue for you, not the dealership. They will always win on a trade-in no matter how good the deal seems to you.

Don't let the salesperson make you think you're in a bidding war for the same car with another customer. This may be true in a few cases, but it may also be a ploy.

Do negotiate without showing emotion and be willing to walk away if it's not the best deal for YOU! Experienced salespeople sense our "impulse to buy now and be in it today".

Don't be a "payment buyer;" focus on the asking price, and then if you're still interested and completed all of your homework on that particular car, negotiate the price down, not the monthly payment. A lower monthly payment only means that you will pay more interest and over a longer term.

Do arrange your own financing before you shop. Get pre-approved for a loan at a competitive rate from a Bank, Savings and Loan, or Credit Union. Don't settle for dealer-arranged or in-house financing.

Do consider a one-owner used car rather than a new one; a used car can be the best value for the money, provided you buy right. The sweet spot for a used car is three years' old and under 50,000 miles driven. You can expect to pay from 40 to 50 percent of what it cost when it was new.

Do ask the dealership if the car you're interested in is being sold by them on a consignment; if they're honest with you and answer yes, you stand a good chance of getting the car at much less than the asking price.

Do use Amortization Schedules to analyze and evaluate a variety of financial hypothetical "what ifs" before you buy.

And finally, Do generate an Amortization Schedule for your auto loan, once you do make your purchase; the schedule will enable you to pay off the loan much faster and avoid paying lots of interest.

> *A Money Sense Quote: The economy depends about as much on economists as the weather does on weather forecasters. - Jean Randy Kauffmann*

Red Flag — Selling on consignment?

DEFINITION —
Consignment: A transaction in which an owner of goods (the consignor) delivers the goods to another (the consignee) for the consignee to sell. The consignee pays the consignor for the goods when the consignee sells the goods. (West's Business Law (Fourth Edition))

But beware: this can be a very tricky proposition if you're selling a big ticket item (e.g., RV, auto, motorcycle, or boat) on consignment. For example, Joe Schmo down the street may be out of work and selling vehicles for friends and neighbors on his front lawn to earn an income. While Joe may be, or seem like, a very nice person and you sort of trust him, Joe may not be the right person for the job nor be located in the safest location in town to sell your vehicle.

Not the right person: Since Joe is doing this on the side, he most likely is not:

a licensed dealer, or

properly insured, or

skilled in sales, or,

dutifully collecting, or paying taxes, or

scam proof, etc.

Not the right location in town: Joe's front lawn or driveway could invite trouble for you in terms of litigation if there's an accident or crime involving your vehicle on Joe's property. Who will answer all the questions regarding the vehicle? Who's responsible for the "test drive"?

And, if you don't know Joe personally, he could be a scam or con-artist himself for all you know or he may even get scammed. So, my best advice is to seek out the licensed, insured, skilled, dutiful, and scam-proof professionals who occupy the best place in town to sell your vehicle: a dealership!

That's right! Selling your vehicle on consignment is a great way to rid yourself of an unwanted monthly bill that you can no longer afford, but still have to pay out each month. In most cases as long as you owe less on the loan than the vehicle is worth, go to and make a deal with either the original dealer you purchased the vehicle from or another authorized dealership in the same line of business and negotiate with and agree to, on paper, a written contract for them to sell your vehicle for you.

ADVANTAGES:
The dealership is going to be licensed and insured, and the sales staff itself has better product knowledge than you do.

The dealership can expedite the sale of your RV, auto, motorcycle, or boat much faster than you can.

The dealership has an incentive to sell your vehicle because they make nothing but pure profit on an item that cost them nothing.

The dealership can maintain and store your vehicle in a safe, well lighted environment indefinitely.

The sales staff does all of the administrative work, title transfer, etc., and pays the lender off in full when the vehicle is sold.

And, you don't need to be present, or on site, or even interact with the buyer during the sales process.

DISADVANTAGES:
You must continue making payments as they become due until the vehicle sells.

You cannot use or operate the vehicle while in consignment.

You may not make as much money when your vehicle finally sells as you might have otherwise made if you sold it yourself.

The dealership may make far more money on the vehicle then you thought it was worth, and you get none of it.

HOW IT WORKS

DEFINITION —
Agreement: A meeting of two or more minds. Often used as a synonym for contract. (West's Business Law (Fourth Edition))

You and the dealership come to an agreement that might go something like this: you need to sell your boat and it's worth $25,000 on the open market. Your loan balance is $18,750. The deal you make with the dealership is:

They get to keep anything they make above $20,000.

You get to keep the difference between the payoff balance and $20,000.

They sell your boat within three weeks for $26,259. You've made another payment since then and they've paid off your $18,300 balance, leaving you with $1,700 cash back. The dealership made $6,259 for selling your boat.

I had to do this myself once. I was living paycheck to paycheck back in the early 1970s and had purchased a brand new motorcycle the year before on a three-year loan. I lost my job about a year later due to a lay-off. I was going to be unable to make the next payment on my bike and my insurance was coming due the following month. I was getting desperate. I didn't want to damage my credit so I approached the dealer I originally purchased the bike from to see if they could sell the bike for me. They agreed to try and the bike was sold by them within one week. I didn't make any money at all on the deal, but the loan was satisfied and my credit was left intact.

If I hadn't been so desperate and had more time, I could have sold the bike myself and gotten back a little more money on the deal, but I didn't. However, allowing the dealer to sell my bike for me on consignment was still a great move on my part.

A Money Sense Quote: I am having an out of money experience. - Author unknown

QUESTION 9 - IF I PURCHASE A CAR FOR ZERO DOWN AND ZERO PERCENT INTEREST WOULD USING AN AMORTIZATION SCHEDULE SERVE ANY PURPOSE?

Yes! Let's say a new car dealership in your area is offering either a double zero loan deal (zero down payment and zero percent interest) or a 2.9 percent interest rate loan for 72 months with a $3,000 cash rebate for certain models. And, let's say you did your homework by getting on the Internet and looking up the best price for one of the models you wanted to purchase. Now you need to know which deal is the best deal, the double zero or the $3,000 cash back. We'll look at each deal separately.

First, the double zero financing generally requires an outstanding credit score. Most people will not qualify for this deal. But if you do qualify, it usually includes financing the Dealer Preparation, Administrative Fees, Sales Tax, License, and Extended Warranty as well. Let's look at it in greater detail.

The Zero Down Payment Zero Percent Interest Rate Loan

Let's say the car you want, along with all the bells and whistles you want too, sells for $18,554.00. The Sales Tax and Dealer Prep come to $1,577.09, the License and all Fees come to $525.34, and you don't want the Extended Warranty. The entire amount financed totals $20,656.43. The loan data would be as follows:

DOUBLE ZERO LOAN DATA FOR 6 YEARS

Loan Amount	$20,656.43
Interest Rate	0%
Scheduled Monthly Payment	$286.89
Term/ Loan Period	72 months
Total Interest Paid	Zero

THE MONTHLY PAYMENTS FOR A:

5-year monthly payment would be $344.27.—Total Interest paid equals 0 percent

4-year monthly payment would be $430.34.—Total Interest paid equals 0 percent

3-year monthly payment would be $573.79.—Total Interest paid equals 0 percent

2-year monthly payment would be $860.68.—Total Interest paid equals 0 percent

1-year monthly payment would be $1,721.37.—Total Interest paid equals 0 percent.

Now, let's look at the 2.9 percent interest rate loan with a $3,000 cash rebate. The difference here might be that the Sales Tax, Dealer Prep, License, Fees, and Extended Warranty all have to be paid up front. And, like the double zero deal, you don't want the Extended Warranty. However, you will have to pay for Tax, Preparation, License, and Fees, out of pocket totaling $2,102.43, but there is no other down payment required. The loan data would be as follows:

2.9 PERCENT INTEREST LOAN FOR 6 YEARS WITH $3000 CASH BACK

Loan Amount	$18,554
Interest Rate	2.9%
Scheduled Monthly Payment	$281.07
Term/loan Period	72 Months
Total Interest Paid	$1,683.34
Total Principal and Interest Paid	$20,237.34
Sales Tax and License Added	$22,339.77
Minus $3,000 Cash Back	$19,339.77
Savings Over The Double Zero Deal	$1,316.66

5-year monthly payment would be $332.57.—Total interest paid equals $1,400.00.

4-year monthly payment would be $430.34.—Total interest paid equals $1,119.32

3-year monthly payment would be $573.79.—Total interest paid equals $841.20

2-year monthly payment would be $860.68.—Total interest paid equals $565.67

1-year monthly payment would be $1,721.37.—Total interest paid equals $292.74

It seems that, at least when the numbers are run for the 72 month term on both loans, the 2.9 percent interest rate loan has a slightly lower total monthly payment amount ($5.82) than the double zero loan. And costs $1,316.66 less total dollars, in the long run, than the double zero loan.

If you generated an Amortization Schedule for the double zero interest rate loan and made a payment for Month Number 1 and then attempted to make a principal payment on Month Number 2 to save money, there is no money to be saved because there is no interest. If you paid the additional $286.89 principal payment for Month Number 2 you only succeed in reducing the term by one additional month and nothing more.

> **Note:** It is not likely that you would ever locate—either on-line or in/with a computer software program anywhere—an Amortization Schedule that would actually run the numbers for a zero percent loan. This is because they're all made to operate with all of the numeric values, including the interest rate, and zero is not a value any schedule program would recognize. You would have to simply do the math yourself by dividing the total loan value by the loan period (i.e., in this case, your $20,656.43 loan divided by the 72 month term which equals a $286.89 monthly payment.) However, if you could find a program that would actually run a schedule for you, it would likely resemble the schedule below.

DOUBLE ZERO AMORTIZATION SCHEDULE

Month Number	Payment Due Date	Beginning Balance	Scheduled Payment	Principal	Interest	Ending Balance
1	1/1/20XX	$20,656.43	$286.89	$286.89	$0.00	$20,369.54
2	2/1	20,369.54	286.89	286.89	0.00	20,082.65
3	3/1	20,082.65	286.89	286.89	0.00	19,795.76
4	4/1	19,795.76	286.89	286.89	0.00	19,508.87
5	5/1	19,508.87	286.89	286.89	0.00	19,221.98
6	6/1	19,221.98	286.89	286.89	0.00	18,935.09
7	7/1	18,935.09	286.89	286.89	0.00	18,648.20
8	8/1	18,648.20	286.89	286.89	0.00	18,361.31
9	9/1	18,361.31	286.89	286.89	0.00	18,074.42
10	10/1	18,074.42	286.89	286.89	0.00	17,787.53
11	11/1	17,787.53	286.89	286.89	0.00	17,500.64
12	12/1	17,500.64	286.89	286.89	0.00	17,213.75
13	1/1/20XX	17,213.75	286.89	286.89	0.00	16,926.86
14	2/1	16,926.86	286.89	286.89	0.00	16,639.97
15	3/1	16,639.97	286.89	286.89	0.00	16,353.08
16	4/1	16,353.08	286.89	286.89	0.00	16,066.19
17	5/1	16,066.19	286.89	286.89	0.00	15,779.30
18	6/1	15,779.30	286.89	286.89	0.00	15,492.41
19	7/1	15,492.41	286.89	286.89	0.00	15,205.52
20	8/1	15,205.52	286.89	286.89	0.00	14,918.63
21	9/1	14,918.63	286.89	286.89	0.00	14,631.74

Month Number	Payment Due Date	Beginning Balance	Scheduled Payment	Principal	Interest	Ending Balance
22	10/1	14,631.74	286.89	286.89	0.00	14,344.85
23	11/1	14,344.85	286.89	286.89	0.00	14,057.96
24	12/1	14,057.96	286.89	286.89	0.00	13,771.07
25	**1/1/20XX**	**13,771.07**	**286.89**	**286.89**	**0.00**	**13,484.18**
26	2/1	13,484.18	286.89	286.89	0.00	13,197.29
27	3/1	13,197.29	286.89	286.89	0.00	12,910.40
28	4/1	12,910.40	286.89	286.89	0.00	12,623.51
29	5/1	12,623.51	286.89	286.89	0.00	12,336.62
30	6/1	12,336.62	286.89	286.89	0.00	12,049.73
31	7/1	12,049.73	286.89	286.89	0.00	11,762.84
32	8/1	11,762.84	286.89	286.89	0.00	11,475.95
33	9/1	11,475.95	286.89	286.89	0.00	11,189.06
34	10/1	11,189.06	286.89	286.89	0.00	10,902.17
35	11/1	10,902.17	286.89	286.89	0.00	10,615.28
36	12/1	10,615.28	286.89	286.89	0.00	10,328.39
37	**1/1/20XX**	**10,328.39**	**286.89**	**286.89**	**0.00**	**10,041.50**
38	2/1	10,041.50	286.89	286.89	0.00	9,754.61
39	3/1	9,754.61	286.89	286.89	0.00	9,467.72
40	4/1	9,467.72	286.89	286.89	0.00	9,180.83
41	5/1	9,180.83	286.89	286.89	0.00	8,893.94
42	6/1	8,893.94	286.89	286.89	0.00	8,607.05
43	7/1	8,607.05	286.89	286.89	0.00	8,320.16
44	8/1	8,320.16	286.89	286.89	0.00	8,033.27
45	9/1	8,033.27	286.89	286.89	0.00	7,746.38
46	10/1	7,746.38	286.89	286.89	0.00	7,459.49
47	11/1	7,459.49	286.89	286.89	0.00	7,172.60
48	6/1	7,172.60	286.89	286.89	0.00	6,885.71
49	**1/1/20XX**	**6,885.71**	**286.89**	**286.89**	**0.00**	**6,598.82**
50	2/1	6,598.82	286.89	286.89	0.00	6,311.93
51	3/1	6,311.93	286.89	286.89	0.00	6,025.04
52	4/1	6,025.04	286.89	286.89	0.00	5,738.15
53	5/1	5,738.15	286.89	286.89	0.00	5,451.26
54	6/1	5,451.26	286.89	286.89	0.00	5,164.37
55	7/1	5,164.37	286.89	286.89	0.00	4,877.48
56	8/1	4,877.48	286.89	286.89	0.00	4,590.59
57	9/1	4,590.59	286.89	286.89	0.00	4,303.70
58	10/1	4,303.70	286.89	286.89	0.00	4,016.81
59	11/1	4,016.81	286.89	286.89	0.00	3,729.92
60	12/1	3,729.92	286.89	286.89	0.00	3,443.03
61	**1/1/20XX**	**3,443.03**	**286.89**	**286.89**	**0.00**	**3,156.14**
62	2/1	3,156.14	286.89	286.89	0.00	2,869.25
63	3/1	2,869.25	286.89	286.89	0.00	2,582.36
64	4/1	2,582.36	286.89	286.89	0.00	2,295.47
65	5/1	2,295.47	286.89	286.89	0.00	2,008.58

Month Number	Payment Due Date	Beginning Balance	Scheduled Payment	Principal	Interest	Ending Balance
66	6/1	2,008.58	286.89	286.89	0.00	1,721.69
67	7/1	1,721.69	286.89	286.89	0.00	1,434.80
68	8/1	1,434.80	286.89	286.89	0.00	1,147.91
69	9/1	1,147.91	286.89	286.89	0.00	861.02
70	10/1	861.02	286.89	286.89	0.00	574.13
71	11/1	574.13	286.89	286.89	0.00	287.24
72	12/1	287.24	286.89	286.89	0.00	0.00

On the other hand, if you generated an Amortization Schedule for the 2.9 percent interest rate loan and then added the principal payments together for Month Numbers 2 through 6. That figure would total $1,189.77. If you then subtracted that figure from $1,316.66 (the amount saved over the double zero interest rate loan) you would have reduced the term on your 2.9 percent interest rate loan by 5 additional months, saved $215.61 more in interest, and have $126.61 left over to go out on the town and celebrate. See the first 6 months below.

Month Number	Payment Due Date	Beginning Balance	Scheduled Payment	Principal	Interest	Ending Balance
1	1/1/XX	$18,554.00	$281.07	$236.24	$44.84	$18,317.76
2	2/1/XX	18,317.76	281.07	236.81	44.27	18,080.96
3	3/1/XX	18,080.96	281.07	237.38	44.70	17,843.58
4	4/1/XX	17843.58	281.07	237.95	43.12	17,605.63
5	5/1/XX	17605.63	281.07	238.53	42.55	17,367.10
6	6/1/XX	17,367.10	281.07	239.10	41.97	17,128.00

THE ENTIRE AMORTIZATION SCHEDULE FOR THIS 2.9 PERCENT LOAN

Month Number	Payment Due Date	Beginning Balance	Scheduled Payment	Principal	Interest	Ending Balance
1	1/1/20XX	$18,554.00	$281.07	$236.24	$44.84	$18,317.76
2	2/1	18,317.76	281.07	236.81	44.27	18,317.76
3	3/1	18,080.96	281.07	237.38	43.70	18,080.96
4	4/1	17,843.58	281.07	237.95	43.12	17,843.58
5	5/1	17,605.63	281.07	238.53	42.55	17,605.63
6	6/1	17,367.10	281.07	239.10	41.97	17,367.10
7	7/1	17,128.00	281.07	239.68	41.39	17,128.00
8	8/1	16,888.32	281.07	240.26	40.81	16,888.32
9	9/1	16,648.05	281.07	240.84	40.23	16,648.05
10	10/1	16,407.21	281.07	241.42	39.65	16,407.21
11	11/1	16,165.79	281.07	242.01	39.07	16,165.79
12	12/1	15,923.78	281.07	242.59	38.48	15,923.78
13	1/1/20XX	15,681.19	281.07	243.18	37.90	15,681.19
14	2/1	15,438.01	281.07	243.77	37.31	15,438.01
15	3/1	15,194.25	281.07	244.35	36.72	15,194.25

Month Number	Payment Due Date	Beginning Balance	Scheduled Payment	Principal	Interest	Ending Balance
16	4/1	14,949.89	281.07	244.95	36.13	14,949.89
17	5/1	14,704.95	281.07	245.54	35.54	14,704.95
18	6/1	14,459.41	281.07	246.13	34.94	14,459.41
19	7/1	14,213.28	281.07	246.73	34.35	14,213.28
20	8/1	13,966.55	281.07	247.32	33.75	13,966.55
21	9/1	13,719.23	281.07	247.92	33.15	13,719.23
22	10/1	13,471.31	281.07	248.52	32.56	13,471.31
23	11/1	13,222.79	281.07	249.12	31.96	13,222.79
24	12/1	12,973.68	281.07	249.72	31.35	12,973.68
25	**1/1/20XX**	**12,723.95**	**281.07**	**250.32**	**30.75**	**12,723.95**
26	2/1	12,473.63	281.07	250.93	30.14	12,473.63
27	3/1	12,222.70	281.07	251.54	29.54	12,222.70
28	4/1	11,971.16	281.07	252.14	28.93	11,971.16
29	5/1	11,719.02	281.07	252.75	28.32	11,719.02
30	6/1	11,466.27	281.07	253.36	27.71	11,466.27
31	7/1	11,212.90	281.07	253.98	27.10	11,212.90
32	8/1	10,958.93	281.07	254.59	26.48	10,958.93
33	9/1	10,704.34	281.07	255.21	25.87	10,704.34
34	10/1	10,449.13	281.07	255.82	25.25	10,449.13
35	11/1	10,193.31	281.07	256.44	24.63	10,193.31
36	12/1	9,936.87	281.07	257.06	24.01	9,936.87
37	**1/1/20XX**	**9,679.81**	**281.07**	**257.68**	**23.39**	**9,679.81**
38	2/1	9,422.13	281.07	258.30	22.77	9,422.13
39	3/1	9,163.82	281.07	258.93	22.15	9,163.82
40	4/1	8,904.90	281.07	259.55	21.52	8,904.90
41	5/1	8,645.34	281.07	260.18	20.89	8,645.34
42	6/1	8,385.16	281.07	260.81	20.26	8,385.16
43	7/1	8,124.35	281.07	261.44	19.63	8,124.35
44	8/1	7,862.91	281.07	262.07	19.00	7,862.91
45	9/1	7,600.84	281.07	262.71	18.37	7,600.84
46	10/1	7,338.13	281.07	263.34	17.73	7,338.13
47	11/1	7,074.79	281.07	263.98	17.10	7,074.79
48	6/1	6,810.82	281.07	264.61	16.46	6,546.20
49	**1/1/20XX**	**6,546.20**	**286.89**	**265.25**	**15.82**	**6,280.95**
50	2/1	6,280.95	281.07	265.90	15.18	6,015.05
51	3/1	6,015.05	281.07	266.54	14.54	5,748.51
52	4/1	5,748.51	281.07	267.18	13.89	5,481.33
53	5/1	5,481.33	281.07	267.83	13.25	5,213.50
54	6/1	5,213.50	281.07	268.47	12.60	4,945.03
55	7/1	4,945.03	281.07	269.12	11.95	4,675.91
56	8/1	4,675.91	281.07	269.77	11.30	4,406.13
57	9/1	4,406.13	281.07	270.43	10.65	4,135.71
58	10/1	4,135.71	281.07	271.08	9.99	3,864.63
59	11/1	3,864.63	281.07	271.73	9.34	3,592.89

Month Number	Payment Due Date	Beginning Balance	Scheduled Payment	Principal	Interest	Ending Balance
60	12/1	3,592.89	281.07	272.39	8.68	3,320.50
61	**1/1/20XX**	**3,320.50**	**281.07**	**273.05**	**8.02**	**3,047.45**
62	2/1	3,047.45	281.07	273.71	7.36	2,773.74
63	3/1	2,773.74	281.07	274.37	6.70	2,499.37
64	4/1	2,499.37	281.07	275.03	6.04	2,224.34
65	5/1	2,224.34	281.07	275.70	5.38	1,948.64
66	6/1	1,948.64	281.07	276.36	4.71	1,672.27
67	7/1	1,672.27	281.07	277.03	4.04	1,395.24
68	8/1	1,395.24	281.07	277.70	3.37	1,117.54
69	9/1	1,117.54	281.07	278.37	2.70	839.16
70	10/1	839.16	281.07	279.05	2.03	560.12
71	11/1	560.12	281.07	279.72	1.35	280.40
72	12/1	280.40	281.07	280.40	0.68	0.00

Quick Review

If you purchase a car for Zero Down and Zero Percent Interest rate, use Amortization Schedules to compare to a Cash Back loan with Interest.

- In the final analysis, if you want to purchase a car and the dealer is offering customers either a zero down payment and zero percent interest rate loan, or a loan at some given interest rate with a cash back offer, using Amortization Schedules will help you determine which loan will save you the most money.

- When you're in the market for an auto, RV, or boat, find the best offers that appear in advertisements and commercials. Use Amortization Schedules to compare deals for any of them.

Examine: How using an Amortization Schedule for a zero down, zero percent interest rate loan can serve any purpose either before or after the deal in Section III.

A Money Sense Quote: Too much money is as demoralizing as too little, and there's no such thing as exactly enough. - Mignon McLaughlin, The second Neurotic's notebook, 1966

Side Bar — *Avoid car loans altogether.*

Typically, car buyers find a car, new or used, and finance either a portion of, or the entire cost of the vehicle. That car loan usually comes with an interest rate of between 0.0 and 25 percent, and the loan period can run up to 84 months.

I would like to suggest that this traditional car buying process be reversed. Here's how: for those of you purchasing a car for the first time and can't wait, buy cheap—not junk—just small and inexpensive, so only a small loan will be needed for a short period of time. Along with your car payment, save an additional dollar amount every month (say, $50-$100) in a savings account dedicated to maintenance and repairs. Once the car has been paid off, keep it, and continue making that same car payment, more if possible, to the maintenance and repair savings account. This account will allow you to maintain your current car while saving for a new one. You're also collecting interest on your maintenance, repair, and car payment account rather than paying interest on a loan while digging deep into your pockets for maintenance and repairs costs.

For those of you who currently have an auto loan payment, repeat the same process as suggested for first time buyers, and like them, once the loan is paid off continue making that same car payment to yourself and in no time you'll be able to pay cash (money you have earned interest on) for a new car. One hundred percent cash up front will always put you in a more strategic negotiating position in terms of the purchase price of the vehicle you want to buy. Once you've purchased your car this way, continue making car payments to yourself for maintenance and repairs, as well as saving for the next new car. In the event you're faced with a financial crisis down the road, simply stop the car payment to yourself without fear of repossession, and resume the payment when the crisis is over.

For more, go to: *AutoFinance101.org.*

A Money Sense Quote: If you think nobody cares if you're alive, try missing a couple of car payments. - Earl Wilson

🚩 RED FLAG — CARS CAN COST YOU ALMOST AS MUCH AS YOUR MORTGAGE WILL IN YOUR LIFETIME.

Think about this: In my view, the most expensive lifetime revolving never-ending expense is the automobile. Why? Because we replace them over and over again. We sell them, trade them in, wear them out, or drive them into the ground, and in many cases, we do this before the last payment is made. Worse yet, almost every car we buy will depreciate in value at a far faster pace than is our ability to pay them off. Then we buy another one only to start the whole car payment process and associated costs all over again.

Along with a never-ending payment cycle are the ever increasing costs associated with driving a car such as maintenance/repairs, auto insurance, and license plates/tabs renewal(s) every year, year after year. Many households own two or more cars at a time that serve different functions/drivers. Add to that parking fees/meters, toll roads, traffic tickets/accidents, and worse yet, the never ending "three steps forward one step back" cost of fuel. And, as taxpayers we all get to pay for more roads and bridges along with maintaining the current ones.

So, be careful not to spend more on revolving car purchases and their associated costs in your lifetime than you would spend for a single home!

A Money Sense Quote: My problem lies in reconciling my gross habits with my net income.
- Errol Flynn

QUESTION 10 - CAN I USE AMORTIZATION SCHEDULES FOR PLANNING "DEBT CONSOLIDATION" STRATEGIES?

Yes! If you're over extended and debt-ridden with financial obligations (i.e., too many credit card bills), a mortgage payment, a car payment, maybe a personal loan or two and a mountain of other small debts, debt consolidation may be for you.

Let's consolidate Judy's debts (excluding her mortgage loan) into a single loan. She must first know the total balances owed on all the debt she wishes to pay-off. It wouldn't hurt her to know the current term periods and interest rates on each of them either. Judy will need to generate several hypothetical Amortization Schedules on the amount she wishes to borrow.

Like Judy, you may want to try running schedules at various terms and interest rates your (regulated) lender offers, to gauge how much your monthly payment might be, and then compare those figures to the total of all the payments you want consolidated, and *only* those debts to actually be consolidated.

Keep in mind, when generating hypothetical Amortization Schedules, try manipulating the term to control your monthly payment rather than setting an ideal low interest rate to control it. Let's examine the debts Judy is considering for consolidation. Her debt balances and monthly payment figures are as follows:

- Credit Card Debt #1 is at a 20.5 percent interest rate, and the unpaid balance on this revolving account is $1,547.34. Her monthly minimum payment is $100.00.

- Credit Card Debt #2 is at a 22.5 percent interest rate, and the unpaid balance on this revolving account is $4,329.02. Her monthly minimum payment is $100.00.

- Auto Loan Debt is at a 9.6 percent interest rate with 25 months remaining. Her unpaid balance is $10,864.04. Her monthly payment is $481.80.

- Personal Loan Debt #1 is at a 25 percent interest rate with 15 months remaining. Her unpaid balance is $2,882.89. Her monthly payment is $159.04.

- Personal Loan Debt #2 is at a 24 percent interest rate with 28 months remaining. Her unpaid balance is $3,111.26. Her monthly payment is $294.25.

- R.V. Loan Debt is at a 12.5 percent interest rate with 59 months remaining. Her unpaid balance is $22,618.41. Her monthly payment is $551.09.

Judy's total unpaid balances for two credit cards and 4 outstanding loans total $45,352.96.

Judy's combined minimum monthly payments for two credit cards and 4 outstanding loans total $1,686.18.

Just to be even clearer about Judy's debts, let's examine them another way with a Table, for a different perspective.

Type of Debt	Interest Rate	Unpaid Balance	Monthly Payment
Credit Card #1	20.5 Percent	$1,547.34	$100.00
Credit Card #2	22.5 Percent	$4,329.02	$100.00
Auto Loan	9.6 Percent	$10,864.04	$481.80
Personal Loan #1	25 Percent	$2,882.89	$159.04
Personal Loan #2	24 Percent	$3,111.26	$294.25
R.V. Loan	12.5 Percent	$22,618.41	$551.09
Totals		$45,352.96	$1,686.18

We now have some quantitative facts to work with. Keep in mind that in order to get a consolidation loan for Judy's debt, she would have to consider obtaining an equity loan against her house since there is probably no other way to secure this loan without collateral.

CAUTION 1:

This can be risky for Judy, because she could be draining all the equity right out of her home and ultimately affecting her long-term financial goals and/or even her retirement.

> Borrowers, in general, should not use their house (like Judy is doing) as a piggy-bank to pull equity out just to pay off debt. Borrowers should first try using schedules to help pay off each debt/loan independently, one at a time and not put their house at risk.

To consolidate all Judy's loans into one, she generates the Loan Data for 3 different hypothetical Amortization Schedules all at a 7.5 percent interest rate. She will change only the term of each to see what happens. She begins with a 15-year term. Examine Loan Data 1 and Month Number 1 of her schedule on the next page:

LOAN DATA 1

Loan Amount	$45,352.96
Annual Interest Rate	7.5%
Scheduled Monthly Payment	$420.42
Term/Period	15 Years
Total Interest Paid	$30,323.42

Note the total interest (over 30 thousand dollars!) Judy would have to pay if she chose this consolidation loan plan. Look at Month Number 1 on her schedule and notice that more than half her first payment is interest.

Month Number	Payment Due Date	Beginning Balance	Scheduled Payment	Principal	Interest	Ending Balance
1	1/1/XX	$45,352.96	$420.42	$136.97	$283.45	$45,069.51

Next, she runs the numbers for a 10 year-term.

LOAN DATA 2

Loan Amount	$45,352.96
Annual Interest Rate	7.5%
Scheduled Monthly Payment	$538.34
Term/Period	10 Years
Total Interest Paid	$19,248.39

The payment would be somewhat higher, but the total interest paid is more than 10 thousand dollars less over the life of the loan. Her monthly payment has increased, but the interest portion in her first payment remained the same.

Month Number	Payment Due Date	Beginning Balance	Scheduled Payment	Principal	Interest	Ending Balance
1	1/1/XX	$45,352.96	$538.34	$254.89	$283.45	$45.098.07

JUDY'S FINAL LOAN IS A 5-YEAR TERM.
LOAN DATA 3

Loan Amount	$45,352.96
Annual Interest Rate	7.5%
Scheduled Monthly Payment	$908.76
Term/Period	5 Years
Total Interest Paid	$9,173.86

The total interest to be paid for this loan would be $9,173.86, over $21,000 less interest than loan #1. Her monthly payment of $908.76 really jumps here, but is still a far cry from the more than $1,600 of combined payments she was paying each month previously.

Month Number	Payment Due Date	Beginning Balance	Scheduled Payment	Principal	Interest	Ending Balance
1	1/1/XX	$45,352.96	$908.76	$625.31	$283.45	$44,727.65

Judy used various term lengths at a constant 7.5 percent interest rate for this imaginary debt scenario. She could have changed interest rates to explore even more options and strategies. Amortization Schedules provide a powerful financial planning tool.

- In the event a consolidation loan would be denied... other planning options might include generating separate schedules for each individual debt. Choose the debt that is the most troubling and make additional principal payments on it until the debt is paid off. Then the next loan, and so on. Continue this process until all the debt is gone.

- In the meantime the trick is to acquire no new debt. Live on a cash basis only, and eventually become debt free.

CAUTION 2:

- Beware of the loan consolidation trap! Consolidation loans are appealing because borrowers are able to combine many loan and credit card payments into one. That single payment is often substantially lower each month than combined payments would be if left scattered out among multiple debt payments each month. The trap occurs after the loan has been consolidated, but new debt is acquired. This consolidation trap could turn into a vicious cycle of spending and consolidating debt and ending up costing them their home or leaving bankruptcy as their only way out.

Exercise: See Judy's Amortization Schedules in Section III to see what other strategies she might have tried.

A Money Sense Quote: Lack of money is the root of all evil. - George Bernard Shaw

 Side Bar — The "Rule of 72".

The "Rule of 72" is a fun, centuries old, formula for quickly approximating, in your head, how soon an investment will double its value for any interest earned at a fixed annual percentage rate (APR) of return on that initial investment.

Here's how it works:

Divide 72 by the APR of interest earned. Regardless of the sum of money you begin with, the interest you earn on your investment determines when that original sum will double: For example:

If your investment is earning 6 percent interest—Divide 72 by 6—the answer is 12, your initial sum will double its value in 12 years.

If it is earning 7 percent interest—Divide 72 by 7—the answer is 10.3, your initial sum will double in 10.3 years.

At 8 percent interest—Divide 72 by 8—the answer is 9, your initial sum will double in 9 years.

At 8.5 percent interest—Divide 72 by 8.5—the answer is 8.5, your initial sum will double in 8.5 years.

If your initial investment is $10,000 and is earning 100 percent interest—Divide 72 by 100—the answer is 7.2, that initial $10,000 will double to $20,000 in 7.2 months. That same $10,000 at 100 percent interest will grow to approximately $33,333.33 in one year.

If your investment is $10,000 and is in a traditional bank account (e.g., a Certificate of Deposit account) today and is earning 2.0 percent interest, divide 72 by 2—the answer is 36, your initial $10,000 will double to $20,000 in 36 years.

The rule of 72 also works even if you want your initial investment dollars to double in value by a certain period of time. Say you have $25,000, and in four years you need $50,000. Now let's say that $25,000 is only earning 6 percent interest annually, the rule shows it will take 12 years for your money to double. But, if you're earning 6 percent already, you can then add to that 6 percent your own annual contribution of 12 percent (1% each month) for an 18 percent total APR and you will double your money in four years.

For example: 6 percent APR + 12 percent annual contributions from YOU equals 18 percent APR. Divide 72 by 18—the answer is 4, your initial $25,000 will double to $50,000 in 4 years.

Keep in mind, this formula is an approximation and works best when calculating growth rates at or below 25 percent but, like horseshoes, is close enough.

The rule of "Rule of 72" also works well for calculating how future inflation could affect you and your wallet. For example: If it now costs you, say, $3,000 a month to live and the inflation rate is currently running at about 4 percent a year—using the rule of 72—divide 72 by 4 and you will know that in 18 years you will need to bring home about $6,000 a month to continue your current lifestyle, provided the inflation rate cooperates and continues to grow at a 4 percent annual rate for the next 18 years. That's not likely, but this rule is very handy for general retirement calculations and planning.

A Money Sense Quote: The safe way to double your money is to fold it over and put it in your pocket. - Frank Hubbard

 RED FLAG — COLLECTION AGENCY BASICS AND FEDERAL LAW

There are more than 5,500 collection agencies in America. Most of them are legitimate and operate within the confines of local, state, and federal law. Collection agencies provide a valuable and needed service. Legitimate agencies strive to commit their employees to high standards and ethical excellence. However, many collection agencies, legitimate and otherwise, have been found guilty of "abusive, deceptive, and unfair collection practices", as seen on three recently televised programs. The first program was a segment presented by NBC's weekly newsmagazine, "Dateline". Another was aired on a program titled the "Clark Howard" show on CNN. And, last but not least, another hour long report, about collection agencies, was broadcast on CNBC. All of the programs demonstrated that many bill collectors employed by questionable agencies tend to be over-zealous when attempting to collect on a debt. Many collectors have been guilty of lying (i.e.., impersonating a Law Enforcement Officer or you or someone close to you), or harassing debtors (i.e., calling at all hours of the day and night and worse.) As a result, all collection agencies have been a federally regulated industry ever since 9/20/1977. It was then that the U.S. Congress approved the Fair Debt Collection Practices Act (FDCPA). This act also governs every action taken by a bill collector. The Federal Trade Commission (FTC) enforces compliance with this act. However, the FTC still received, from 2009 thru 2011, more complaints about collection agencies from the public for non-compliance with the law than it did for any other industry in America.

If a debt collector makes contact with you and fails to comply with the law, they can be held personally liable. If an agency is legitimate, a debtor should expect a collector to be accurate, businesslike, composed, decisive, detached, fair, flexible, honest, logical, mature, polite, tactful, understanding, and nothing less. Please refer to the entire FDCPA document for a more complete and thorough understanding of this consumer credit protection law.

Most collection agencies maintain a low profile (i.e., no public advertising and no exterior signage), especially agencies that operate illegally off shore or in back allies. Most of us would never know a legal agency existed in our city even if we were standing directly in front of one. A typical collection agency performs their work in a hubbub of fast-paced and intense boiler-room pandemonium. Collectors themselves work in small groups called pods, and there may be many pods within an agency. A supervisor is assigned to each pod and shares in the collection duties. Several supervisors typically report to one manager. Pods usually specialize in client types (e.g., utility companies, banks, retail stores, etc.).

In a typical work day collectors contact debtors, locally and across country, in the morning hours no sooner than 8 a.m. debtor's time. Collectors then relax in the middle part of their day searching for new debtors that may be hard to locate. They do this by "skip-tracing", which is a means of cross referencing known facts and information about a debtor in the event they have either moved, changed jobs, changed names, gone into hiding, etc. They end their day contacting more debtors, but no later than 9 p.m. debtor's time.

Individual collectors are paid an hourly base rate, which may be slightly above state minimum wage requirements. Collectors also earn a commission based on his or her success at collecting debt for clients. Commissions can double a collector's weekly take-home pay, and this is the driving force behind all the effort collectors put into their work. Unscrupulous and scavenger collection agencies tend to hire the young and energetic, money motivated, and preferably the "psychopathic" types.

Special Warning: According to "The American Heritage Collage Dictionary" a psychopath is a person with an antisocial personality disorder, manifested in aggressive, perverted, or criminal behavior without <u>empathy or remorse</u>.

We often think of psychopaths as extremely violent, dangerous, and irrational people, and indeed some exhibit these characteristics. It is estimated that one in one hundred people is a psychopath, but only a small number of them are actually violent, dangerous, and irrational. However, all of them behave without empathy or remorse and many psychopaths work for most of the unscrupulous and scavenger collection agencies scattered throughout the western hemisphere. These companies allow, if not encourage, these psychotic bill collectors to manipulate, scheme, scam, curse at, threaten, and intimidate those they call. Sometimes they even state that they're going to show up at the debtor's front door before the day is out to collect on a debt, or else! If these collectors fail to consistently collect debt, by any means, they're replaced by another psychopath immediately.

There is no education or other special requirements to be a bill collector, beyond a GED or high school diploma. However, most agencies do require completion of a one to two-week training period before new employees' man the phones. Legitimate agencies even offer ongoing training. Many agencies, especially the unscrupulous and scavenger ones don't really care about work experience. Few even require drug testing. Collectors with serious money and debt management issues of their own often get hired by agencies with a reputation for tripping over the law. In fact, few collectors working in these questionable agencies know little about the correct use of money at all, but that doesn't stop them from yelling and screaming into the phone at debtors.

If you're overwhelmed by debt and having a difficult time paying your bills in the current economic slowdown, there's no need to fret about a collection agency onslaught if you know the law. The law states that you cannot be contacted by a collection agency unless you are more than 180 days delinquent. If an agency has made recent contact with you, or you expect a call soon, be extremely careful! Collection agencies call to get payment in full just about any way they can. Collectors will often recommend the following as quick sources of money:

Bank Accounts	Bonuses/Pension/Profit Sharing Plan
Friends and Relatives	Military Reserve Pay/Vacation Pay
Credit Card Loans	Deferred Car Payment
Unemployment or Welfare Checks	Stocks and Bonds (sell)
Bank, Credit Union or Student Loans	Home Mortgages and Equity Loans (refinance).
Cash on Hand	Sale of Personal Property
Overtime or Salary Advances	Tax Refunds and much more!

Before a collection agency calls you, contact your creditor(s) in person or by phone to arrange a pay-off strategy that will work for you. Don't allow a collection agency to talk you into doing something that can potentially lead to financial instability, personal bankruptcy, loss of employment, and/or an invasion of your privacy.

A Money Sense Quote: I'm so poor I can't even pay attention. - Ron Kittle, 1987

QUESTION 11 - CAN AMORTIZATION SCHEDULES PROVIDE ME WITH FINANCIAL PLANNING STRATEGIES FOR RENTAL/INVESTMENT PROPERTY.

Yes, before and after the loan! First narrow your rental/investment property search to a *specific area* and explore that particular market to the nth degree, (e.g., local economy/history, prime locations, zoning/taxes, asking prices, structures/land, rental histories and property management agencies). Hypothetical Amortization Schedules should be the starting point for all of your potential rental/investment property strategies.

Ray and Jackie are married and in their late 50s. Their children are grown and have since left the nest. Both are coming up on retirement but lost more than 60 percent of their 401(k) retirement savings when the stock market took a recent and deep nose dive. Fortunately, they have been saving money in a bank account over the years. Unfortunately though, the account is now paying only about 0.30 percent interest.

Ray and Jackie realize that if they are going to have enough money to retire they will have to take a chance and do something now! They decide to purchase a rental house. They'll do all the necessary prep work, as previously suggested, and then generate some hypothetical Amortization Schedules, as an additional step to help them evaluate what their best loan borrowing options will be.

Ray and Jackie own their home free and clear and have about $75,000 in the bank. This gives them a great deal of financial flexibility. They've concluded that if they were going to purchase a rental house, they would use the equity in their home to acquire a loan. They would also avoid a 4 to 6 week waiting period for a conventional mortgage loan to close once they made an offer on a piece of property. With all of their prep work completed, they know they can get an 80 percent equity loan from the bank on their current home, which has a current downgraded assessment value of $250,000 because of the on-going decline in the Real Estate market coupled with the economic downturn. Their bank currently offers equity loans at a 6.22 percent annual interest rate over a 20 year maximum term with no closing costs. With a $200,000 loan, combined with the $75,000 in the bank, they can purchase a $275,000 house including closing costs.

Ray and Jackie generate a hypothetical Amortization Schedule for a $200,000 loan at 6.22 percent interest rate over a 20-year term to see what their payments would be. The schedule shows the payment would be $1,458.36 a month.

Month Number	Payment Due Date	Beginning Balance	Scheduled Payment	Principal	Interest	Ending Balance
1	1/1/XX	$200,000.00	$1,458.36	$421.69	$1,036.67	$199,578.31

Their prep work that was completed earlier indicates that the local economy in the area in which they want to make their purchase will not support rents that go much above $1,000 a month.

They generate another hypothetical schedule for $90,000, same interest rate and term, and *that* payment drops to $656.26 per month.

Month Number	Payment Due Date	Beginning Balance	Scheduled Payment	Principal	Interest	Ending Balance
1	1/1/XX	$90,000.00	$656.26	$189.26	$466.50	$89,810.24

This $90,000 loan combined with their $75,000 in the Bank would give them $165,000 total, if needed, to purchase a rental house. Ray and Jackie want to purchase a house that will rent for under $1,000, but above $656 a month, and still be able to make a profit in the long run. They have also decided to keep a $25,000 minimum cushion in the bank for emergencies, after the purchase is made. Now with the minimum and maximum rent parameters established they must examine some of their other prep work before they actually borrow the $90,000.

Let's take a look on the next page at some of their concerns if they borrow $90,000 at a 6.22 percent interest rate over 20 years.

Here are the expenses Ray and Jackie think they need to recover in rent payments each month.

Loan Payment	Property Taxes	Water & Garbage	Home Owners Insurance	Property Management Fees
$656.26	$100.00	$82.90	$39.00	$91.10

It looks as though they need to collect a grand total of $969.26 in rent per month to stay even. This looks worse than it really is, and here is why.

- Ray and Jackie do not have to recover the *principal* portion of their loan payment in the rent they collect which, in this case according to their schedule, begins at $189.26. The principal portion of their loan is money only needed to pay their loan balance down. They will, or at least should, recover their entire principal when the property is sold at a later date. So, they can reduce the total rent by this principal amount, if they wish, and still make a profit down the road. Confused?

- Let's say you paid $100,000 cash for a $100,000 rental house. You now own the house outright. Would you need to recover any of that money in your rent? No, of course not! Again as stated above, hopefully the house would increase in value over the years, so not only would you get your $100,000 back when you sold the property, but you would earn a nice profit as well. If, on the other hand, the renters are paying part of, or the entire principal, it's as though they're buying the house for you. Whether principal is paid all at once in cash, or is paid back in increments over time, or any amount of additional principal is paid in advance...not one red cent of principal has to be made up in rent.

- All Ray and Jackie's expenses, such as repairs and maintenance, property tax, water & garbage, management fees, etc., can be written off on their Federal Income Taxes. If need be, Ray and Jackie can lower the rent even more and *still* make a profit. They would require no Private Mortgage Insurance since the rental property would be paid for in cash and they still maintain well over 20 percent equity in their own house.

- There is also depreciation on the rental house and interest on the loan that can be written off on their taxes. Important: Interest on loans of this type can only be written off up to a $100,000 loan. For more information on interest deductions contact a tax advisor or an accountant.

- Rental property should always be held inside a Limited Liability Company (LLC) to protect all of your other assets from any liabilities. You should also retain a (minimum) three million dollar umbrella insurance policy.

While Ray and Jackie were doing their research, they discovered the area where they hope to purchase has increased in value, on average, 7 percent annually over a recent

14-year period. The house prices in this area have since fallen. Homes there are now listing for about 15 percent lower than just 2 years ago, but have recently stabilized.

Now, with the aid of hypothetical Amortization Schedules to help them complete their prep work, Ray and Jackie go ahead and borrow the $90,000 equity loan from their bank. In the meantime they start looking at properties in the area in which they want to buy. Ray and Jackie begin by looking at houses on the market offered at $165,000 or less. They feel strongly that even though an asking price may be in the $165,000 range, they can make an offer of less than $140,000 to a motivated seller looking to make a quick cash deal and a fast closing. They find a 3-bedroom rambler in good shape offered at $151,500. They make an offer of $134,500 and emphasize they have cash in hand. A counter offer comes back from the seller the next day at $142,000. Ray and Jackie know their cash offer might be too irresistible and counter with a $139,500 final offer. The seller accepts their final offer because the cash deal will allow the closing to occur in days rather than weeks. In fact, the closing will happen so quickly that the seller will need to rent his own house from Ray and Jackie for the remainder of the month thereby insuring their first monthly payment and allowing their just-hired property manager time to find a renter. Their $90,000 loan closes within days of their offer and the closing on the rental property takes place a few days after that.

Here is Ray and Jackie's entire Amortization Schedule for their new loan.

Loan Data for a 20-year Loan

Loan Amount	$90,000.00
Interest Rate	6.22%
Scheduled Monthly Payment	$656.26
Term/ Loan Period	20 Years
Total Interest Paid	$67,503.03

See their complete schedule on the next page.

A Money Sense Quote: Inflation is when you pay fifteen dollars for a haircut you used to get for five dollars when you had hair. – Sam Uwing

20 year Amortization Schedule

Month Number	Payment Due Date	Beginning Balance	Scheduled Payment	Principal	Interest	Ending Balance
1	1/1/20XX	$90,000.00	$656.26	$189.76	$466.50	$89,810.24
2	2/1	89,810.24	656.26	190.75	465.52	89,619.49
3	3/1	89,619.49	656.26	191.73	464.53	89,427.76
4	4/1	89,427.76	656.26	192.73	463.53	89,235.03
5	5/1	89,235.03	656.26	193.73	462.53	89,041.30
6	6/1	89,041.30	656.26	194.73	461.53	88,846.57
7	7/1	88,846.57	656.26	195.74	460.52	88,650.83
8	8/1	88,650.83	656.26	196.76	459.51	88,454.07
9	9/1	88,454.07	656.26	197.78	458.49	88,256.29
10	10/1	88,256.29	656.26	198.80	457.46	88,057.49
11	11/1	88,057.49	656.26	199.83	456.43	87,857.66
12	12/1	87,857.66	656.26	200.87	455.40	87,656.80
13	1/1/20XX	87,656.80	656.26	201.91	454.35	87,454.89
14	2/1	87,454.89	656.26	202.95	453.31	87,251.93
15	3/1	87,251.93	656.26	204.01	452.26	87,047.93
16	4/1	87,047.93	656.26	205.06	451.20	86,842.86
17	5/1	86,842.86	656.26	206.13	450.14	86,636.73
18	6/1	86,636.73	656.26	207.20	449.07	86,429.54
19	7/1	86,429.54	656.26	208.27	447.99	86,221.27
20	8/1	86,221.27	656.26	209.35	446.91	86,011.92
21	9/1	86,011.92	656.26	210.43	445.83	85,801.49
22	10/1	85,801.49	656.26	211.52	444.74	85,589.96
23	11/1	85,589.96	656.26	212.62	443.64	85,377.34
24	12/1	85,377.34	656.26	213.72	442.54	85,163.62
25	1/1/20XX	85,163.62	656.26	214.83	441.43	84,948.79
26	2/1	84,948.79	656.26	215.94	440.32	84,732.84
27	3/1	84,732.84	656.26	217.06	439.20	84,515.78
28	4/1	84,515.78	656.26	218.19	438.07	84,297.59
29	5/1	84,297.59	656.26	219.32	436.94	84,078.27
30	6/1	84,078.27	656.26	220.46	435.81	83,857.81
31	7/1	83,857.81	656.26	221.60	434.66	83,636.21
32	8/1	83,636.21	656.26	222.75	433.51	83,413.46
33	9/1	83,413.46	656.26	223.90	432.36	83,189.56
34	10/1	83,189.56	656.26	225.06	431.20	82,964.50
35	11/1	82,964.50	656.26	226.23	430.03	82,738.27
36	12/1	82,738.27	656.26	227.40	428.86	82,510.86
37	1/1/20XX	82,510.86	656.26	228.58	427.68	82,282.28
38	2/1	82,282.28	656.26	229.77	426.50	82,052.52
39	3/1	82,052.52	656.26	230.96	425.31	81,821.56
40	4/1	81,821.56	656.26	232.15	424.11	81,589.40
41	5/1	81,589.40	656.26	233.36	422.91	81,356.05
42	6/1	81,356.05	656.26	234.57	421.70	81,121.48

Month Number	Payment Due Date	Beginning Balance	Scheduled Payment	Principal	Interest	Ending Balance
43	7/1	$81,121.48	$656.26	$235.78	$420.48	$80,885.70
44	8/1	80,885.70	656.26	237.01	419.26	80,648.69
45	9/1	80,648.69	656.26	238.23	418.03	80,410.46
46	10/1	80,410.46	656.26	239.47	416.79	80,170.99
47	11/1	80,170.99	656.26	240.71	415.55	79,930.28
48	6/1	79,930.28	656.26	241.96	414.31	79,688.32
49	**1/1/20XX**	**79,688.32**	**656.26**	**243.21**	**413.05**	**79,445.11**
50	2/1	79,445.11	656.26	244.47	411.79	79,200.64
51	3/1	79,200.64	656.26	245.74	410.52	78,954.90
52	4/1	78,954.90	656.26	247.01	409.25	78,707.89
53	5/1	78,707.89	656.26	248.29	407.97	78,459.59
54	6/1	78,459.59	656.26	249.58	406.68	78,210.01
55	7/1	78,210.01	656.26	250.87	405.39	77,959.14
56	8/1	77,959.14	656.26	252.17	404.09	77,706.96
57	9/1	77,706.96	656.26	253.48	402.78	77,453.48
58	10/1	77,453.48	656.26	254.80	401.47	77,198.69
59	11/1	77,198.69	656.26	256.12	400.15	76,942.57
60	12/1	76,942.57	656.26	257.44	398.82	76,685.13
61	**1/1/20XX**	**76,685.13**	**656.26**	**258.78**	**397.48**	**76,426.35**
62	2/1	76,426.35	656.26	260.12	396.14	76,166.23
63	3/1	76,166.23	656.26	261.47	394.79	75,904.76
64	4/1	75,904.76	656.26	262.82	393.44	75,641.94
65	5/1	75,641.94	656.26	264.19	392.08	75,377.75
66	6/1	75,377.75	656.26	265.55	390.71	75,112.20
67	7/1	75,112.20	656.26	266.93	389.33	74,845.27
68	8/1	74,845.27	656.26	268.31	387.95	74,576.95
69	9/1	74,576.95	656.26	269.71	386.56	74,307.25
70	10/1	74,307.25	656.26	271.10	385.16	74,036.15
71	11/1	74,036.15	656.26	272.51	383.75	73,763.64
72	12/1	73,763.64	656.26	273.92	382.34	73,489.72
73	**1/1/20XX**	**73,489.72**	**656.26**	**275.34**	**380.92**	**73,214.37**
74	2/1	73,214.37	656.26	276.77	379.49	72,937.61
75	3/1	72,937.61	656.26	278.20	378.06	72,659.40
76	4/1	72,659.40	656.26	279.64	376.62	72,379.76
77	5/1	72,379.76	656.26	281.09	375.17	72,098.66
78	6/1	72,098.66	656.26	282.55	373.71	71,816.11
79	7/1	71,816.11	656.26	284.02	372.25	71,532.10
80	8/1	71,532.10	656.26	285.49	370.77	71,246.61
81	9/1	71,246.61	656.26	286.97	369.29	70,959.64
82	10/1	70,959.64	656.26	288.46	367.81	70,671.19
83	11/1	70,671.19	656.26	289.95	366.31	70,381.24
84	12/1	70,381.24	656.26	291.45	364.81	70,089.78
85	**1/1/20XX**	**70,089.78**	**656.26**	**292.96**	**363.30**	**69,796.82**
86	2/1	69,796.82	656.26	294.48	361.78	69,502.34

Month Number	Payment Due Date	Beginning Balance	Scheduled Payment	Principal	Interest	Ending Balance
87	3/1	$69,502.34	$656.26	$296.01	$360.25	$69,206.33
88	4/1	69,206.33	656.26	297.54	358.72	68,908.79
89	5/1	68,908.79	656.26	299.09	357.18	68,609.70
90	6/1	68,609.70	656.26	300.64	355.63	68,309.06
91	7/1	68,309.06	656.26	302.19	354.07	68,006.87
92	8/1	68,006.87	656.26	303.76	352.50	67,703.11
93	9/1	67,703.11	656.26	305.33	350.93	67,397.77
94	10/1	67,397.77	656.26	306.92	349.35	67,090.86
95	11/1	67,090.86	656.26	308.51	347.75	66,782.35
96	6/1	66,782.35	656.26	310.11	346.16	66,472.24
97	**1/1/20XX**	**66,472.24**	**656.26**	**311.71**	**344.55**	**66,472.24**
98	2/1	66,160.53	656.26	313.33	342.93	66,160.53
99	3/1	65,847.20	656.26	314.95	341.31	65,847.20
100	4/1	65,532.24	656.26	316.59	339.68	65,532.24
101	5/1	65,215.65	656.26	318.23	338.03	65,215.65
102	6/1	64,897.43	656.26	319.88	336.38	64,897.43
103	7/1	64,577.55	656.26	321.54	334.73	64,577.55
104	8/1	64,256.01	656.26	323.20	333.06	64,256.01
105	9/1	63,932.81	656.26	324.88	331.39	63,932.81
106	10/1	63,607.93	656.26	326.56	329.70	63,607.93
107	11/1	63,281.37	656.26	328.25	328.01	63,281.37
108	12/1	62,953.12	656.26	329.96	326.31	62,953.12
109	**1/1/20XX**	**62,623.16**	**656.26**	**331.67**	**324.60**	**62,623.16**
110	2/1	62,291.50	656.26	333.39	322.88	62,291.50
111	3/1	61,958.11	656.26	335.11	321.15	61,958.11
112	4/1	61,623.00	656.26	336.85	319.41	61,623.00
113	5/1	61,286.15	656.26	338.60	317.67	61,286.15
114	6/1	60,947.55	656.26	340.35	315.91	60,947.55
115	7/1	60,607.20	656.26	342.12	314.15	60,607.20
116	8/1	60,265.08	656.26	343.89	312.37	60,265.08
117	9/1	59,921.20	656.26	345.67	310.59	59,921.20
118	10/1	59,575.53	656.26	347.46	308.80	59,575.53
119	11/1	59,228.06	656.26	349.26	307.00	59,228.06
120	12/1	58,878.80	656.26	351.07	305.19	58,878.80
121	**1/1/20XX**	**58,527.72**	**656.26**	**352.89**	**303.37**	**58,527.72**
122	2/1	58,174.83	656.26	354.72	301.54	58,174.83
123	3/1	57,820.11	656.26	356.56	299.70	57,820.11
124	4/1	57,463.55	656.26	358.41	297.85	57,463.55
125	5/1	57,105.14	656.26	360.27	295.99	57,105.14
126	6/1	56,744.87	656.26	362.14	294.13	56,744.87
127	7/1	56,382.73	656.26	364.01	292.25	56,382.73
128	8/1	56,018.72	656.26	365.90	290.36	56,018.72
129	9/1	55,652.82	656.26	367.80	288.47	55,652.82
130	10/1	55,285.03	656.26	369.70	286.56	55,285.03

Month Number	Payment Due Date	Beginning Balance	Scheduled Payment	Principal	Interest	Ending Balance
131	11/1	$54,915.32	$656.26	$371.62	$284.64	$54,915.32
132	12/1	54,543.71	656.26	373.54	282.72	54,543.71
133	**1/1/20XX**	**54,170.16**	**656.26**	**375.48**	**280.78**	**54,170.16**
134	2/1	53,794.68	656.26	377.43	278.84	53,794.68
135	3/1	53,417.25	656.26	379.38	276.88	53,417.25
136	4/1	53,037.87	656.26	381.35	274.91	53,037.87
137	5/1	52,656.52	656.26	383.33	272.94	52,656.52
138	6/1	52,273.19	656.26	385.31	270.95	52,273.19
139	7/1	51,887.88	656.26	387.31	268.95	51,887.88
140	8/1	51,500.57	656.26	389.32	266.94	51,500.57
141	9/1	51,111.25	656.26	391.34	264.93	51,111.25
142	10/1	50,719.92	656.26	393.36	262.90	50,719.92
143	11/1	50,326.55	656.26	395.40	260.86	50,326.55
144	12/1	49,931.15	656.26	397.45	258.81	49,533.70
145	**1/1/20XX**	**49,533.70**	**656.26**	**399.51**	**256.75**	**49,533.70**
146	2/1	49,134.18	656.26	401.58	254.68	49,134.18
147	3/1	48,732.60	656.26	403.67	252.60	48,732.60
148	4/1	48,328.93	656.26	405.76	250.50	48,328.93
149	5/1	47,923.18	656.26	407.86	248.40	47,923.18
150	6/1	47,515.32	656.26	409.97	246.29	47,515.32
151	7/1	47,105.34	656.26	412.10	244.16	47,105.34
152	8/1	46,693.24	656.26	414.24	242.03	46,693.24
153	9/1	46,279.01	656.26	416.38	239.88	46,279.01
154	10/1	45,862.62	656.26	418.54	237.72	45,862.62
155	11/1	45,444.08	656.26	420.71	235.55	45,444.08
156	12/1	45,023.37	656.26	422.89	233.37	45,023.37
157	**1/1/20XX**	**44,600.48**	**656.26**	**425.08**	**231.18**	**44,600.48**
158	2/1	44,175.39	656.26	427.29	228.98	44,175.39
159	3/1	43,748.11	656.26	429.50	226.76	43,748.11
160	4/1	43,318.61	656.26	431.73	224.53	43,318.61
161	5/1	42,886.88	656.26	433.97	222.30	42,886.88
162	6/1	42,452.91	656.26	436.22	220.05	42,452.91
163	7/1	42,016.70	656.26	438.48	217.79	42,016.70
164	8/1	41,578.22	656.26	440.75	215.51	41,578.22
165	9/1	41,137.47	656.26	443.03	213.23	41,137.47
166	10/1	40,694.44	656.26	445.33	210.93	40,694.44
167	11/1	40,249.11	656.26	447.64	208.62	40,249.11
168	12/1	39,801.47	656.26	449.96	206.30	39,801.47
169	**1/1/20XX**	**39,351.51**	**656.26**	**452.29**	**203.97**	**39,351.51**
170	2/1	38,899.22	656.26	454.63	201.63	38,899.22
171	3/1	38,444.59	656.26	456.99	199.27	38,444.59
172	4/1	37,987.60	656.26	459.36	196.90	37,987.60
173	5/1	37,528.24	656.26	461.74	194.52	37,528.24
174	6/1	37,066.49	656.26	464.13	192.13	37,066.49

Month Number	Payment Due Date	Beginning Balance	Scheduled Payment	Principal	Interest	Ending Balance
175	7/1	$36,602.36	$656.26	$466.54	$189.72	$36,602.36
176	8/1	36,135.82	656.26	468.96	187.30	36,135.82
177	9/1	35,666.86	656.26	471.39	184.87	35,666.86
178	10/1	35,195.47	656.26	473.83	182.43	35,195.47
179	11/1	34,721.64	656.26	476.29	179.97	34,721.64
180	12/1	34,245.35	656.26	478.76	177.51	34,245.35
181	**1/1/20XX**	**33,766.59**	**656.26**	**481.24**	**175.02**	**33,766.59**
182	2/1	33,285.35	656.26	483.73	172.53	33,285.35
183	3/1	32,801.62	656.26	486.24	170.02	32,801.62
184	4/1	32,315.38	656.26	488.76	167.50	32,315.38
185	5/1	31,826.62	656.26	491.29	164.97	31,826.62
186	6/1	31,335.32	656.26	493.84	162.42	31,335.32
187	7/1	30,841.48	656.26	496.40	159.86	30,841.48
188	8/1	30,345.08	656.26	498.97	157.29	30,345.08
189	9/1	29,846.11	656.26	501.56	154.70	29,846.11
190	10/1	29,344.55	656.26	504.16	152.10	29,344.55
191	11/1	28,840.39	656.26	506.77	149.49	28,840.39
192	12/1	28,333.61	656.26	509.40	146.86	27,824.21
193	**1/1/20XX**	**27,824.21**	**656.26**	**512.04**	**144.22**	**27,312.17**
194	2/1	27,312.17	656.26	514.69	141.57	26,797.48
195	3/1	26,797.48	656.26	517.36	138.90	26,280.12
196	4/1	26,280.12	656.26	520.04	136.22	25,760.07
197	5/1	25,760.07	656.26	522.74	133.52	25,237.33
198	6/1	25,237.33	656.26	525.45	130.81	24,711.88
199	7/1	24,711.88	656.26	528.17	128.09	24,183.71
200	8/1	24,183.71	656.26	530.91	125.35	23,652.80
201	9/1	23,652.80	656.26	533.66	122.60	23,119.14
202	10/1	23,119.14	656.26	536.43	119.83	22,582.71
203	11/1	22,582.71	656.26	539.21	117.05	22,043.50
204	12/1	22,043.50	656.26	542.00	114.26	21,501.50
205	**1/1/20XX**	**21,501.50**	**656.26**	**544.81**	**111.45**	**20,956.68**
206	2/1	20,956.68	656.26	547.64	108.63	20,409.05
207	3/1	20,409.05	656.26	550.48	105.79	19,858.57
208	4/1	19,858.57	656.26	553.33	102.93	19,305.24
209	5/1	19,305.24	656.26	556.20	100.07	18,749.04
210	6/1	18,749.04	656.26	559.08	97.18	18,189.96
211	7/1	18,189.96	656.26	561.98	94.28	17,627.99
212	8/1	17,627.99	656.26	564.89	91.37	17,063.09
213	9/1	17,063.09	656.26	567.82	88.44	16,495.28
214	10/1	16,495.28	656.26	570.76	85.50	15,924.51
215	11/1	15,924.51	656.26	573.72	82.54	15,350.79
216	12/1	15,350.79	656.26	576.69	79.57	14,774.10
217	**1/1/20XX**	**14,774.10**	**656.26**	**579.68**	**76.58**	**14,194.42**
218	2/1	14,194.42	656.26	582.69	73.57	13,611.73

Month Number	Payment Due Date	Beginning Balance	Scheduled Payment	Principal	Interest	Ending Balance
219	3/1	$13,611.73	$656.26	$585.71	$70.55	$13,026.02
220	4/1	13,026.02	656.26	588.74	67.52	12,437.27
221	5/1	12,437.27	656.26	591.80	64.47	11,845.48
222	6/1	11,845.48	656.26	594.86	61.40	11,250.61
223	7/1	11,250.61	656.26	597.95	58.32	10,652.67
224	8/1	10,652.67	656.26	601.05	55.22	10,051.62
225	9/1	10,051.62	656.26	604.16	52.10	9,447.46
226	10/1	9,447.46	656.26	607.29	48.97	8,840.17
227	11/1	8,840.17	656.26	610.44	45.82	8,229.73
228	12/1	8,229.73	656.26	613.61	42.66	7,616.12
229	**1/1/20XX**	**7,616.12**	**656.26**	**616.79**	**39.48**	**6,999.33**
230	2/1	6,999.33	656.26	619.98	36.28	6,379.35
231	3/1	6,379.35	656.26	623.20	33.07	5,756.16
232	4/1	5,756.16	656.26	626.43	29.84	5,129.73
233	5/1	5,129.73	656.26	629.67	26.59	4,500.05
234	6/1	4,500.05	656.26	632.94	23.33	3,867.12
235	7/1	3,867.12	656.26	636.22	20.04	3,230.90
236	8/1	3,230.90	656.26	639.52	16.75	2,591.38
237	9/1	2,591.38	656.26	642.83	13.43	1,948.55
238	10/1	1,948.55	656.26	646.16	10.10	1,302.39
239	11/1	1,302.39	656.26	649.51	6.75	652.88
240	12/1	652.88	656.26	652.88	3.38	0.00

Ray and Jackie bought the right house at the right time for the right price. Even if the house drops a little more in value things will eventually level off and, in time, begin to rise in value again.

Ray and Jackie's first tenants sign a 1-year lease and will pay $995.00 a month. Ray and Jackie will continue to use their Amortization Schedule for the purpose of making additional principal payments garnered from the positive cash flow of their rental property investment.

Quick Review

Amortization Schedules can provide you with Financial Planning Strategies for Rental/Investment Property.

- Ray and Jackie realized this and then generated some hypothetical Amortization Schedules, as an additional step to help them evaluate what their best loan borrowing options would be.
- They began by generating hypothetical schedules and using them to set the best high and low parameters for an equity loan they could afford to repay easily.
- Ray and Jackie also used schedules to help them set an ideal rent for the area in which they intended to purchase property.

- And finally, they will use their actual Amortization Schedule for their equity loan to pay it off early.

IMPORTANT REMINDER

The following bears partial repeating from question 1. Principal—The amount of money in each regularly scheduled payment applied to a loan amount is money that goes directly into your equity/investment. If your investment is an asset, such as real estate, you should recover all this money, no matter *when or how much you paid in*, including *all* additional principal payments when you sell that asset.

If you're thinking about purchasing rental property, you might begin your search by visiting: www.rentometer.com. This Web site compares rent in areas in which you may want to invest.

A Money Sense Quote: We all know how the size of sums of money appears to vary in a remarkable way according as they are being paid in or paid out. - Julian Huxley, Essays of a Biologist, 1923

Side Bar — Why not use Amortization Schedule programs and become a lender for the sale of your own house?

I'm sure you've seen this sign many times before, "For Sale By Owner" (FSBO). Many homeowners attempt to sell their home on their own. Their primary incentive is to avoid paying a real estate commission and fees. But when a buyer is found, many homeowners fail to take the next logical step, which is to offer owner financing! If you own your home outright and want to sell it, it may be difficult to find a buyer today who has easy access to credit. Why not use Amortization Schedule programs and become a lender for the sale of your own house?

For example, Lois and Jacob are retired and own their home outright. They want to sell it themselves, because they don't need all the money at once, and if they had it all now, it would just sit in the bank CD earning about 1.5 percent interest. So they've decided to carry their own real estate contract. By doing this, Lois and Jacob feel they will accomplish several things:

- They stand a greater chance of selling their house faster in a down real estate market.
- They will determine who qualifies to purchase their house.
- They will have more flexibility in the asking price.
- They can ask for a slightly higher interest rate than commercial lenders.

- The closing costs for both parties would be extremely low or non-existent.
- They can set up a loan agreement that outlines the conditions of the loan itself (i.e., the down payment amount, any pre-payment penalties in the event the buyer wants to pay the loan off quick, the length of the loan term, and so on).
- They will earn a greater amount of interest on their money than if it sat in the bank.
- They will receive a monthly income well into the foreseeable future.

Ray and Jackie did their own local real estate market research and analysis. As a result they appraised their house for $145,500. After turning down several offers, Ray and Jackie accepted an offer from Jim and Mary. The amount offered was $143,400. Jim and Mary agreed to put $43,000 down and pay their own share of the closing costs in cash. They financed their loan portion with Ray and Jackie for the remaining $100,000 at 6.15 percent interest over 30 years. Both parties have an Amortization Schedule for the loan, and Jim and Mary will not be permitted to make additional principal payments towards their loan until payment number 121. That's because Ray and Jackie included a pre-payment penalty clause dis-allowing any additional principal payments to be made prior to payment number 120. This will insure that most of the money Ray and Jackie receive in the first 10 years will come in the form of interest with the bulk of the principal, $84,948.06 still left to be paid, with 20 years on the loan remaining. Because of Ray and Jackie's ages they also had a will written to protect their interest in this house.

> I am not recommending that everyone sell their house "FSBO." Real estate companies provide a valuable and needed service in this arena and have many more resources available to work with than do homeowners. However, I am suggesting that for those who can, why not consider taking the next logical step and become the lender? Your house may sell much faster if you carry the contract. All that is really needed is the ability to generate Amortization Schedules, and some good intestinal fortitude.

To examine more information about the pros and cons about FSBO's, visit the following websites:

www.bankarte.com/brm/news/real-estate/fsbo1.asp

www.forsalebyowner.com/home-selling-tips.html

www.relocation.com/library/real_estate_guide/seller_guide/fsbo.html

A Money Sense Quote: I once met an economist who believed that everything was fungible for money, so I suggested he enclose himself in a large bell-jar with as much money as he wanted and see how long he lasted. - Amory Lovins

QUESTION 12 - CAN AMORTIZATION SCHEDULES HELP ELIMINATE MY CREDIT CARD DEBT?

Yes! Amortization Schedules are the perfect _control_ tool for this kind of debt.

For example, Randy and Kelly have Credit Card Debt! They owe $9,000 on a single credit card and pay 19.5 percent interest. Due to a poor credit rating, they're unable to transfer their balance to a credit card with a lower interest rate or take out a short-term, low interest loan to pay their card off. So, together they worked out a payoff strategy that will eliminate their credit card debt once-and-for-all!

They started out by examining their monthly income and expenses. Randy and Kelly found they could only afford to pay an extra $250 over and above the $100 minimum payment they had already been making. They agreed they could apply $350 a month total to the debt until it was paid in full. Now, with their monthly payment for the card established, the remaining questions to be answered were: how long would the term need to be to reflect their allotted payment, and how much interest would they ultimately have to pay?

To take full advantage of the $350 allotted for their credit card, Randy and Kelly used a computer software program to generate _several_ hypothetical Amortization Schedules. They began with a 4-year schedule and discovered their payment would be $271.48 a month..."too low" they thought. Next they tried a 3-year schedule and found that payment would be $332.18 per month. This was close, but still too low. Finally they tried tweaking out 2 months from the 3-year schedule down to 34 months and to their surprise, that schedule was perfect! Their payment would be $349.72 per month. Needless to say, they chose to use the 34-month schedule. Now they knew how long the term was going to be and how much interest they would ultimately pay. Examine a brief summary below of the three schedules Randy and Kelly generated.

SCHEDULE SUMMARY

Schedules Examined	Total Payment they can make	Projected Payment	Projected Interest
4-Year Term	$350.00	$271.48	$4,031.11
3-Year Term	$350.00	$332.18	$2,958.62
34 Month Term	$350.00	$346.72	$2,751.32

THE 4-YEAR AMORTIZATION SCHEDULE

Month Number	Payment Due Date	Beginning Balance	Scheduled Payment	Principal	Interest	Ending Balance
1	1/1/20XX	$9,000.00	$271.48	$125.23	$146.25	$8,874.77
2	2/1	8,874.77	271.48	127.27	144.21	8,747.50
3	3/1	8,747.50	271.48	129.33	142.15	8,618.17
4	4/1	8,618.17	271.48	131.44	140.05	8,486.73
5	5/1	8,486.73	271.48	133.57	137.91	8,353.16
6	6/1	8,353.16	271.48	135.74	135.74	8,217.42
7	7/1	8,217.42	271.48	137.95	133.53	8,079.47

Month Number	Payment Due Date	Beginning Balance	Scheduled Payment	Principal	Interest	Ending Balance
8	8/1	$8,079.47	$271.48	$140.19	$131.29	$7,939.28
9	9/1	7,939.28	271.48	142.47	129.01	7,796.81
10	10/1	7,796.81	271.48	144.78	126.70	7,652.03
11	11/1	7,652.03	271.48	147.14	124.35	7,504.89
12	12/1	7,504.89	271.48	149.53	121.95	7,355.36
13	**1/1/20XX**	**7,355.36**	**271.48**	**151.96**	**119.52**	**7,203.41**
14	2/1	7,203.41	271.48	154.43	117.06	7,048.98
15	3/1	7,048.98	271.48	156.94	114.55	6,892.05
16	4/1	6,892.05	271.48	159.49	112.00	6,732.56
17	5/1	6,732.56	271.48	162.08	109.40	6,570.48
18	6/1	6,570.48	271.48	164.71	106.77	6,405.77
19	7/1	6,405.77	271.48	167.39	104.09	6,238.38
20	8/1	6,238.38	271.48	170.11	101.37	6,068.28
21	9/1	6,068.28	271.48	172.87	98.61	5,895.40
22	10/1	5,895.40	271.48	175.68	95.80	5,719.72
23	11/1	5,719.72	271.48	178.54	92.95	5,541.19
24	12/1	5,541.19	271.48	181.44	90.04	5,359.75
25	**1/1/20XX**	**5,359.75**	**271.48**	**184.39**	**87.10**	**5,175.36**
26	2/1	5,175.36	271.48	187.38	84.10	4,987.98
27	3/1	4,987.98	271.48	190.43	81.05	4,797.56
28	4/1	4,797.56	271.48	193.52	77.96	4,604.04
29	5/1	4,604.04	271.48	196.67	74.82	4,407.37
30	6/1	4,407.37	271.48	199.86	71.62	4,207.51
31	7/1	4,207.51	271.48	203.11	68.37	4,004.40
32	8/1	4,004.40	271.48	206.41	65.07	3,797.99
33	9/1	3,797.99	271.48	209.76	61.72	3,588.22
34	10/1	3,588.22	271.48	213.17	58.31	3,375.05
35	11/1	3,375.05	271.48	216.64	54.84	3,158.41
36	12/1	3,158.41	271.48	220.16	51.32	2,938.26
37	**1/1/20XX**	**2,938.26**	**271.48**	**223.73**	**47.75**	**2,714.52**
38	2/1	2,714.52	271.48	227.37	44.11	2,487.15
39	3/1	2,487.15	271.48	231.07	40.42	2,256.09
40	4/1	2,256.09	271.48	234.82	36.66	2,021.27
41	5/1	2,021.27	271.48	238.64	32.85	1,782.63
42	6/1	1,782.63	271.48	242.51	28.97	1,540.12
43	7/1	1,540.12	271.48	246.45	25.03	1,293.66
44	8/1	1,293.66	271.48	250.46	21.02	1,043.20
45	9/1	1,043.20	271.48	254.53	16.95	788.67
46	10/1	788.67	271.48	258.67	12.82	530.01
47	11/1	530.01	271.48	262.87	8.61	267.14
48	6/1	267.14	271.48	267.14	4.34	0.00

THE 3-YEAR AMORTIZATION SCHEDULE

Month Number	Payment Due Date	Beginning Balance	Scheduled Payment	Principal	Interest	Ending Balance
1	1/1/20XX	$9,000.00	$332.18	$185.93	$146.25	$8,814.07
2	2/1	8,814.07	33.18	188.96	143.23	8,625.11
3	3/1	8,625.11	33.18	192.03	140.16	8,433.09
4	4/1	8,433.09	33.18	195.15	137.04	8,237.94
5	5/1	8,237.94	33.18	198.32	133.87	8,039.62
6	6/1	8,039.62	33.18	201.54	130.64	7,838.08
7	7/1	7,838.08	33.18	204.81	127.37	7,633.27
8	8/1	7,633.27	33.18	208.14	124.04	7,425.12
9	9/1	7,425.12	33.18	211.53	120.66	7,213.60
10	10/1	7,213.60	33.18	214.96	117.22	6,998.64
11	11/1	6,998.64	33.18	218.46	113.73	6,780.18
12	12/1	6,780.18	33.18	222.01	110.18	6,558.17
13	1/1/20XX	6,558.17	33.18	225.61	106.57	6,332.56
14	2/1	6,332.56	33.18	229.28	102.90	6,103.28
15	3/1	6,103.28	33.18	233.01	99.18	5,870.27
16	4/1	5,870.27	33.18	236.79	95.39	5,633.48
17	5/1	5,633.48	33.18	240.64	91.54	5,392.84
18	6/1	5,392.84	33.18	244.55	87.63	5,148.29
19	7/1	5,148.29	33.18	248.52	83.66	4,899.77
20	8/1	4,899.77	33.18	252.56	79.62	4,647.21
21	9/1	4,647.21	33.18	256.67	75.52	4,390.54
22	10/1	4,390.54	33.18	260.84	71.35	4,129.70
23	11/1	4,129.70	33.18	265.08	67.11	3,864.63
24	12/1	3,864.63	33.18	269.38	62.80	3,595.24
25	1/1/20XX	3,595.24	33.18	273.76	58.42	3,321.48
26	2/1	3,321.48	33.18	278.21	53.97	3,043.27
27	3/1	3,043.27	33.18	282.73	49.45	2,760.54
28	4/1	2,760.54	33.18	287.32	44.86	2,473.22
29	5/1	2,473.22	33.18	291.99	40.19	2,181.22
30	6/1	2,181.22	33.18	296.74	35.44	1,884.48
31	7/1	1,884.48	33.18	301.56	30.62	1,582.92
32	8/1	1,582.92	33.18	306.46	25.72	1,276.46
33	9/1	1,276.46	33.18	311.44	20.74	965.02
34	10/1	965.02	33.18	316.50	15.68	648.52
35	11/1	648.52	33.18	321.65	10.54	326.87
36	12/1	326.87	33.18	326.87	5.31	0.00

See the 34-month schedule on the next page.

THE 34-MONTH AMORTIZATION SCHEDULE

Month Number	Payment Due Date	Beginning Balance	Scheduled Payment	Principal	Interest	Ending Balance
1	1/1/20XX	$9,000.00	$346.62	$200.37	$146.25	$8,799.63
2	2/1	8,799.63	346.62	203.63	142.99	8,596.00
3	3/1	8,596.00	346.62	206.94	139.69	8,389.06
4	4/1	8,389.06	346.62	210.30	136.32	8,178.76
5	5/1	8,178.76	346.62	213.72	132.90	7,965.05
6	6/1	7,965.05	346.62	217.19	129.43	7,747.86
7	7/1	7,747.86	346.62	220.72	125.90	7,527.14
8	8/1	7,527.14	346.62	224.31	122.32	7,302.83
9	9/1	7,302.83	346.62	227.95	118.67	7,074.88
10	10/1	7,074.88	346.62	231.66	114.97	6,843.22
11	11/1	6,843.22	346.62	235.42	111.20	6,607.80
12	12/1	6,607.80	346.62	239.25	107.38	6,368.56
13	1/1/20XX	6,368.56	346.62	243.13	103.49	6,125.43
14	2/1	6,125.43	346.62	247.08	99.54	5,878.34
15	3/1	5,878.34	346.62	251.10	95.52	5,627.24
16	4/1	5,627.24	346.62	255.18	91.44	5,372.06
17	5/1	5,372.06	346.62	259.33	87.30	5,112.74
18	6/1	5,112.74	346.62	263.54	83.08	4,849.20
19	7/1	4,849.20	346.62	267.82	78.80	4,581.37
20	8/1	4,581.37	346.62	272.17	74.45	4,309.20
21	9/1	4,309.20	346.62	276.60	70.02	4,032.60
22	10/1	4,032.60	346.62	281.09	65.53	3,751.51
23	11/1	3,751.51	346.62	285.66	60.96	3,465.85
24	12/1	3,465.85	346.62	290.30	56.3)	3,175.55
25	1/1/20XX	3,175.55	346.62	295.02	51.60	2,880.53
26	2/1	2,880.53	346.62	299.81	46.81	2,580.71
27	3/1	2,580.71	346.62	304.69	41.94	2,276.03
28	4/1	2,276.03	346.62	309.64	36.99	1,966.39
29	5/1	1,966.39	346.62	314.67	31.95	1,651.72
30	6/1	1,651.72	346.62	319.78	26.84	1,331.94
31	7/1	1,331.94	346.62	324.98	21.64	1,006.96
32	8/1	1,006.96	346.62	330.26	16.36	676.71
33	9/1	676.71	346.62	335.63	11.00	341.08
34	10/1	341.08	346.62	341.08	5.54	00.0

Credit card debt and Amortization Schedules go hand-in-hand and work very well together. Randy and Kelly discovered schedules can be easily customized and tailor-made to work for this kind of debt repayment. All they had to do was get serious about paying their credit card off. Having made that commitment, the schedules provided the control tool needed to accomplish their goal.

Quick Review

After determining how much additional money they could pay each month, Randy and Kelly used three different Amortization Schedules to gauge a perfect term.

- First, they tried a 4-year Amortization Schedule term to see if they were relatively close to their budgeted amount. That schedule put them in the ballpark with room to spare.

- Schedule number two was used to work backwards--or to shorten the term to three years. They still did not go over their budgeted amount.

- A third schedule was generated that was two months shorter and they *still* didn't go over their budget.

In addition to knowing exactly how much they would have to pay each and every month, they also now know *when* the card is going to be paid off and how much total interest it's going to cost them, right down to the penny. In the end, the schedules made all the difference. No other financial planning tool can offer this ability to both strategically plan and effectively control credit card debt.

A Money Sense Quote: Money may be the husk of many things but not the kernel. It brings you food, but not appetite; medicine, but not health; acquaintance, but not friends; servants, but not loyalty; days of joy, but not peace or happiness. - Henrik Ibsen

 Side Bar — Multiple Credit-Card Balances

There are many ways for credit card holders to pay off multiple credit cards, some good, and some not so good! Many personal financial advisors suggest that the best way to begin is to pay down the card with the highest interest rate while continuing to make the minimum payments on the other cards, then the next highest card, and so on, until all the cards are paid off.

Other advisors suggest card holders attack the credit card with the highest balance first, while continuing to make minimum payments on the other cards, then the next highest card, and so on, until all the cards are paid off.

My suggestion is to begin with the credit card with the lowest balance, regardless of the interest rate, while continuing to make the minimum payments on the other cards, then the next lowest card, and so on, until all the cards are paid off.

Here's why! The average household owes more than $10,000 on credit cards. Much of that debt, for many consumers, is scattered out among 4, 5, 6 or more cards. Let's say you have outstanding balances on five credit cards. Your lowest card has a balance of $500, and your highest card has a balance of, say, $5,000. Now, let's say your credit card statements arrive in the mail and you have an extra $100 left over at the end of the month. You should pay that $100 to the card with the lowest balance. Repeat that behavior as often as possible until that credit card is completely paid off, at which point, do not cancel, but instead, destroy that card. Now you have four cards to pay off rather than five. Just repeat the process on the card with the next lowest balance, and before you know it, you're down to a single credit card. Mathematically the first two ways to pay off multiple credit cards, suggested earlier, may save you a little more money, but throwing $100 extra each month at a $5,000 credit card balance, even at a low interest rate, will keep five credit cards in flux, and take a psychological toll on your psyche for as long as it takes to pay off the card with the highest balance and/or interest.

To be sure you're taking the most cost effective approach, try running Amortization Schedules on each card to develop the best pay off strategy for every credit card balance and interest rate.

NOTES:

A Money Sense Quote: It's good to have money and the things that money can buy, but it's good, too, to check up once and awhile and make sure that you haven't lost the thing that money can't buy. - George Horace Lorimer

 RED FLAG — CREDIT CARDS HAVE "NO TERM LIMIT," THAT IS, NO PAY-OFF DATE!

Credit Cards, unlike typical installment loans, which do have term limits, operate on a revolving or never-ending basis. And, as a result, the principal balance can change upwards monthly if the card is used for any additional purchases.

If you choose to use an Amortization Schedule to help pay off a credit card debt, you won't be able to use that particular card again until the debt is paid – in full! Here's why; that particular schedule you created was designed for use until the debt is paid off. To continue to use the card would render that particular Amortization Schedule useless. Also, a single Amortization Schedule cannot be generated on combined credit cards, that is, one schedule for two separate cards. If you wish to pay off two cards using this method you must generate a separate schedule for each card. Three cards, three schedules and so on. They're all separate debts with different balances and interest rates and cannot be co-mingled onto a single Amortization Schedule.

For credit-card comparison calculators that actually compare credit cards to each other go to:

www.lowcards.com

www.bankrate.com

www.federalreserve.gov

If you're having trouble making payments on Credit Card Debt, and are well beyond using Amortization Schedules and comparison calculators as a payoff strategy, go to *www.helpwithmycredit.org* for help. This Web site has been set up by the major credit-card companies to offer assistance in this regard.

> *A Money Sense Quote: The only reason a great many American families don't own an elephant is that they have never been offered an elephant for a dollar down and easy weekly payments.*
> *- Mad Magazine*

QUESTION 13 - CAN AN AMORTIZATION SCHEDULE HELP ME GET RID OF PRIVATE MORTGAGE INSURANCE (PMI)?

Yes! Why should you pay out good hard-earned money for something you don't want and don't need? The cost, *to you*, for PMI can be more than twice as much as what you might pay for homeowners insurance each year, which you <u>do</u> want and <u>do</u> need! PMI premiums can add anywhere from $100 to $200 or more per month to your mortgage payment. The sooner you achieve the 20 percent equity level in your home, the sooner you can cancel that nasty PMI.

PMI is paid by the homeowner to protect the lender in the event the homeowner defaults on the mortgage loan. PMI does not relieve the homeowner of the obligation to pay the loan back. PMI is not life or disability insurance designed to pay off a mortgage in the event of disability or death of the homeowner. PMI can be cancelled by the homeowner when 20 percent equity has been established in the property. This occurs either because the property has increased in value by 20 percent over time, or the homeowner has paid down 20 percent of the principal on the loan over time, or a combination of the two equals slightly over a 20 percent equity on the home's total value.

Let's examine how one couple used an Amortization Schedule on their loan to plan a strategy to get rid of their PMI as quickly as possible.

Fred and Nancy purchased a home after the housing bust for a depreciated value of $175,500. It was offered on the market just a short time before for $265,900. Oh my, how things can fall apart in a hurry. Back to Fred and Nancy.

They only had a 5 percent down payment, which came to $8,775 after paying closing costs. They acquired a $166,725 mortgage at 7.25 percent interest rate over a 30-year period. Their lender required they get PMI. This added $109 a month to their monthly $1,137.36 mortgage payment for a total payment of $1,246.36. They had to get their loan balance down to $140,400 to get their PMI cancelled. Fred and Nancy examined an Amortization Schedule they received from their lender on their loan and discovered the following:

If they don't utilize their schedule <u>and</u> take no other action <u>at all</u>, they would have to:

- Make 133 scheduled payments, equal to 11+ years, before reaching the 20 percent equity level necessary to cancel the PMI.

- Pay $14,497 for PMI over those 133 scheduled payments.

- Pay $124,943.88 in Interest over those 133 scheduled payments. See below.

Total Monthly Payment With PMI	Regular Payments with PMI Total 133	Total Paid to PMI over 133 Months	Total Interest Paid over 133 Months
$1,246.36	$165,765.88	$14,497.00	$124,943.88

Since getting to scheduled payment number 133 (the 20 percent equity level) is critical to getting rid of their PMI, Fred and Nancy will use their Amortization Schedule to their advantage to help them get there much faster.

They decide to make 2 additional principal payments on their schedule (right to the penny) with every regular scheduled payment they make.

Examine how they do this in a brief Amortization Schedule summary below.

Month Number	Payment Due Date	Beginning Balance	Scheduled Payment	Principal	Interest	Ending Balance
1	9/1/XX	$166,725.00	$1,137.36	$130.06	$1,007.30	$166,594.94
2	10/1/XX	166,594.94	1,137.36	130.85	1,006.51	166,464.09
3	11/1/XX	166,464.09	1,137.36	131.64	1,005.72	166,332.45

Step 1. They will make their scheduled payment on their payment date for Month Number 1 as scheduled.

Step 2. They will include with their scheduled payment for Month Number 1, an additional $130.85 and $131.64 (under the Principal column) for Months Numbered 2 and 3. By doing this they will avoid paying $1,006.51 and $1005.72 (under the interest column) for Months Numbered 2 and 3--forever!

Step 3. They will check off and date their scheduled payment (e.g., Month Number 1) in black for record keeping.

Step 4. They will check off and date in red their additional principal payments (e.g., Months Numbered 2 & 3) for record keeping.

Step 5. They will indicate on their payment coupon or the return portion of their statement that the additional money included is to be applied to <u>Principal</u>.

Step 6. They will repeat this process for payment numbers 4, 5 and 6 on their next payment date (the date payment 2 is due) and again, on payment numbers 7, 8 and 9 and so on until they reach payment/Month Number 133.

In doing this they will arrive at payment or Month Number 133 in 45 months -or 88 payments ahead of schedule.

When they arrive at their scheduled payment or Month Number 133:

- They will have paid only $4,905 for PMI – a $9,592 savings.
- They will have paid only $60,992.50 in Interest – a $63,951.38 savings.
- Their combined PMI and Interest saved will total $73,543.38.
- Their house payment will drop from $1,246.36 with PMI back to $1,137.36 without PMI.
- They will have accumulated $35,100 equity in their home in 45 months.
- In just 45 months they will have reduced their total number of scheduled payments by 133 months and have less than 19 years remaining on their mortgage loan.
- Their savings in interest and PMI alone would be equivalent to earning $8.84 an hour, for 40 hours a week for the next 45 months!

Quick Review

AMORTIZATION SCHEDULES CAN HELP YOU GET RID OF YOUR PMI.

- Amortization Schedules afford you the ability to create and customize a financial strategy that will save you money like nothing else will. Fred and Nancy *could* have decided to use their schedule *just long enough* to recoup the $14,497 lost to PMI by making enough extra principal payments and avoiding the interest for those payments. In fact, the possibilities for saving them money by using their schedule are almost endless.

- Amortization Schedules can help any borrower get rid of PMI and save thousands and thousands of dollars in the process. Additional principal payments also reduce the length of the loan and the total amount of interest a borrower would otherwise have to pay. With Amortization Schedules helping the borrower strategize, they are only limited by how creatively they use one.

- Many lenders force homebuyers to purchase PMI if they make less than the required 20 percent down payment. PMI, unlike homeowner's insurance, does nothing to protect the borrower or their investment. It just protects the lender in the event the homeowner defaults and the loan goes into foreclosure. The law says the lender must send homebuyers paying PMI an *annual* reminder that they have this insurance, plus information about how to cancel it.

A Money Sense Quote: A nickel ain't worth a dime anymore. - Yogi Berra @&#$! Huh?*

  Side Bar — Caution, PMI rules vary from lender to lender.

Private Mortgage Insurance rules may vary on mortgage loans from lender to lender, and loan type (e.g., FHA Loan, Conventional Loan, etc.). Talk to your Loan Officer or lender if you have any questions about your PMI. Note: If you're a veteran and decide to purchase a home with a VA loan, you are not required to have PMI, even if you have no down payment. For VA loan information about PMI requirements or additional rules for VA loan eligibility, go to: *www.homeloans.va.gov*.

The only other way to avoid paying for PMI, with less than a 20 percent down payment, is to acquire a piggy-back loan for the down payment. However, piggy-back loans for this purpose are extremely rare now since the mortgage meltdown in 2008. That's good for the borrower, because piggy-back loans only add to their debt load and a borrower could still be paying on that loan long after they would have established a 20 percent equity in their home to eliminate PMI.

A Money Sense Quote: Wallets are the fabricated items into which we put our fabricated money, which most people believe to be their possession of the realest value. - The Quote Garden

QUESTION 14 - I'M NOT ABLE TO KEEP PACE WITH THE EXTRA PRINCIPAL PAYMENTS ON MY AMORTIZATION SCHEDULE. WHAT SHOULD I DO?

First, you don't need an Amortization Schedule to pay-down a loan—any loan. You're free to pay extra principal whenever you choose, provided there is no early pay-off penalty in your loan agreement (well, you *could* still pay extra principal in that case, but be prepared to also pay the penalty, which could be quite steep.) However, if there is no early pay-off penalty and you want total control of your loan, meaning the ability to strategize, and to always know your pay-off balance, and how much interest you can or will save, you will need a schedule. Here's what you can do if you have an Amortization Schedule, but aren't able to keep pace with the principal payments.

For many people, trying to keep up with an Amortization Schedule can be quite daunting. The extra principal payments either start out too high in the beginning or they accelerate so quickly that it becomes impossible to continue them as they increase over time.

For example, Simon finances $21,500 at a 9.0 percent interest rate over 4 years for a new car. He generates his own Amortization Schedule for his loan and the first five months of his schedule are as follows:

AMORTIZATION SCHEDULE 1

Month Number	Payment Due Date	Beginning Balance	Scheduled Payment	Principal	Interest	Ending Balance
1	1/1/XX	$21,500.00	$535.03	$373.78	$161.25	21,126.22
2	1/2/XX	21,126.22	535.03	376.58	158.45	20,749.64
3	1/3/XX	20,749.64	535.03	379.41	155.62	20,370.23
4	1/4/XX	20,370.23	535.03	382.25	152.78	19,987.98
5	1/5/XX	19,987.98	535.03	385.12	149.91	19,602.86

As you can see, Simon's first scheduled payment for Month Number 1 would be $535.03. His principal payment for Month Number 2 would be $376.58. If Simon were to attempt to pay both his regular payment and his next principal payment, his combined payment would be $911.61. If he wanted to continue making one regular payment and one principal payment every month, the combined payment would accelerate even faster.

Simon can still make extra principal payments using an Amortization Schedule program that features an *extra* payment option. An extra payment schedule will allow Simon to set a fixed extra principal payment amount of his choosing (e.g., $100 a month). And, this fixed amount will remain constant throughout the life of the loan, or until he changes the extra payment amount or cancels it altogether on his Amortization Schedule. This feature allows for any borrower to pay just one constant total payment amount each and every month until the loan is paid in full. The extra payment schedule will automatically adjust to this additional principal payment by shortening the term of the loan and advancing the pay-off date of the original loan contract. The extra payment amount can be changed or discontinued at any time and a new Amortization Schedule can be generated to reflect a new principal payment amount.

Let's generate a new Amortization Schedule for Simon's car loan with the same loan data, but with the extra payment option. Let's stay with our $100 extra principal payment used in the previous example.

A BRIEF SUMMARY OF AMORTIZATION SCHEDULE 2

Month Number	Payment Due Date	Beginning Balance	Scheduled Payment	**Extra Payment**	**Total Payment**	Principal	Interest	Ending Balance
1	1/1/XX	$21,500.00	$535.03	**$100.00**	**$635.03**	$473.78	$161.25	$21,026.22
2	2/1/XX	21,026.22	$535.03	**$100.00**	**$635.03**	477.33	157.70	20,391.19

Note: Simon would still have to indicate on his payment coupon that the extra $100 amount sent with your payment is to be applied to Principal.

As you can see, in schedule 2, with the extra principal payment feature, the extra principal payment of $100 and the regular payment of $535.03 combine to form a constant Total Payment of $635.03 a month. If Simon continues his payments at this pace he will reduce his term by 8 months and avoid paying $785.56 in interest for his loan. Simon can stop, change or eliminate the extra payment by generating a new schedule at any time.

Quick Review

To keep pace with the principal payments on your Amortization Schedule, use a schedule with an extra payment option.

- Amortization Schedule number 1 is the typical schedule discussed throughout this publication, in which the borrower makes regular scheduled payments according to the Month Number and Due Date.

    o Additional principal payments may be added in any order or whenever possible to avoid paying interest for any given month.

    o As additional principal payments are made, the term of the loan shortens.

- Amortization Schedule number 2 is identical to schedule number 1 in every way, except:

    o You can *pre-set* a built-in and fixed extra principal payment amount which will remain constant throughout the entire loan period or until the extra payment amount is changed or is canceled altogether on your Amortization Schedule.

- o The extra payment will automatically reduce the term of the loan according to those extra payments. You would still, however, have to indicate on your payment coupon that the extra money sent in with your payment is to be applied to Principal.

Note: the scheduled monthly payment can never be less than the original loan agreement.

A Money Sense Quote: Do not virtue money for any more nor any less than it is worth; it is a good servant but a bad master. - Alexandre Dumas fils, Camille, 1852

SIDE BAR — IS THERE ANY OTHER WAY TO PAY DOWN MY MORTGAGE, OR ANY OTHER LOAN, FASTER WITHOUT USING AN AMORTIZATION SCHEDULE?

Yes! You do not need an Amortization Schedule to pay down any loan faster. You're free to pay extra principal towards any loan you want, at any time, provided there is no pre-payment penalty.

For example, if you have a set mortgage payment every month and have an extra $100.00 at the end of the month, send it in with your house payment as an additional principal payment. The following month you may have only $25 left over. Send it in too! Any amount of extra money you want to pay towards any loan is a good thing. It not only pays your house or other loans off sooner, but it lessens your debt load faster and saves you some interest. Just remember to indicate on your payment coupon that the extra money is to be applied to principal.

A Money Sense Quote: But tell me: how did gold get to the highest value? Because it is uncommon and useless and gleaming and gentle in its brilliance; It always gives itself. Only as an image of the highest virtue did gold get to be the highest value. The giver's glance gleams like gold. A golden brilliance concludes peace between the moon and the sun. Uncommon is the highest virtue and useless, it is gleaming and gentle in its brilliance: a gift-giving virtue is the highest virtue. - Friedrich Nietzsche

Red Flag — Deficit Spending Gone Mad, Your Tax Dollars and the threat of future Hyper-Inflation?

In 2009 the federal government spent approximately $787 Billion tax-payer dollars for the Troubled Asset Relief Program, better known as (TARP), in an effort to revive our economy; however the economy still continues to experience the greatest recession since "The Great Depression".

You may ask - what happened to cause this great recession? The economy seemed to have been buzzing along just fine, and then - out of the blue, in mid-September, 2008, the economic world was tilted on its polar axis and everything came crashing down. Overnight millions of American families lost a combined total of $11 Trillion worth of value in their homes. The real estate bubble popped. What on earth happened to cause this? Well... to put it a nutshell, the big picture goes something like this. The economic dominoes began to wobble decades ago when congress either relaxed or eliminated many of the regulations enacted to establish proper principles, practices and policies to better control all financial activities on Wall Street after the Great Depression.

With many regulations now repealed or at least allocated to the back burner our big investment banks and other financial institutions on Wall Street got very creative. Their ultimate goal was to eliminate risk on loans. To accomplish this, the big banks basically side-stepped existing regulations (regulatory arbitrage/black box) to create an altered and extremely complex derivatives market (e.g., leveraged swaps and bets) out of the view of regulators and born from this were very exotic and extremely toxic mortgage securities. And who was going to carry all of the risk? A very large insurance company called the American International Group (AIG).

The first domino fell, when In early September, 2008 a world class investment bank on Wall Street was on the verge of failing when the feds stepped in, with tax-payer dollars, and rescued it.

The second domino fell, when the announcement came in mid-September, 2008 that another world class investment bank on Wall Street failed and there was going to be no rescue at all from the feds.

Suddenly there was a great deal of panic in the financial community because the investment banking chiefs were now confused, "Would they (the banks) be rescued by the feds in the event of eminent failure or not?" Suddenly, economic dominos began to fall in England, Ireland, Italy, Greece and other large economies throughout the rest of the world. The entire nation of Iceland eventually went bankrupt. More nations may still fail as well.

Since AIG was on the hook for bailing out the banks for billions upon billions of dollars' worth of worthless toxic mortgage assets, it was ultimately rescued, with your money, by the feds. This was done to prevent systemic failure. And instead of making the " too big to fail" banks morally responsible (moral hazard) for their actions the feds instead force-fed them billions and billions of tax-payer dollars to honor AIG's backing of the banks and their failed toxic mortgages.

This infusion of tax-payer dollars pumped into the investment banks came with absolutely no strings attached. The banks were still allowed to conduct business as usual and to this day no single major investment banking chief has ever been prosecuted or even been brought to trial for creating this economic disaster.

Back to: TARP, the once mighty dollar, hyper-inflation and new tax ploys aimed at you and me.

A good portion of those TARP dollars was also spent to bail out many other Wall Street financial institutions as well. Even the Detroit auto industry was bailed out. This was done to eliminate systemic risk to giant corporations that could fail, theoretically causing other corporations to fail, and they, in turn, causing even more corporations to fail until the entire economic system in America collapsed. Add those bail-out dollars to the current federal deficit and the money we owe to ourselves is now in the double digit trillions of dollars bracket and growing larger every day. In fact, if the federal government were to print out every single dollar bill that it owes at the speed of light, it would have to print $186,000 per second (equivalent to $670 Billion or just under one TARP per hour) 24/7 for almost 3 years non-stop to cover just the principal portion of the national debt fiasco. It would cost each and every working tax-payer $138,000 – or – every man, woman, and child living in America today, more than $50,000 each to pay off the debt. Our government, right now, either borrows money from other nations (with interest due) or prints currency to cover its annual short fall and over-spending practices. The fed spends far more money than it takes in. Even in the years when there's been a surplus in tax revenue, that surplus was returned to taxpayers in the form of lower taxes rather than used to pay down our national debt. The once-powerful dollar is becoming more de-valued every day and as a result, hyper-inflation—like we have never witnessed in our history—is poised to attack our wallets when we least expect it. If you thought that high gas prices are bad now, much higher prices for all goods and services will explode in the faces of our children and grandchildren in the very near future. The federal government doesn't have a monopoly on deficit-spending practices; our states, cities, counties, and the individual consumer are all guilty as well.

For example:

47 states in the U.S. recently ran combined deficits approaching $145 billion. California, the eighth largest economy in the world, led them all with a $26 billion deficit.

49 states had total tax revenue fall in 2009 and 36 of those states reported double-digit declines.

Then there were and still are all of the city and county governments that are falling far short of needed revenue by the millions as well.

And finally, there are the American consumers, who, combined, owe more than a $2 trillion in consumer debt, which equals 140 percent of our combined annual incomes.

What's the bottom line? In my view, the future for our once-great nation is looking very bleak. Our entire nation is still at risk of systemic failure! The risk is very real and you can be sure the various governments that could be affected by such an event will find new ways and/or reasons to raise taxes to meet future revenue shortfalls. They may disguise many tax increases with non-voter approved ploys and deceptions. In the future, taxpayers may experience clandestine tax raising methods by using euphemisms such as tolls, fees, penalties, surcharges, and other decoy words to feed their insatiable need for more government. It occurs to me that similar money-raising tactics were used by the credit card companies before the passage of H.R. 627 protecting us from these very same governmental ploys and deception tactics they want to use on us.

As consumers and taxpayers, we are victims of both kinds of debt, personal and governmental debt at every level. So as a private citizen, your safest financial footprint if it all comes crashing down, is to have none, and eliminate all of your personal debt before it's too late. As a taxpayer, remember the federal government can de-value the dollar all it needs to, by either printing more and/or borrowing more from foreign nations. States can and will create new tax schemes to milk the middle class for the money they need to meet their revenue needs (i.e., along with current sin taxes might come sweet tax, fat tax, fast food tax, pop tax, grocery bag tax, etc.) and all of us will be left with new taxes to pay while at the same time being faced with future skyrocketing inflation. Be prepared financially to survive future economic socialism at one extreme or an economic collapse at the other extreme if we fail to change our current personal spending habits, as well as our local, state and federal government spending habits! None of these habits are good for the middle class.

The following is a sampling of some of the crazy taxes we pay each month just on our Phone Bill:

Federal Tax	Telephone Assistance Program
Federal Subscriber Line	City Sales Tax
Federal USF Recovery Charge	City Utility Tax
HSI Surcharge	State and Local 911 Surcharge
State Sales Tax	State and County 911 surcharge
State Telecom Relay Service and Equipment	

Every utility bill comes with a similar multi-layer tax structure. Check all of your bills and see if you and/or your utility company can make any sense of them.

A Money Sense Quote: If all the economists were laid end to end, they'd never reach a conclusion. - George Bernard Shaw

Section II in Review

The core of this book began with questions and answers about Amortization Schedules programs and how to use them to create options, and "what if" strategies and scenarios to pay down and eliminate all debt.

- Question 1 — Answered in great detail what Amortization Schedules are and how they break an entire loan down into all of its essential components (e.g., Month Number, Beginning Balance, Scheduled Payment, Principal, Interest, and Ending Balance). It also went on further to explain how the Amortization Schedule computer programs that produce these schedules have built-in formulas, require no mathematical expertise, and are very easy to use.

- Question 2 — Answered why everyone should use Amortization Schedule computer programs. It also explains why they are the best personal financial tool ever created for quantitative analysis of personal debt. And if you use them wisely you'll be able to pay off *all of your debt* and stay relatively debt free leading into your retirement years.

- Question 3 — Answered how Amortization Schedules can not only tell you what you *do* know about your loan, but also what you don't know, such as: how much of each monthly payment applies to the principal amount of your loan, how much applies to interest in that same payment, at what point half the interest will be paid on your loan, and at what point half the balance is paid. And much more!

- Question 4 — Answered how the "Term" is the period of time agreed on by all legal parties to repay a loan. You learned that not only does the Term determine the amount of each payment, but also how much total interest will be paid on a particular loan during that Term. You learned that the Term on a loan contract will have as much bearing, if not more, on the total interest paid as the "Interest Rate" itself.

- Question 5 — Answered how Amortization Schedules can help you convert your 30-year mortgage into a 15-year mortgage without refinancing. You learned that Amortization Schedule computer programs can easily help you choose a 25, 20, 15, 10, or 5-year Term or anything between. And you learned there's no re-financing involved and no need to contact your lender.

- Question 6 — Answered how using Amortization Schedule computer programs can help you determine when and how to make a down payment on a house or condo.

- Question 7 — Answered how to use Amortization Schedules if you're planning to refinance. You learned that running an Amortization Schedule program enables you to plan the best strategy for your situation—like refinancing an adjustable-rate mortgage (ARM) or combining two mortgages into one. You learned how Amortization Schedules also provide you with the ability to look at other loan options available beyond refinancing an entire new loan using hypothetical loan schedules to help choose which loan option was best for you before signing on the dotted line.

- Question 8 — Answered how you can use an Amortization Schedule before and after you buy a car. You learned that before you buy a car, schedules can help you determine the best loan. You learned that you can use Amortization Schedules after your purchase to save lots of money even if you made a bad deal to start with.

- Question 9 — Answered how using an Amortization Schedule, even if you purchase a car for Zero Down and Zero Percent Interest, could still serve a purpose to save you money either before or after the deal.

- Question 10 — Answered how to use Amortization Schedules for planning "Debt Consolidation" strategies. And how even if you're over extended and debt-ridden with financial obligations (i.e., too many credit card bills), a mortgage payment, a car payment, maybe a personal loan or two, and a mountain of other small debts, debt consolidation may be for you.

- Question 11 — Answered how Amortization Schedules provide Financial Planning Strategies for Rental or Investment Properties. You know how schedules can be used before or after the loan! You learned how Hypothetical Amortization Schedules should be the starting point for all of your potential rental/investment property strategies.

- Question 12 — Answered how Amortization Schedules help eliminate Credit Card Debt and how they're the perfect _control_ tool for this kind of debt.

- Question 13 — Answered how an Amortization Schedule can help get rid of Private Mortgage Insurance (PMI), and why you should not have to pay out good hard-earned money for something you don't want and don't need.

- Question 14 — Answered how you can keep pace with the principal payments on your Amortization Schedule. And you learned how you don't even need an Amortization Schedule to pay-down a loan—any loan. You learned that you're free to pay extra principal whenever you choose, provided there is no early pay-off penalty in your loan agreement.

Section III

Amortization Schedules Illustrated

As mentioned in the introduction, this section contains several of the Amortization Schedules discussed in Section II for study and examination. These schedules, along with all the valuable information you learned in section II, will help put you on a road to financial recovery and/or help you avoid financial ruin. Again, use them to practice your own "what if" strategies and scenarios. Remember, unless you are out of debt and own outright every asset you have in your possession, there may be nothing tangible or concrete waiting for you in your future if our economic system eventually collapses.

Quick Review from Question 2, Section II

Luke and Maria just purchased a condominium.

Remember our discussion about Luke and Maria acquiring a $150,000 loan at 7.0 percent interest over 30 years for a condominium. And, if they pay for their condo over the 30-year term it will cost them exactly $359,263.35. See below.

Original Loan Amount	$150,000.00
Accrued Interest Paid	$209,263.35
360 Payments Made	$359,263.35

Exercise 1

1. If Luke and Maria paid an additional 10 extra principal payments along with their first regular payment, how much extra money would they have to pay? And, how much interest would they save?

2. If Luke and Maria paid an additional 10 extra principal payments along with their regular payment beginning their 29th year, how much extra money would they have to pay? And, how much interest would they save?

3. In what month will the principal portion of Luke and Maria's house payment finally be greater than the interest portion?

4. In what year of Luke and Maria's term will they pay more than half the interest on this loan, which equals to $104,631.67?

5. How many years will it take Luke and Maria to have reached the halfway point of paying off their $150,000 mortgage?

6. How much total absolute interest will Luke and Maria have to pay over the lifetime of their mortgage?

7. If Luke and Maria sell their house in 30 years, how much money would they need to sell it for to break even?

The answers to these questions are located at the end of this Amortization Schedule.

LUKE AND MARIA'S ENTIRE AMORTIZATION SCHEDULE

Month Number	Payment Due Date	Beginning Balance	Scheduled Payment	Principal	Interest	Ending Balance
1	9/1/20XX	$150,000.00	$997.95	$122.95	$875.00	$149,877.05
2	10/1	149,877.05	997.95	123.67	874.28	149,753.38
3	11/1	149,753.38	997.95	124.39	873.56	149,628.98
4	12/1	149,628.98	997.95	125.12	872.84	149,503.87
5	1/1/20XX	149,503.87	997.95	125.85	872.11	149,378.02
6	2/1	149,378.02	997.95	126.58	871.37	149,251.44
7	3/1	149,251.44	997.95	127.32	870.63	149,124.12
8	4/1	149,124.12	997.95	128.06	869.89	148,996.05
9	5/1	148,996.05	997.95	128.81	869.14	148,867.24
10	6/1	148,867.24	997.95	129.56	868.39	148,737.68
11	7/1	148,737.68	997.95	130.32	867.64	148,607.36
12	8/1	148,607.36	997.95	131.08	866.88	148,476.29
13	9/1	148,476.29	997.95	131.84	866.11	148,344.44
14	10/1	148,344.44	997.95	132.61	865.34	148,211.83
15	11/1	148,211.83	997.95	133.38	864.57	148,078.45
16	12/1	148,078.45	997.95	134.16	863.79	147,944.28
17	1/1/20XX	147,944.28	997.95	134.95	863.01	147,809.34
18	2/1	147,809.34	997.95	135.73	862.22	147,673.61
19	3/1	147,673.61	997.95	136.52	861.43	147,537.08
20	4/1	147,537.08	997.95	137.32	860.63	147,399.76
21	5/1	147,399.76	997.95	138.12	859.83	147,261.64
22	6/1	147,261.64	997.95	138.93	859.03	147,122.71
23	7/1	147,122.71	997.95	139.74	858.22	146,982.98
24	8/1	146,982.98	997.95	140.55	857.40	146,842.42
25	9/1	146,842.42	997.95	141.37	856.58	146,701.05
26	10/1	146,701.05	997.95	142.20	855.76	146,558.85
27	11/1	146,558.85	997.95	143.03	854.93	146,415.82
28	12/1	146,415.82	997.95	143.86	854.09	146,271.96
29	1/1/20XX	146,271.96	997.95	144.70	853.25	146,127.26
30	2/1	146,127.26	997.95	145.54	852.41	145,981.72
31	3/1	145,981.72	997.95	146.39	851.56	145,835.32
32	4/1	145,835.32	997.95	147.25	850.71	145,688.08
33	5/1	145,688.08	997.95	148.11	849.85	145,539.97
34	6/1	145,539.97	997.95	148.97	848.98	145,391.00
35	7/1	145,391.00	997.95	149.84	848.11	145,241.16
36	8/1	145,241.16	997.95	150.71	847.24	145,090.45
37	9/1	145,090.45	997.95	151.59	846.36	144,938.85
38	10/1	144,938.85	997.95	152.48	845.48	144,786.38
39	11/1	144,786.38	997.95	153.37	844.59	144,633.01
40	12/1	144,633.01	997.95	154.26	853.69	144,478.75
41	1/1/20XX	144,478.75	997.95	155.16	842.79	144,323.59
42	2/1	144,323.59	997.95	156.07	841.89	144,167.25
43	3/1	144,167.25	997.95	156.98	840.98	144,010.55

Month Number	Payment Due Date	Beginning Balance	Scheduled Payment	Principal	Interest	Ending Balance
44	4/1	$144,010.55	$997.95	$157.89	$840.06	$143,852.65
45	5/1	143,852.65	997.95	158.81	839.14	143,693.84
46	6/1	143,693.84	997.95	159.74	838.21	143,534.10
47	7/1	143,534.10	997.95	160.67	837.28	143,373.43
48	8/1	143,373.43	997.95	161.61	836.35	143,211.82
49	9/1	143,211.82	997.95	162.55	835.40	143,049.27
50	10/1	143,049.27	997.95	163.50	834.45	142,885.77
51	11/1	142,885.77	997.95	164.45	833.50	142,721.32
52	12/1	142,721.32	997.95	165.41	832.54	142,555.90
53	**1/1/20XX**	**142,555.90**	**997.95**	**166.38**	**831.58**	**142,389.53**
54	2/1	142,389.53	997.95	167.35	830.61	142,222.18
55	3/1	142,222.18	997.95	168.32	829.63	142,053.85
56	4/1	142,053.85	997.95	169.31	828.65	141,884.55
57	5/1	141,884.55	997.95	170.29	827.66	141,714.25
58	6/1	141,714.25	997.95	171.29	826.67	141,542.97
59	7/1	141,542.97	997.95	172.29	825.67	141,370.68
60	8/1	141,370.68	997.95	173.29	824.66	141,197.39
61	9/1	141,197.39	997.95	174.30	823.65	141,023.09
62	10/1	141,023.09	997.95	175.32	822.63	140,847.77
63	11/1	140,847.77	997.95	176.34	821.61	140,671.43
64	12/1	140,671.43	997.95	177.37	820.58	140,494.05
65	**1/1/20XX**	**140,494.05**	**997.95**	**178.41**	**819.55**	**140,315.65**
66	2/1	140,315.65	997.95	179.45	818.51	140,136.20
67	3/1	140,136.20	997.95	180.49	817.46	139,955.71
68	4/1	139,955.71	997.95	181.55	816.41	139,774.17
69	5/1	139,774.17	997.95	182.60	815.35	139,591.56
70	6/1	139,591.56	997.95	183.67	814.28	139,407.89
71	7/1	139,407.89	997.95	184.74	813.21	139,223.15
72	8/1	139,223.15	997.95	185.82	812.14	139,037.33
73	9/1	139,037.33	997.95	186.90	811.05	138,850.43
74	10/1	138,850.43	997.95	187.99	809.96	138,662.44
75	11/1	138,662.44	997.95	189.09	808.86	138,473.34
76	12/1	138,473.34	997.95	190.19	807.76	138,283.15
77	**1/1/20XX**	**138,283.15**	**997.95**	**191.30**	**806.65**	**138,091.85**
78	2/1	138,091.85	997.95	192.42	805.54	137,899.43
79	3/1	137,899.43	997.95	193.54	804.41	137,705.89
80	4/1	137,705.89	997.95	194.67	803.28	137,511.23
81	5/1	137,511.23	997.95	195.80	802.15	137,315.42
82	6/1	137,315.42	997.95	196.95	801.01	137,118.47
83	7/1	137,118.47	997.95	198.10	799.86	136,920.38
84	8/1	136,920.38	997.95	199.25	798.70	136,721.13
85	9/1	136,721.13	997.95	200.14	797.54	136,520..71
86	10/1	136,520..71	997.95	201.58	796.37	136,319.13
87	11/1	136,319.13	997.95	202.76	795.19	136,116.37

Month Number	Payment Due Date	Beginning Balance	Scheduled Payment	Principal	Interest	Ending Balance
88	12/1	$136,116.37	$997.95	$203.94	$794.01	$135,912.43
89	**1/1/20XX**	**135,912.43**	**997.95**	**205.13**	**792.82**	**135,707.30**
90	2/1	135,707.30	997.95	206.33	791.63	135,500.97
91	3/1	135,500.97	997.95	207.53	790.42	135,293.44
92	4/1	135,293.44	997.95	208.74	789.21	135,084.70
93	5/1	135,084.70	997.95	209.96	787.99	134,874.74
94	6/1	134,874.74	997.95	211.18	786.77	134,663.55
95	7/1	134,663.55	997.95	212.42	785.54	134,451.14
96	8/1	134,451.14	997.95	213.66	784.30	134,237.48
97	9/1	134,237.48	997.95	214.90	783.05	134,022.58
98	10/1	134,022.58	997.95	216.16	781.80	133,806.42
99	11/1	133,806.42	997.95	217.42	780.54	133,589.01
100	12/1	133,589.01	997.95	218.68	779.27	133,370.32
101	**1/1/20XX**	**133,370.32**	**997.95**	**219.96**	**777.99**	**133,150.36**
102	2/1	133,150.36	997.95	221.24	776.71	132,929.11
103	3/1	132,929.11	997.95	222.53	775.42	132,706.58
104	4/1	132,706.58	997.95	223.83	774.12	132,482.75
105	5/1	132,482.75	997.95	225.14	772.82	132,257.61
106	6/1	132,257.61	997.95	226.45	771.50	132,031.16
107	7/1	132,031.16	997.95	227.77	770.18	131,803.39
108	8/1	131,803.39	997.95	229.10	768.85	131,574.29
109	9/1	131,574.29	997.95	230.44	767.52	131,343.85
110	10/1	131,343.85	997.95	231.78	766.17	131,112.07
111	11/1	131,112.07	997.95	233.13	764.82	130,878.93
112	12/1	130,878.93	997.95	234.49	763.46	130,644.44
113	**1/1/20XX**	**130,644.44**	**997.95**	**235.86**	**762.09**	**130,408.58**
114	2/1	130,408.58	997.95	237.24	760.72	130,171.34
115	3/1	130,171.34	997.95	238.62	759.33	129,932.72
116	4/1	129,932.72	997.95	240.01	757.94	129,692.71
117	5/1	129,692.71	997.95	241.41	756.54	129,451.30
118	6/1	129,451.30	997.95	242.82	755.13	129,208.47
119	7/1	129,208.47	997.95	244.24	753.72	128,964.24
120	8/1	128,964.24	997.95	245.66	752.29	128,718.57
121	9/1	128,718.57	997.95	247.10	750.86	128,471.48
122	10/1	128,471.48	997.95	248.54	749.42	128,222.94
123	11/1	128,222.94	997.95	249.99	747.97	127,972.96
124	12/1	127,972.96	997.95	251.44	746.51	127,721.51
125	**1/1/20XX**	**127,721.51**	**997.95**	**252.91**	**745.04**	**127,468.60**
126	2/1	127,468.60	997.95	254.39	743.57	127,214.21
127	3/1	127,214.21	997.95	255.87	742.08	126,958.34
128	4/1	126,958.34	997.95	257.36	740.59	126,700.98
129	5/1	126,700.98	997.95	258.86	739.09	126,442.11
130	6/1	126,442.11	997.95	260.37	737.58	126,181.74
131	7/1	126,181.74	997.95	261.89	736.06	125,919.85

Month Number	Payment Due Date	Beginning Balance	Scheduled Payment	Principal	Interest	Ending Balance
132	8/1	$125,919.85	$997.95	$263.42	$734.53	$125,656.42
133	9/1	125,656.42	997.95	264.96	733.00	125,391.47
134	10/1	125,391.47	997.95	266.50	731.45	125,124.96
135	11/1	125,124.96	997.95	268.06	729.90	124,856.90
136	12/1	124,856.90	997.95	269.62	728.33	124,587.28
137	**1/1/20XX**	**124,587.28**	**997.95**	**271.19**	**726.76**	**124,316.09**
138	2/1	124,316.09	997.95	272.78	725.18	124,043.31
139	3/1	124,043.31	997.95	274.37	723.59	123,768.94
140	4/1	123,768.94	997.95	275.97	721.99	123,492.98
141	5/1	123,492.98	997.95	277.58	720.38	123,215.40
142	6/1	123,215.40	997.95	279.20	718.76	122,936.20
143	7/1	122,936.20	997.95	280.83	717.13	122,655.37
144	8/1	122,655.37	997.95	282.46	715.49	122,372.91
145	9/1	122,372.91	997.95	284.11	713.84	122,088.80
146	10/1	122,088.80	997.95	285.77	712.18	121,803.03
147	11/1	121,803.03	997.95	287.44	710.52	121,515.59
148	12/1	121,515.59	997.95	289.11	708.84	121,226.48
149	**1/1/20XX**	**121,226.48**	**997.95**	**290.80**	**707.15**	**120,935.68**
150	2/1	120,935.68	997.95	292.50	705.46	120,643.19
151	3/1	120,643.19	997.95	294.20	703.75	120,348.98
152	4/1	120,348.98	997.95	295.92	702.04	120,053.07
153	5/1	120,053.07	997.95	297.64	700.31	119,755.43
154	6/1	119,755.43	997.95	299.38	698.57	119,456.05
155	7/1	119,456.05	997.95	301.13	696.83	119,154.91
156	8/1	119,154.91	997.95	302.88	695.07	118,852.03
157	9/1	118,852.03	997.95	304.65	693.30	118,547.38
158	10/1	118,547.38	997.95	306.43	691.53	118,240.95
159	11/1	118,240.95	997.95	308.21	689.74	117,932.74
160	12/1	117,932.74	997.95	310.01	687.94	117,622.73
161	**1/1/20XX**	**117,622.73**	**997.95**	**311.82**	**686.13**	**117,310.90**
162	2/1	117,310.90	997.95	313.64	684.31	116,997.28
163	3/1	116,997.28	997.95	315.47	682.48	116,681.81
164	4/1	116,681.81	997.95	317.31	680.64	116,364.50
165	5/1	116,364.50	997.95	319.16	678.79	116,045.34
166	6/1	116,045.34	997.95	321.02	676.93	115,724.31
167	7/1	115,724.31	997.95	322.90	675.06	115,401.42
168	8/1	115,401.42	997.95	324.78	673.17	115,076.64
169	9/1	115,076.64	997.95	326.67	671.28	114,749.97
170	10/1	114,749.97	997.95	328.58	669.37	114,421.39
171	11/1	114,421.39	997.95	330.50	667.46	114,090.89
172	12/1	114,090.89	997.95	332.42	665.53	113,758.47
173	**1/1/20XX**	**113,758.47**	**997.95**	**334.36**	**663.59**	**113,424.11**
174	2/1	113,424.11	997.95	336.31	661.64	113,087.79
175	3/1	113,087.79	997.95	338.27	659.68	112,749.52

Month Number	Payment Due Date	Beginning Balance	Scheduled Payment	Principal	Interest	Ending Balance
176	4/1	$112,749.52	$997.95	$340.25	$657.71	$112,409.27
177	5/1	112,409.27	997.95	342.23	655.72	112,067.04
178	6/1	112,067.04	997.95	344.23	651.72	111,722.81
179	7/1	111,722.81	997.95	346.24	649.70	111,376.57
180	8/1	111,376.57	997.95	348.26	647.67	111,028.31
181	9/1	111,028.31	997.95	350.29	645.62	110,678.02
182	10/1	110,678.02	997.95	352.33	643.57	110,325.69
183	11/1	110,325.69	997.95	354.39	641.50	109,971.31
184	12/1	109,971.31	997.95	356.45	639.42	109,614.85
185	**1/1/20XX**	**109,614.85**	**997.95**	**358.53**	**637.33**	**109,256.32**
186	2/1	109,256.32	997.95	360.63	635.22	108,895.69
187	3/1	108,895.69	997.95	362.73	633.11	108,532.96
188	4/1	108,532.96	997.95	364.84	630.98	108,168.12
189	5/1	108,168.12	997.95	366.97	628.84	107,801.15
190	6/1	107,801.15	997.95	369.11	626.69	107,432.03
191	7/1	107,432.03	997.95	371.27	624.52	107,060.77
192	8/1	107,060.77	997.95	373.43	622.34	106,687.32
193	9/1	106,687.32	997.95	370.96	626.99	106,311.71
194	10/1	106,311.71	997.95	372.81	625.14	105,933.90
195	11/1	105,933.90	997.95	374.66	623.29	105,553.90
196	12/1	105,553.90	997.95	376.51	621.44	105,171.68
197	**1/1/20XX**	**105,171.68**	**997.95**	**378.36**	**619.59**	**104,787.22**
198	2/1	104,787.22	997.95	380.21	617.74	104,400.53
199	3/1	104,400.53	997.95	382.06	615.89	104,011.58
200	4/1	104,011.58	997.95	383.91	614.04	103,620.36
201	5/1	103,620.36	997.95	385.76	612.19	103,226.86
202	6/1	103,226.86	997.95	387.61	610.34	102,831.06
203	7/1	102,831.06	997.95	389.46	608.49	102,432.95
204	8/1	102,432.95	997.95	391.31	606.64	102,032.53
205	9/1	102,032.53	997.95	393.16	604.79	101,629.76
206	10/1	101,629.76	997.95	395.01	602.94	101,224.65
207	11/1	101,224.65	997.95	396.86	601.09	100,817.17
208	12/1	100,817.17	997.95	398.71	599.24	100,407.32
209	**1/1/20XX**	**100,407.32**	**997.95**	**400.56**	**597.39**	**99,995.07**
210	2/1	99,995.07	997.95	402.41	595.54	99,580.42
211	3/1	99,580.42	997.95	404.26	593.69	99,163.36
212	4/1	99,163.36	997.95	406.11	591.84	98,743.86
213	5/1	98,743.86	997.95	407.96	589.99	98,321.91
214	6/1	98,321.91	997.95	409.81	588.14	97,897.50
215	7/1	97,897.50	997.95	411.66	586.29	97,470.61
216	8/1	97,470.61	997.95	413.51	584.44	97,041.24
217	9/1	97,041.24	997.95	415.36	582.59	96,609.36
218	10/1	96,609.36	997.95	417.21	580.74	96,174.96
219	11/1	96,174.96	997.95	419.06	578.89	95,738.03

Month Number	Payment Due Date	Beginning Balance	Scheduled Payment	Principal	Interest	Ending Balance
220	12/1	$95,738.03	$997.95	$420.91	$577.04	$95,298.54
221	**1/1/20XX**	**95,298.54**	**997.95**	**422.76**	**575.19**	**94,856.50**
222	2/1	94,856.50	997.95	444.62	553.33	94,411.87
223	3/1	94,411.87	997.95	447.22	550.74	93,964.66
224	4/1	93,964.66	997.95	449.82	548.15	93,514.83
225	5/1	93,514.83	997.95	452.42	545.56	93,062.38
226	6/1	93,062.38	997.95	455.02	542.97	92,607.29
227	7/1	92,607.29	997.95	457.62	540.38	92,149.54
228	8/1	92,149.54	997.95	460.22	537.79	91,689.13
229	9/1	91,689.13	997.95	462.82	535.20	91,226.03
230	10/1	91,226.03	997.95	465.42	532.61	90,760.23
231	11/1	90,760.23	997.95	468.02	530.02	90,291.71
232	12/1	90,291.71	997.95	470.62	527.43	89,820.46
233	**1/1/20XX**	**89,820.46**	**997.95**	**473.22**	**524.84**	**89,346.46**
234	2/1	89,346.46	997.95	475.82	522.25	88,869.69
235	3/1	88,869.69	997.95	478.42	519.66	88,390.14
236	4/1	88,390.14	997.95	481.02	517.07	87,907.80
237	5/1	87,907.80	997.95	483.62	514.38	87,422.64
238	6/1	87,422.64	997.95	486.22	511.89	86,934.65
239	7/1	86,934.65	997.95	488.82	509.30	86,443.82
240	8/1	86,443.82	997.95	491.42	506.71	85,950.12
241	9/1	85,950.12	997.95	494.02	504.12	85,453.54
242	10/1	85,453.54	997.95	499.22	501.53	84,954.06
243	11/1	84,954.06	997.95	501.82	498.94	84,451.68
244	12/1	84,451.68	997.95	504.42	496.35	83,946.38
245	**1/1/20XX**	**83,946.38**	**997.95**	**507.02**	**493.76**	**83,438.11**
246	2/1	83,438.11	997.95	509.62	491.17	82,926.88
247	3/1	82,926.88	997.95	512.22	488.58	82,412.67
248	4/1	82,412.67	997.95	514.82	485.99	81,895.46
249	5/1	81,895.46	997.95	517.42	483.40	81,375.20
250	6/1	81,375.20	997.95	517.42	480.81	80,851.94
251	7/1	80,851.94	997.95	520.02	478.22	80,325.62
252	8/1	80,325.62	997.95	522.62	475.63	79,796.23
253	9/1	79,796.23	997.95	525.22	473.04	79,263.76
254	10/1	79,263.76	997.95	527.82	470.45	78,728.17
255	11/1	78,728.17	997.95	530.42	467.86	78,189.47
256	12/1	78,189.47	997.95	533.02	465.27	77,647.62
257	**1/1/20XX**	**77,647.62**	**997.95**	**535.62**	**462.68**	**77,102.61**
258	2/1	77,102.61	997.95	538.22	460.09	76,554.42
259	3/1	76,554.42	997.95	540.82	457.50	76,003.03
260	4/1	76,003.03	997.95	543.42	454.91	75,448.43
261	5/1	75,448.43	997.95	546.02	452.32	74,890.59
262	6/1	74,890.59	997.95	548.62	449.73	74,329.50
263	7/1	74,329.50	997.95	551.22	447.14	73,765.14

Month Number	Payment Due Date	Beginning Balance	Scheduled Payment	Principal	Interest	Ending Balance
264	8/1	$73,765.14	$997.95	$553.82	$444.55	$73,197.48
265	9/1	73,197.48	997.95	556.42	441.96	72,626.51
266	10/1	72,626.51	997.95	559.02	439.37	72,052.21
267	11/1	72,052.21	997.95	561.62	436.78	71,474.56
268	12/1	71,474.56	997.95	564.22	434.19	70,893.55
269	**1/1/20XX**	**70,893.55**	**997.95**	**566.82**	**431.60**	**70,309.14**
270	2/1	70,309.14	997.95	569.42	429.01	69,721.32
271	3/1	69,721.32	997.95	572.02	426.42	69,130.07
272	4/1	69,130.07	997.95	574.62	423.83	68,535.38
273	5/1	68,535.38	997.95	577.22	421.24	67,937.21
274	6/1	67,937.21	997.95	579.82	418.65	67,335.56
275	7/1	67,335.56	997.95	582.42	416.06	66,730.40
276	8/1	66,730.40	997.95	585.02	413.47	66,121.71
277	9/1	66,121.71	997.95	587.62	410.88	65,509.46
278	10/1	65,509.46	997.95	590.22	408.29	64,893.65
279	11/1	64,893.65	997.95	592.82	405.70	64,274.24
280	12/1	64,274.24	997.95	623.02	374.93	63,651.22
281	**1/1/20XX**	**63,651.22**	**997.95**	**626.65**	**371.30**	**63,024.56**
282	2/1	63,024.56	997.95	630.28	367.67	62,394.25
283	3/1	62,394.25	997.95	633.91	364.04	61,760.27
284	4/1	61,760.27	997.95	637.54	360.41	61,122.58
285	5/1	61,122.58	997.95	641.17	356.78	59,836.03
286	6/1	59,836.03	997.95	644.80	353.15	59,187.12
287	7/1	59,187.12	997.95	648.43	349.52	58,534.42
288	8/1	58,534.42	997.95	652.06	345.89	57,887.92
289	9/1	57,887.92	997.95	655.69	342.26	57,217.59
290	10/1	57,217.59	997.95	659.32	338.63	56,553.40
291	11/1	56,553.40	997.95	662.95	335.00	55,885.34
292	12/1	55,885.34	997.95	666.58	331.37	55,213.39
293	**1/1/20XX**	**55,213.39**	**997.95**	**670.21**	**327.74**	**54,537.51**
294	2/1	54,537.51	997.95	673.84	324.11	53,857.69
295	3/1	53,857.69	997.95	677.47	320.48	53,173.91
296	4/1	53,173.91	997.95	681.10	316.85	52,486.14
297	5/1	52,486.14	997.95	684.73	313.22	51,794.35
298	6/1	51,794.35	997.95	688.36	309.59	51,098.53
299	7/1	51,098.53	997.95	691.99	305.96	59,836.03
300	8/1	59,836.03	997.95	695.62	302.13	50,398.65
301	9/1	50,398.65	997.95	699.25	298.08	49,694.69
302	10/1	49,694.69	997.95	702.88	295.07	48,986.62
303	11/1	48,986.62	997.95	706.51	291.44	48,274.43
304	12/1	48,274.43	997.95	710.14	287.81	47,558.07
305	**1/1/20XX**	**47,558.07**	**997.95**	**713.77**	**284.18**	**46,837.54**
306	2/1	46,837.54	997.95	717.40	280.55	46,112.81
307	3/1	46,112.81	997.95	721.03	276.92	45,383.84

Month Number	Payment Due Date	Beginning Balance	Scheduled Payment	Principal	Interest	Ending Balance
308	4/1	$45,383.84	$997.95	$724.66	$273.29	$44,650.63
309	5/1	44,650.63	997.95	728.29	269.66	43,913.14
310	6/1	43,913.14	997.95	731.92	266.03	43,171.34
311	7/1	43,171.34	997.95	735.55	262.40	42,425.22
312	8/1	42,425.22	997.95	739.18	258.77	41,674.75
313	9/1	41,674.75	997.95	742.81	255.14	40,919.90
314	10/1	40,919.90	997.95	746.44	251.51	40,160.64
315	11/1	40,160.64	997.95	750.07	247.88	39,396.96
316	12/1	39,396.96	997.95	753.70	244.25	38,628.82
317	**1/1/20XX**	**38,628.82**	**997.95**	**757.33**	**240.62**	**37,856.20**
318	2/1	37,856.20	997.95	760.96	236.99	37,079.08
319	3/1	37,079.08	997.95	764.59	233.36	36,297.42
320	4/1	36,297.42	997.95	768.22	229.73	35,511.20
321	5/1	35,511.20	997.95	771.85	226.10	34,720.39
322	6/1	34,720.39	997.95	775.48	222.47	33,924.98
323	7/1	33,924.98	997.95	779.11	218.84	33,124.92
324	8/1	33,124.92	997.95	782.74	215.21	32,320.19
325	9/1	32,320.19	997.95	786.37	211.58	31,510.77
326	10/1	31,510.77	997.95	790.00	207.95	30,696.63
327	11/1	30,696.63	997.95	793.63	204.32	29,877.74
328	12/1	29,877.74	997.95	797.26	200.69	29,054.08
329	**1/1/20XX**	**29,054.08**	**997.95**	**800.89**	**197.06**	**28,225.60**
330	2/1	28,225.60	997.95	804.52	193.43	27,392.30
331	3/1	27,392.30	997.95	808.15	189.80	26,554.13
332	4/1	26,554.13	997.95	811.78	186.17	25,711.08
333	5/1	25,711.08	997.95	815.41	182.54	24,863.11
334	6/1	24,863.11	997.95	819.04	178.91	23,152.29
335	7/1	23,152.29	997.95	822.67	171.65	22,289.40
336	8/1	22,289.40	997.95	826.30	168.02	21,421.46
337	9/1	21,421.46	997.95	829.93	124.96	20,548.47
338	10/1	20,548.47	997.95	873.00	119.87	19,670.38
339	11/1	19,670.38	997.95	878.09	114.74	18,787.17
340	12/1	18,787.17	997.95	883.21	109.59	17,898.81
341	**1/1/20XX**	**17,898.81**	**997.95**	**888.36**	**104.41**	**17,005.26**
342	2/1	17,005.26	997.95	893.54	99.20	16,106.51
343	3/1	16,106.51	997.95	898.76	99.20	15,202.51
344	4/1	15,202.51	997.95	904.00	93.95	14,293.24
345	5/1	14,293.24	997.95	909.27	88.68	13,378.66
346	6/1	13,378.66	997.95	914.58	83.38	12,458.75
347	7/1	12,458.75	997.95	919.91	78.04	11,533.47
348	8/1	11,533.47	997.95	925.28	72.68	10,602.80
349	9/1	10,602.80	997.95	930.68	67.28	23,152.29
350	10/1	23,152.29	997.95	936.10	61.85	9,666.69
351	11/1	9,666.69	997.95	941.56	56.39	8,725.13

Month Number	Payment Due Date	Beginning Balance	Scheduled Payment	Principal	Interest	Ending Balance
352	12/1	$8,725.13	$997.95	$947.06	$50.90	$7,778.07
353	**1/1/20XX**	**7,778.07**	**997.95**	**952.58**	**45.37**	**6,825.49**
354	2/1	6,825.49	997.95	958.14	39.82	5,867.35
355	3/1	5,867.35	997.95	963.73	34.23	4,903.62
356	4/1	4,903.62	997.95	969.35	28.60	3,934.27
357	5/1	3,934.27	997.95	975.00	22.95	2,959.27
358	6/1	2,959.27	997.95	980.69	17.26	1,978.58
359	7/1	1,978.58	997.95	986.41	11.54	992.17
360	8/1	992.17	997.95	992.17	5.79	0.00

ANSWERS TO THE QUESTIONS IN EXERCISE 1

1. If Luke and Maria paid an additional 10 extra principal payments along with their first regular payment, how much extra money would they have to pay? *They would pay $1,269.68 and reduce their term by 10 months.* And, how much interest would they save? *They would save $8,709.85 in interest they would never have to pay.*

2. If Luke and Maria paid an additional 10 extra principal payments along with their regular payment beginning their 29th year, how much extra money would they have to pay? *They would have to pay $9,666.69 and reduce their term by 10 months. And, how much interest would they save? They would only save $312.85. This is why it is so important to make principal payments in the beginning while the principal payments are low and the interest you can save is so high.*

3. In what month will the principal portion of Luke and Maria's house payment finally be greater than the interest portion? *This would not occur until month 243, or 20 years into the term of their mortgage.*

4. In what year of Luke and Maria's term will they pay more than half the interest on this loan, which equals to $104,631.67? *They will pay 50 percent of their interest in the first 11 years.*

5. How many years will it take Luke and Maria to have reached the halfway point of paying off their $150,000 mortgage? *It will take them 22 years to pay off half the original loan if they only make regular scheduled payments.*

6. How much total absolute interest will Luke and Maria have to pay over the lifetime of their mortgage? *They will pay 139.51 percent on this 7.0 percent loan over the 30-year term period.*

7. If Luke and Maria sell their house in 30 years, how much money would they need to sell it for to break even? *They would have to sell it for $359,263.35 to recoup all of the interest and principal they paid.*

Put Luke and Maria's Amortization Schedule to work as though this was your mortgage; what would you do with it to save money?

QUICK REVIEW FROM QUESTION 4, SECTION II

How will the "Term" on a loan affect my payment?

Remember I mentioned earlier in question 4 that the "Term" is the period of time agreed on by all legal parties to repay a loan. And, that it not only determines the amount of each payment, but also how much total interest will be paid on a particular loan during that Term. The "Term" that is assigned to any loan contract will have as much bearing, if not more, on the total interest paid as the "Interest Rate" itself.

I generated four Amortization Schedules for this demonstration, two of which are 1 year terms, one for $100 and one for $100,000, and two additional schedules for the same values but for a 15-year-term period. All of the schedules are at a 10 percent interest rate. Let's see what happens:

LOAN DATA 1
FOR A $100 LOAN AT A 10% INTEREST RATE
1 YEAR TERM

Loan Amount	$100.00
Annual Interest Rate	10%
Scheduled Monthly Payment	$8.79
Term/Period	1 Year
Total Interest Paid	$5.50

Now examine the entire Amortization Schedule below to see how it all breaks down.

1 YEAR AMORTIZATION SCHEDULE FOR A $100 LOAN AT A 10% INTEREST RATE

Month Number	Payment Due Date	Beginning Balance	Scheduled Payment	Principal	Interest	Ending Balance
1	1/1/20XX	$100.00	$8.79	$7.96	$0.83	$92.04
2	2/1	92.04	8.79	8.02	0.77	84.02
3	3/1	84.02	8.79	8.09	0.70	75.93
4	4/1	75.93	8.79	8.16	0.63	67.77
5	5/1	67.77	8.79	8.23	0.56	59.54
6	6/1	59.54	8.79	8.30	0.50	51.24
7	7/1	51.24	8.79	8.36	0.43	42.88
8	8/1	42.88	8.79	8.43	0.36	34.45
9	9/1	34.45	8.79	8.50	0.29	25.94
10	10/1	25.94	8.79	8.58	0.22	17.37
11	11/1	17.37	8.79	8.65	0.14	8.72
12	12/1	8.72	8.79	8.72	0.07	00.0

Note: With a one year term you would only pay 5.5 percent absolute interest or $5.50 for a $100 loan, even though it's really a 10 percent loan.

Let's examine the same 10 percent loan but only change the term period from 1 year to 15 years and see what happens.

LOAN DATA 2
FOR A $100 LOAN AT A 10% INTEREST RATE
15 YEAR TERM

Loan Amount	$100.00
Annual Interest Rate	10%
Scheduled Monthly Payment	$1.07
Term/Period	15 Year
Total Interest Paid	$93.43

Note in Loan Data 2 that the Monthly Payment drops from $8.79 which appeared in loan data 1 to $1.07 and the total interest you would have to pay jumps to $93.43—that's 93.43 percent absolute interest you would have to pay for a 10 percent loan.

Now examine the entire Amortization Schedule below to see how it all breaks down.

15-YEAR AMORTIZATION SCHEDULE FOR A $100 LOAN AT A 10% INTEREST RATE

Month Number	Payment Due Date	Beginning Balance	Scheduled Payment	Principal	Interest	Ending Balance
1	1/1/20XX	$100.00	$1.07	$0.24	$0.83	$99.76
2	2/1	99.76	1.07	0.24	0.83	99.52
3	3/1	99.52	1.07	0.25	0.83	99.27
4	4/1	99.27	1.07	0.25	0.83	99.02
5	5/1	99.02	1.07	0.25	0.83	98.77
6	6/1	98.77	1.07	0.25	0.82	98.52
7	7/1	98.52	1.07	0.25	0.82	98.27
8	8/1	98.27	1.07	0.26	0.82	98.01
9	9/1	98.01	1.07	0.26	0.82	97.75
10	10/1	97.75	1.07	0.26	0.81	97.49
11	11/1	97.49	1.07	0.26	0.81	97.23
12	12/1	97.23	1.07	0.26	0.81	96.97
13	1/1/20XX	96.97	1.07	0.27	0.81	96.70
14	2/1	96.70	1.07	0.27	0.81	96.43
15	3/1	96.43	1.07	0.27	0.80	96.16
16	4/1	96.16	1.07	0.27	0.80	95.89
17	5/1	95.89	1.07	0.28	0.80	95.61
18	6/1	95.61	1.07	0.28	0.80	95.34
19	7/1	95.34	1.07	0.28	0.79	95.06
20	8/1	95.06	1.07	0.28	0.79	94.77
21	9/1	94.77	1.07	0.28	0.79	94.49
22	10/1	94.49	1.07	0.29	0.79	94.20
23	11/1	94.20	1.07	0.29	0.79	93.91
24	12/1	93.91	1.07	0.29	0.78	93.62
25	1/1/20XX	93.62	1.07	0.29	0.78	93.32

Month Number	Payment Due Date	Beginning Balance	Scheduled Payment	Principal	Interest	Ending Balance
26	2/1	$93.32	$1.07	$0.30	$0.78	$93.03
27	3/1	93.03	1.07	0.30	0.78	92.73
28	4/1	92.73	1.07	0.30	0.77	92.43
29	5/1	92.43	1.07	0.30	0.77	92.12
30	6/1	92.12	1.07	0.31	0.77	91.82
31	7/1	91.82	1.07	0.31	0.77	91.51
32	8/1	91.51	1.07	0.31	0.76	91.19
33	9/1	91.19	1.07	0.31	0.76	90.88
34	10/1	90.88	1.07	0.32	0.76	90.56
35	11/1	90.56	1.07	0.32	0.75	90.24
36	12/1	90.24	1.07	0.32	0.75	89.92
37	**1/1/20XX**	**89.92**	**1.07**	**0.33**	**0.75**	**89.59**
38	2/1	89.59	1.07	0.33	0.75	89.27
39	3/1	89.27	1.07	0.33	0.74	88.94
40	4/1	88.94	1.07	0.33	0.74	88.60
41	5/1	88.60	1.07	0.34	0.74	88.27
42	6/1	88.27	1.07	0.34	0.74	87.93
43	7/1	87.93	1.07	0.34	0.73	87.58
44	8/1	87.58	1.07	0.34	0.73	87.24
45	9/1	87.24	1.07	0.35	0.73	86.89
46	10/1	86.89	1.07	0.35	0.72	86.54
47	11/1	86.54	1.07	0.35	0.72	86.19
48	6/1	86.19	1.07	0.36	0.72	85.83
49	**1/1/20XX**	**85.83**	**1.07**	**0.36**	**0.72**	**85.47**
50	2/1	85.47	1.07	0.36	0.71	85.11
51	3/1	85.11	1.07	0.37	0.71	84.74
52	4/1	84.74	1.07	0.37	0.71	84.38
53	5/1	84.38	1.07	0.37	0.70	84.01
54	6/1	84.01	1.07	0.37	0.70	83.63
55	7/1	83.63	1.07	0.38	0.70	83.25
56	8/1	83.25	1.07	0.38	0.69	82.87
57	9/1	82.87	1.07	0.38	0.69	82.49
58	10/1	82.49	1.07	0.39	0.69	82.10
59	11/1	82.10	1.07	0.39	0.68	81.71
60	12/1	81.71	1.07	0.39	0.68	81.32
61	**1/1/20XX**	**81.32**	**1.07**	**0.40**	**0.68**	**80.92**
62	2/1	80.92	1.07	0.40	0.67	80.52
63	3/1	80.52	1.07	0.40	0.67	80.12
64	4/1	80.12	1.07	0.41	0.67	79.71
65	5/1	79.71	1.07	0.41	0.66	79.30
66	6/1	79.30	1.07	0.41	0.66	78.88
67	7/1	78.88	1.07	0.42	0.66	78.47
68	8/1	78.47	1.07	0.42	0.65	78.05
69	9/1	78.05	1.07	0.42	0.65	77.62

Month Number	Payment Due Date	Beginning Balance	Scheduled Payment	Principal	Interest	Ending Balance
70	10/1	$77.62	$1.07	$0.43	$0.65	$77.19
71	11/1	77.19	1.07	0.43	0.64	76.76
72	12/1	76.76	1.07	0.43	0.64	76.33
73	**1/1/20XX**	**76.33**	**1.07**	**0.44**	**0.64**	**75.89**
74	2/1	75.89	1.07	0.44	0.63	75.45
75	3/1	75.45	1.07	0.45	0.63	75.00
76	4/1	75.00	1.07	0.45	0.63	74.55
77	5/1	74.55	1.07	0.45	0.62	74.10
78	6/1	74.10	1.07	0.46	0.62	73.64
79	7/1	73.64	1.07	0.46	0.61	73.18
80	8/1	73.18	1.07	0.46	0.61	72.72
81	9/1	72.72	1.07	0.47	0.61	72.25
82	10/1	72.25	1.07	0.47	0.60	71.78
83	11/1	71.78	1.07	0.48	0.60	71.30
84	12/1	71.30	1.07	0.48	0.59	70.82
85	**1/1/20XX**	**70.82**	**1.07**	**0.48**	**0.59**	**70.33**
86	2/1	70.33	1.07	0.49	0.59	69.85
87	3/1	69.85	1.07	0.49	0.58	69.35
88	4/1	69.35	1.07	0.50	0.58	68.86
89	5/1	68.86	1.07	0.50	0.57	68.36
90	6/1	68.36	1.07	0.50	0.57	67.85
91	7/1	67.85	1.07	0.51	0.57	67.34
92	8/1	67.34	1.07	0.51	0.56	66.83
93	9/1	66.83	1.07	0.52	0.56	66.31
94	10/1	66.31	1.07	0.52	0.55	65.79
95	11/1	65.79	1.07	0.53	0.55	65.26
96	6/1	65.26	1.07	0.53	0.54	64.73
97	**1/1/20XX**	**64.73**	**1.07**	**$0.54**	**0.54**	**64.20**
98	2/1	64.20	1.07	0.54	0.53	63.66
99	3/1	63.66	1.07	0.54	0.53	63.11
100	4/1	63.11	1.07	0.55	0.53	62.56
101	5/1	62.56	1.07	0.55	0.52	62.01
102	6/1	62.01	1.07	0.56	0.52	61.45
103	7/1	61.45	1.07	0.56	0.51	60.89
104	8/1	60.89	1.07	0.57	0.51	60.32
105	9/1	60.32	1.07	0.57	0.50	59.75
106	10/1	59.75	1.07	0.58	0.50	59.17
107	11/1	59.17	1.07	0.58	0.49	58.59
108	12/1	58.59	1.07	0.59	0.49	58.01
109	**1/1/20XX**	**58.01**	**1.07**	**0.59**	**0.48**	**57.41**
110	2/1	57.41	1.07	0.60	0.48	56.82
111	3/1	56.82	1.07	0.60	0.47	56.22
112	4/1	56.22	1.07	0.61	0.47	55.61
113	5/1	55.61	1.07	0.61	0.46	55.00

Month Number	Payment Due Date	Beginning Balance	Scheduled Payment	Principal	Interest	Ending Balance
114	6/1	$55.00	$1.07	$0.62	$0.46	$54.38
115	7/1	54.38	1.07	0.62	0.45	53.76
116	8/1	53.76	1.07	0.63	0.45	53.14
117	9/1	53.14	1.07	0.63	0.44	52.50
118	10/1	52.50	1.07	0.64	0.44	51.87
119	11/1	51.87	1.07	0.64	0.43	51.22
120	12/1	51.22	1.07	0.65	0.43	50.58
121	**1/1/20XX**	**50.58**	**1.07**	**0.65**	**0.42**	**49.92**
122	2/1	49.92	1.07	0.66	0.42	49.26
123	3/1	49.26	1.07	0.66	0.41	48.60
124	4/1	48.60	1.07	0.67	0.41	47.93
125	5/1	47.93	1.07	0.68	0.40	47.26
126	6/1	47.26	1.07	0.68	0.39	46.58
127	7/1	46.58	1.07	0.69	0.39	45.89
128	8/1	45.89	1.07	0.69	0.54	45.20
129	9/1	45.20	1.07	0.70	0.53	44.50
130	10/1	44.50	1.07	0.70	0.53	43.79
131	11/1	43.79	1.07	0.71	0.53	43.09
132	12/1	43.09	1.07	0.72	0.52	42.37
133	**1/1/20XX**	**42.37**	**1.07**	**0.72**	**0.52**	**41.65**
134	2/1	41.65	1.07	0.73	0.51	40.92
135	3/1	40.92	1.07	0.73	0.51	40.19
136	4/1	40.19	1.07	0.74	0.50	39.45
137	5/1	39.45	1.07	0.75	0.50	38.70
138	6/1	38.70	1.07	0.75	0.49	37.95
139	7/1	37.95	1.07	0.76	0.49	37.19
140	8/1	37.19	1.07	0.76	0.48	36.43
141	9/1	36.43	1.07	0.77	0.48	35.66
142	10/1	35.66	1.07	0.78	0.47	34.88
143	11/1	34.88	1.07	0.78	0.47	34.09
144	12/1	34.09	1.07	0.79	0.46	33.30
145	**1/1/20XX**	**$33.30**	**$1.07**	**$0.80**	**$0.38**	**$32.51**
146	2/1	32.51	1.07	0.80	0.38	31.70
147	3/1	31.70	1.07	0.81	0.37	30.89
148	4/1	30.89	1.07	0.82	0.36	30.07
149	5/1	30.07	1.07	0.82	0.36	29.25
150	6/1	29.25	1.07	0.83	0.35	28.42
151	7/1	28.42	1.07	0.84	0.35	27.58
152	8/1	27.58	1.07	0.84	0.34	26.74
153	9/1	26.74	1.07	0.85	0.33	25.89
154	10/1	25.89	1.07	0.86	0.33	25.03
155	11/1	25.03	1.07	0.87	0.32	24.16
156	12/1	24.16	1.07	0.87	0.32	23.29
157	**1/1/20XX**	**23.29**	**1.07**	**0.88**	**0.31**	**22.41**

Month Number	Payment Due Date	Beginning Balance	Scheduled Payment	Principal	Interest	Ending Balance
158	2/1	$22.41	$1.07	$0.89	$0.30	$21.52
159	3/1	21.52	1.07	0.90	0.30	20.62
160	4/1	20.62	1.07	0.90	0.29	19.72
161	5/1	19.72	1.07	0.91	0.28	18.81
162	6/1	18.81	1.07	0.92	0.28	17.89
163	7/1	17.89	1.07	0.93	0.27	16.97
164	8/1	16.97	1.07	0.93	0.26	16.03
165	9/1	16.03	1.07	0.94	0.26	15.09
166	10/1	15.09	1.07	0.95	0.25	14.14
167	11/1	14.14	1.07	0.96	0.24	13.19
168	12/1	13.19	1.07	0.96	0.24	12.22
169	**1/1/20XX**	**12.22**	**1.07**	**0.97**	**0.23**	**11.25**
170	2/1	11.25	1.07	0.98	0.22	10.27
171	3/1	10.27	1.07	0.99	0.22	9.28
172	4/1	9.28	1.07	1.00	0.21	8.28
173	5/1	8.28	1.07	1.01	0.20	7.28
174	6/1	7.28	1.07	1.01	0.19	6.26
175	7/1	6.26	1.07	1.02	0.19	5.24
176	8/1	5.24	1.07	1.03	0.18	4.21
177	9/1	4.21	1.07	1.04	0.17	3.17
178	10/1	3.17	1.07	1.05	0.16	2.12
179	11/1	2.12	1.07	1.06	0.16	1.07
180	12/1	1.07	1.07	1.07	0.15	0.00

Now let's examine two loans for $100,000, one set for a one year term and the other for a 15-year term, to see what happens.

LOAN DATA 3
FOR A $100,000 LOAN AT A10% INTEREST RATE
1-YEAR TERM

Loan Amount	$100,000
Annual Interest Rate	10%
Scheduled Monthly Payment	$8,791.57
Term/Period	1 Year
Total Interest Paid	$5,499.06

Note: Again, with a one-year term you would only pay 5.5 percent absolute interest or $5,499.06 for a $100,000 loan, even though it's a 10 percent loan.

Now examine the entire Amortization Schedule on the next page to see how it all breaks down.

1-YEAR AMORTIZATION SCHEDULE FOR A $100,000 LOAN AT A 10% INTEREST RATE

Month Number	Payment Due Date	Beginning Balance	Scheduled Payment	Principal	Interest	Ending Balance
1	1/1/20XX	$100,000.00	$8,791.57	$7,958.26	$833.33	$92,041.74
2	2/1	92,041.74	8,791.57	8,024.57	767.01	84,017.17
3	3/1	84,017.17	8,791.57	8,091.45	700.14	75,925.72
4	4/1	75,925.72	8,791.57	8,158.87	632.71	67,766.85
5	5/1	67,766.85	8,791.57	8,226.86	564.72	59,539.99
6	6/1	59,539.99	8,791.57	8,295.42	496.17	51,244.56
7	7/1	51,244.56	8,791.57	8,364.55	427.04	42,880.01
8	8/1	42,880.01	8,791.57	8,434.26	357.33	34,445.76
9	9/1	34,445.76	8,791.57	8,504.54	287.05	25,941.22
10	10/1	25,941.22	8,791.57	8,575.41	216.18	17,365.80
11	11/1	17,365.80	8,791.57	8,646.87	144.72	8,718.93
12	12/1	8,718.93	8,791.57	8,718.93	72.66	92,041.74

As you can see, the Term affects the total amount paid back regardless of the 10 percent fixed Interest Rate.

Let's examine the same 10 percent loan but only change the term period from 1 year to 15 years and see what happens.

LOAN DATA 4
FOR A $100,000 LOAN AT A10% INTEREST RATE
15-YEAR TERM

Loan Amount	$100,000
Annual Interest Rate	10%
Scheduled Monthly Payment	$1.074.61
Term/Period	1 Year
Total Interest Paid	$93,428.93

Note in Loan Data 4 that the Monthly Payment drops from $8,791.57 which appeared in loan data 3 to $1,074.61 and the total interest you would have to pay jumps to $93,428.93—that's 93.43 percent absolute interest you would have to pay for this 10 percent loan.

Now examine the entire Amortization Schedule below to see how it all breaks down.

15-YEAR AMORTIZATION SCHEDULE FOR A $100,000 LOAN AT A 10% INTEREST RATE

Month Number	Payment Due Date	Beginning Balance	Scheduled Payment	Principal	Interest	Ending Balance
1	1/1/20XX	$100,000.00	$1.074.61	$241.27	$833.33	$99,758.73
2	2/1	99,758.73	1.074.61	243.28	831.32	99,515.45
3	3/1	99,515.45	1.074.61	245.31	829.30	99,270.14
4	4/1	99,270.14	1.074.61	247.35	827.25	99,022.78
5	5/1	99,022.78	1.074.61	249.42	825.19	98,773.37

Month Number	Payment Due Date	Beginning Balance	Scheduled Payment	Principal	Interest	Ending Balance
6	6/1	$98,773.37	$1.074.61	$251.49	$823.11	$98,521.87
7	7/1	98,521.87	1.074.61	253.59	821.02	98,268.28
8	8/1	98,268.28	1.074.61	255.70	818.90	98,012.58
9	9/1	98,012.58	1.074.61	257.83	816.77	97,754.75
10	10/1	97,754.75	1.074.61	259.98	814.62	97,494.77
11	11/1	97,494.77	1.074.61	262.15	812.46	97,232.62
12	12/1	97,232.62	1.074.61	264.33	810.27	96,968.28
13	**1/1/20XX**	**96,968.28**	**1.074.61**	**266.54**	**808.07**	**96,701.75**
14	2/1	96,701.75	1.074.61	268.76	805.85	96,432.99
15	3/1	96,432.99	1.074.61	271.00	803.61	96,161.99
16	4/1	96,161.99	1.074.61	273.26	801.35	95,888.74
17	5/1	95,888.74	1.074.61	275.53	799.07	95,613.21
18	6/1	95,613.21	1.074.61	277.83	796.78	95,335.38
19	7/1	95,335.38	1.074.61	280.14	794.46	95,055.23
20	8/1	95,055.23	1.074.61	282.48	792.13	94,772.76
21	9/1	94,772.76	1.074.61	284.83	789.77	94,487.92
22	10/1	94,487.92	1.074.61	287.21	787.40	94,200.72
23	11/1	94,200.72	1.074.61	289.60	785.01	93,911.12
24	12/1	93,911.12	1.074.61	292.01	782.59	93,619.11
25	**1/1/20XX**	**93,619.11**	**1.074.61**	**294.45**	**780.16**	**93,324.66**
26	2/1	93,324.66	1.074.61	296.90	777.71	93,027.76
27	3/1	93,027.76	1.074.61	299.37	775.23	92,728.39
28	4/1	92,728.39	1.074.61	301.87	772.74	92,426.52
29	5/1	92,426.52	1.074.61	304.38	770.22	92,122.13
30	6/1	92,122.13	1.074.61	306.92	767.68	91,815.21
31	7/1	91,815.21	1.074.61	309.48	765.13	91,505.73
32	8/1	91,505.73	1.074.61	312.06	762.55	91,193.68
33	9/1	91,193.68	1.074.61	314.66	759.95	90,879.02
34	10/1	90,879.02	1.074.61	317.28	757.33	90,561.74
35	11/1	90,561.74	1.074.61	319.92	754.68	90,241.82
36	12/1	90,241.82	1.074.61	322.59	752.02	89,919.23
37	**1/1/20XX**	**89,919.23**	**1.074.61**	**325.28**	**749.33**	**89,593.95**
38	2/1	89,593.95	1.074.61	327.99	746.62	89,265.96
39	3/1	89,265.96	1.074.61	330.72	743.88	88,935.24
40	4/1	88,935.24	1.074.61	333.48	741.13	88,601.76
41	5/1	88,601.76	1.074.61	336.26	738.35	88,265.50
42	6/1	88,265.50	1.074.61	339.06	735.55	87,926.44
43	7/1	87,926.44	1.074.61	341.88	732.72	87,584.56
44	8/1	87,584.56	1.074.61	344.73	729.87	87,239.82
45	9/1	87,239.82	1.074.61	347.61	727.00	86,892.22
46	10/1	86,892.22	1.074.61	350.50	724.10	86,541.71
47	11/1	86,541.71	1.074.61	353.42	721.18	86,188.29
48	6/1	86,188.29	1.074.61	356.37	718.24	85,831.92
49	**1/1/20XX**	**$85,831.92**	**$1.074.61**	**$362.33**	**$715.27**	**$85,472.58**

Month Number	Payment Due Date	Beginning Balance	Scheduled Payment	Principal	Interest	Ending Balance
50	2/1	$85,472.58	$1.074.61	$365.35	$712.27	$85,110.25
51	3/1	85,110.25	1.074.61	368.40	709.25	84,744.89
52	4/1	84,744.89	1.074.61	371.47	706.21	84,376.50
53	5/1	84,376.50	1.074.61	374.56	703.14	84,005.03
54	6/1	84,005.03	1.074.61	377.68	700.04	83,630.47
55	7/1	83,630.47	1.074.61	380.83	696.92	83,252.78
56	8/1	83,252.78	1.074.61	384.01	693.77	82,871.95
57	9/1	82,871.95	1.074.61	387.21	690.60	82,487.94
58	10/1	82,487.94	1.074.61	390.43	687.40	82,100.74
59	11/1	82,100.74	1.074.61	393.69	684.17	81,710.31
60	12/1	81,710.31	1.074.61	396.97	680.92	81,316.62
61	**1/1/20XX**	**81,316.62**	**1.074.61**	**400.27**	**677.64**	**80,919.65**
62	2/1	80,919.65	1.074.61	403.61	674.33	80,519.38
63	3/1	80,519.38	1.074.61	406.97	670.99	80,115.77
64	4/1	80,115.77	1.074.61	410.37	667.63	79,708.79
65	5/1	79,708.79	1.074.61	413.78	664.24	79,298.43
66	6/1	79,298.43	1.074.61	417.23	660.82	78,884.64
67	7/1	78,884.64	1.074.61	420.71	657.37	78,467.41
68	8/1	78,467.41	1.074.61	424.22	653.90	78,046.70
69	9/1	78,046.70	1.074.61	427.75	650.39	77,622.49
70	10/1	77,622.49	1.074.61	431.32	646.85	77,194.73
71	11/1	77,194.73	1.074.61	434.91	643.29	76,763.42
72	12/1	76,763.42	1.074.61	438.53	639.70	76,328.51
73	**1/1/20XX**	**76,328.51**	**1.074.61**	**442.19**	**636.07**	**75,889.97**
74	2/1	75,889.97	1.074.61	445.87	632.42	75,447.79
75	3/1	75,447.79	1.074.61	449.59	628.73	75,001.91
76	4/1	75,001.91	1.074.61	453.34	625.02	74,552.32
77	5/1	74,552.32	1.074.61	457.11	621.27	74,098.99
78	6/1	74,098.99	1.074.61	460.92	617.49	73,641.87
79	7/1	73,641.87	1.074.61	464.76	613.68	73,180.95
80	8/1	73,180.95	1.074.61	468.64	609.84	72,716.19
81	9/1	72,716.19	1.074.61	472.54	605.97	72,247.55
82	10/1	72,247.55	1.074.61	476.48	602.06	71,775.01
83	11/1	71,775.01	1.074.61	480.45	598.13	71,298.53
84	12/1	71,298.53	1.074.61	484.45	594.15	70,818.08
85	**1/1/20XX**	**70,818.08**	**1.074.61**	**488.49**	**590.15**	**70,333.62**
86	2/1	70,333.62	1.074.61	492.56	586.11	69,845.13
87	3/1	69,845.13	1.074.61	496.67	582.04	69,352.57
88	4/1	69,352.57	1.074.61	500.81	577.94	68,855.90
89	5/1	68,855.90	1.074.61	504.98	573.80	68,355.10
90	6/1	68,355.10	1.074.61	509.19	569.63	67,850.12
91	7/1	67,850.12	1.074.61	513.43	565.42	67,340.93
92	8/1	67,340.93	1.074.61	517.71	561.17	66,827.50
93	9/1	66,827.50	1.074.61	522.02	556.90	66,309.79

Month Number	Payment Due Date	Beginning Balance	Scheduled Payment	Principal	Interest	Ending Balance
94	10/1	$66,309.79	$1.074.61	$526.37	$552.58	$65,787.76
95	11/1	65,787.76	1.074.61	530.76	548.23	65,261.39
96	6/1	65,261.39	1.074.61	362.33	543.84	64,730.63
97	**1/1/20XX**	**64,730.63**	**1.074.61**	**535.18**	**539.42**	**64,195.45**
98	2/1	64,195.45	1.074.61	539.64	534.96	63,655.80
99	3/1	63,655.80	1.074.61	544.14	530.47	63,111.66
100	4/1	63,111.66	1.074.61	548.67	525.93	62,562.99
101	5/1	62,562.99	1.074.61	553.25	521.36	62,009.74
102	6/1	62,009.74	1.074.61	557.86	516.75	61,451.89
103	7/1	61,451.89	1.074.61	562.51	512.10	60,889.38
104	8/1	60,889.38	1.074.61	567.19	507.41	60,322.19
105	9/1	60,322.19	1.074.61	571.92	502.68	59,750.27
106	10/1	59,750.27	1.074.61	576.69	497.92	59,173.58
107	11/1	59,173.58	1.074.61	581.49	493.11	58,592.09
108	12/1	58,592.09	1.074.61	586.34	488.27	58,005.75
109	**1/1/20XX**	**58,005.75**	**1.074.61**	**591.22**	**483.38**	**57,414.53**
110	2/1	57,414.53	1.074.61	596.15	478.45	56,818.38
111	3/1	56,818.38	1.074.61	601.12	473.49	56,217.26
112	4/1	56,217.26	1.074.61	606.13	468.48	55,611.13
113	5/1	55,611.13	1.074.61	611.18	463.43	54,999.95
114	6/1	54,999.95	1.074.61	616.27	458.33	54,383.68
115	7/1	54,383.68	1.074.61	621.41	453.20	53,762.27
116	8/1	53,762.27	1.074.61	626.59	448.02	53,135.68
117	9/1	53,135.68	1.074.61	631.81	442.80	52,503.88
118	10/1	52,503.88	1.074.61	637.07	437.53	51,866.80
119	11/1	51,866.80	1.074.61	642.38	432.22	51,224.42
120	12/1	51,224.42	1.074.61	647.73	426.87	50,576.69
121	**1/1/20XX**	**50,576.69**	**1.074.61**	**653.13**	**421.47**	**49,923.55**
122	2/1	49,923.55	1.074.61	658.58	416.03	49,264.98
123	3/1	49,264.98	1.074.61	664.06	410.54	48,600.91
124	4/1	48,600.91	1.074.61	669.60	405.01	47,931.32
125	5/1	47,931.32	1.074.61	675.18	399.43	47,256.14
126	6/1	47,256.14	1.074.61	680.80	393.80	46,575.34
127	7/1	46,575.34	1.074.61	686.48	388.13	45,888.86
128	8/1	45,888.86	1.074.61	692.20	382.41	45,196.66
129	9/1	45,196.66	1.074.61	697.97	376.64	44,498.69
130	10/1	44,498.69	1.074.61	703.78	370.82	43,794.91
131	11/1	43,794.91	1.074.61	709.65	364.96	43,085.26
132	12/1	43,085.26	1.074.61	715.56	359.04	42,369.70
133	**1/1/20XX**	**42,369.70**	**1.074.61**	**721.52**	**353.08**	**41,648.18**
134	2/1	41,648.18	1.074.61	727.54	347.07	40,920.64
135	3/1	40,920.64	1.074.61	733.60	341.01	40,187.04
136	4/1	40,187.04	1.074.61	739.71	334.89	39,447.33
137	5/1	39,447.33	1.074.61	745.88	328.73	38,701.45

Month Number	Payment Due Date	Beginning Balance	Scheduled Payment	Principal	Interest	Ending Balance
138	6/1	$38,701.45	$1.074.61	$752.09	$322.51	$37,949.36
139	7/1	37,949.36	1.074.61	758.36	316.24	37,191.00
140	8/1	37,191.00	1.074.61	764.68	309.92	36,426.32
141	9/1	36,426.32	1.074.61	771.05	303.55	35,655.27
142	10/1	35,655.27	1.074.61	777.48	297.13	34,877.79
143	11/1	34,877.79	1.074.61	783.96	290.65	34,093.83
144	12/1	34,093.83	1.074.61	790.49	284.12	33,303.34
145	**1/1/20XX**	**33,303.34**	**1.074.61**	**797.08**	**277.53**	**32,506.26**
146	2/1	32,506.26	1.074.61	803.72	270.89	31,702.54
147	3/1	31,702.54	1.074.61	810.42	264.19	30,892.13
148	4/1	30,892.13	1.074.61	817.17	257.43	30,074.96
149	5/1	30,074.96	1.074.61	823.98	250.62	29,250.98
150	6/1	29,250.98	1.074.61	830.85	243.76	28,420.13
151	7/1	28,420.13	1.074.61	837.77	236.83	27,582.36
152	8/1	27,582.36	1.074.61	844.75	229.85	26,737.61
153	9/1	26,737.61	1.074.61	851.79	222.81	25,885.81
154	10/1	25,885.81	1.074.61	858.89	215.72	25,026.92
155	11/1	25,026.92	1.074.61	866.05	208.56	24,160.88
156	12/1	24,160.88	1.074.61	873.26	201.34	23,287.61
157	**1/1/20XX**	**23,287.61**	**1.074.61**	**880.54**	**194.06**	**22,407.07**
158	2/1	22,407.07	1.074.61	887.88	186.73	21,519.19
159	3/1	21,519.19	1.074.61	895.28	179.33	20,623.91
160	4/1	20,623.91	1.074.61	902.74	171.87	19,721.17
161	5/1	19,721.17	1.074.61	910.26	164.34	18,810.91
162	6/1	18,810.91	1.074.61	917.85	156.76	17,893.06
163	7/1	17,893.06	1.074.61	925.50	149.11	16,967.57
164	8/1	16,967.57	1.074.61	933.21	141.40	16,034.36
165	9/1	16,034.36	1.074.61	940.99	133.62	15,093.37
166	10/1	15,093.37	1.074.61	948.83	125.78	14,144.55
167	11/1	14,144.55	1.074.61	956.73	117.87	13,187.81
168	12/1	13,187.81	1.074.61	964.71	109.90	12,223.10
169	**1/1/20XX**	**12,223.10**	**1.074.61**	**972.75**	**101.86**	**11,250.36**
170	2/1	11,250.36	1.074.61	980.85	93.75	10,269.51
171	3/1	10,269.51	1.074.61	989.03	85.58	9,280.48
172	4/1	9,280.48	1.074.61	997.27	77.34	8,283.21
173	5/1	8,283.21	1.074.61	1,005.58	69.03	7,277.63
174	6/1	7,277.63	1.074.61	1,013.96	60.65	6,263.68
175	7/1	6,263.68	1.074.61	1,022.41	52.20	5,241.27
176	8/1	5,241.27	1.074.61	1,030.93	43.68	4,210.34
177	9/1	4,210.34	1.074.61	1,039.52	35.09	3,170.82
178	10/1	3,170.82	1.074.61	1,048.18	26.42	2,122.64
179	11/1	2,122.64	1.074.61	1,056.92	17.69	1,065.72
180	12/1	1,065.72	1.074.61	1,065.72	8.88	32,506.26

Let's try two $100 loans, one at 2 Percent for a 10 year term, and one at 10 percent for a two year term to see what happens.

LOAN DATA 1
FOR A $100 LOAN AT A 2% INTEREST RATE
10-YEAR TERM

Loan Amount	$100.00
Annual Interest Rate	2%
Scheduled Monthly Payment	$0/92
Term/Period	10 Year
Total Interest Paid	$10.42

LOAN DATA 2
FOR A $100 LOAN AT A10% INTEREST RATE
2-YEAR TERM

Loan Amount	$100.00
Annual Interest Rate	10%
Scheduled Monthly Payment	$4.61
Term/Period	2 Year
Total Interest Paid	$10.75

Note: Just by flip-flopping the interest rates and the terms for the same $100 loan you'll pay roughly the same total absolute interest on each loan. It's only the Scheduled Monthly Payment that changes dramatically for each loan. So remember, if all else is equal except the term, a longer term will always cost you more dollars in absolute interest.

As I extend the loan beyond 24 months, any interest rate becomes less of a great deal. However, the monthly payment does come down as the term lengthens on all loans.

Again, this is why a used-car salesperson may ask, "How much do you want to pay each month"? They will control not just the interest rate you ultimately get, but the term, as well, to get that payment you want. So don't be fooled into thinking that the "Interest Rate" alone will determine the total dollars you will ultimately pay in interest.

Credit cards are even worse because they have you on both counts: high interest and virtually an infinite term because cardholders keep their account revolving with new debt. Imagine paying 39 percent interest on a revolving (no term limit) credit card that you only make minimum payments on each month. (Most people do this, in fact.)

Generate your own hypothetical Amortization Schedules at various "Terms" before you borrow money. In doing this you can determine your own term and payment before you make a loan agreement.

QUICK REVIEW FROM QUESTION 6, SECTION II

With the help of Amortization Schedules, can Terry and Elaine determine the down payment they should make on their house?

Remember earlier, Terry and Elaine made an offer on a house. They then generated a few Amortization Schedules to help them determine down payment options on their mortgage. After careful consideration they've decided to make a zero percent down payment and finance 100 percent of the mortgage. This strategy will enable them to use the $20,000 they had originally set aside for a down payment as one additional gigantic principal payment to be paid along with their first scheduled payment. They will:

- Cut their remaining balance to slightly less than $80,000.00.
- Reduce their term by about 146 months with about 214 months remaining.
- Pay just a little more than $72,000 total interest over the remaining loan period.
- Avoid paying approximately $55,000.00 in interest for month numbers 2 through 146.
- Have their PMI canceled because they would have a 20 percent equity stake in the house.

Examine these key points in their Amortization Schedule below.

PAYMENT STRATEGY
0 PERCENT DOWN AND 100 PERCENT FINANCED

Scheduled Monthly Payment	$632.07
Total Interest to be Paid (Approx.)	$72,000
Remaining Payments (Approx.)	214
Private Mortgage Insurance Required	For 1 month maybe?

TERRY AND ELAINE'S AMORTIZATION SCHEDULE FOR THIS LOAN

Month Number	Payment Due Date	Beginning Balance	Scheduled Payment	Principal	Interest	Ending Balance
1	1/1/20XX	$100,000.00	$632.07	$90.40	$541.67	$99,909.60
2	2/1	99,909.60	632.07	90.89	541.18	99,818.71
3	3/1	99,818.71	632.07	91.38	540.68	99,727.32
4	4/1	99,727.32	632.07	91.88	540.19	99,635.45
5	5/1	99,635.45	632.07	92.38	539.69	99,543.07
6	6/1	99,543.07	632.07	92.88	539.19	99,450.19
7	7/1	99,450.19	632.07	93.38	538.69	99,356.81
8	8/1	99,356.81	632.07	93.89	538.18	99,262.93
9	9/1	99,262.93	632.07	94.39	537.67	99,168.53
10	10/1	99,168.53	632.07	94.91	537.16	99,073.63

Month Number	Payment Due Date	Beginning Balance	Scheduled Payment	Principal	Interest	Ending Balance
11	11/1	$99,073.63	$632.07	$95.42	$536.65	$98,978.21
12	12/1	98,978.21	632.07	95.94	536.13	98,882.27
13	**1/1/20XX**	**98,882.27**	**632.07**	**96.46**	**535.61**	**98,785.82**
14	2/1	98,785.82	632.07	96.98	535.09	98,688.84
15	3/1	98,688.84	632.07	97.50	534.56	98,591.34
16	4/1	98,591.34	632.07	98.03	534.04	98,493.31
17	5/1	98,493.31	632.07	98.56	533.51	98,394.74
18	6/1	98,394.74	632.07	99.10	532.97	98,295.65
19	7/1	98,295.65	632.07	99.63	532.43	98,196.01
20	8/1	98,196.01	632.07	100.17	531.90	98,095.84
21	9/1	98,095.84	632.07	100.72	531.35	97,995.12
22	10/1	97,995.12	632.07	101.26	530.81	97,893.86
23	11/1	97,893.86	632.07	101.81	530.26	97,792.05
24	12/1	97,792.05	632.07	102.36	529.71	97,689.69
25	**1/1/20XX**	**97,689.69**	**632.07**	**102.92**	**529.15**	**97,586.78**
26	2/1	97,586.78	632.07	103.47	528.60	97,483.30
27	3/1	97,483.30	632.07	104.03	528.03	97,379.27
28	4/1	97,379.27	632.07	104.60	527.47	97,274.67
29	5/1	97,274.67	632.07	105.16	526.90	97,169.51
30	6/1	97,169.51	632.07	105.73	526.33	97,063.78
31	7/1	97,063.78	632.07	106.31	525.76	96,957.47
32	8/1	96,957.47	632.07	106.88	525.19	96,850.59
33	9/1	96,850.59	632.07	107.46	524.61	96,743.13
34	10/1	96,743.13	632.07	108.04	524.03	96,635.09
35	11/1	96,635.09	632.07	108.63	523.44	96,526.46
36	12/1	96,526.46	632.07	109.22	522.85	96,417.24
37	**1/1/20XX**	**96,417.24**	**632.07**	**109.81**	**522.26**	**96,307.43**
38	2/1	96,307.43	632.07	110.40	521.67	96,197.03
39	3/1	96,197.03	632.07	111.00	521.07	96,086.03
40	4/1	96,086.03	632.07	111.60	520.47	95,974.43
41	5/1	95,974.43	632.07	112.21	519.86	95,862.22
42	6/1	95,862.22	632.07	112.81	519.25	95,749.41
43	7/1	95,749.41	632.07	113.43	518.64	95,635.98
44	8/1	95,635.98	632.07	114.04	518.03	95,521.94
45	9/1	95,521.94	632.07	114.66	517.41	95,407.28
46	10/1	95,407.28	632.07	115.28	516.79	95,292.01
47	11/1	95,292.01	632.07	115.90	516.17	95,176.10
48	6/1	95,176.10	632.07	116.53	515.54	95,059.57
49	**1/1/20XX**	**95,059.57**	**632.07**	**117.16**	**514.91**	**94,942.41**
50	2/1	94,942.41	632.07	117.80	514.27	94,824.61
51	3/1	94,824.61	632.07	118.43	513.63	94,706.18
52	4/1	94,706.18	632.07	119.08	512.99	94,587.10
53	5/1	94,587.10	632.07	119.72	512.35	94,467.38
54	6/1	94,467.38	632.07	120.37	511.70	94,347.01

Month Number	Payment Due Date	Beginning Balance	Scheduled Payment	Principal	Interest	Ending Balance
55	7/1	$94,347.01	$632.07	$121.02	$511.05	$94,225.99
56	8/1	94,225.99	632.07	121.68	510.39	94,104.31
57	9/1	94,104.31	632.07	122.34	509.73	93,981.98
58	10/1	93,981.98	632.07	123.00	509.07	93,858.98
59	11/1	93,858.98	632.07	123.67	508.40	93,735.31
60	12/1	93,735.31	632.07	124.34	507.73	93,610.98
61	**1/1/20XX**	**93,610.98**	**632.07**	**125.01**	**507.06**	**93,485.97**
62	2/1	93,485.97	632.07	125.69	506.38	93,360.28
63	3/1	93,360.28	632.07	126.37	505.70	93,233.92
64	4/1	93,233.92	632.07	127.05	505.02	93,106.87
65	5/1	93,106.87	632.07	127.74	504.33	92,979.13
66	6/1	92,979.13	632.07	128.43	503.64	92,850.70
67	7/1	92,850.70	632.07	129.13	502.94	92,721.57
68	8/1	92,721.57	632.07	129.83	502.24	92,591.74
69	9/1	92,591.74	632.07	130.53	501.54	92,461.21
70	10/1	92,461.21	632.07	131.24	500.83	92,329.98
71	11/1	92,329.98	632.07	131.95	500.12	92,198.03
72	12/1	92,198.03	632.07	132.66	499.41	92,065.37
73	**1/1/20XX**	**92,065.37**	**632.07**	**133.38**	**498.69**	**91,931.99**
74	2/1	91,931.99	632.07	134.10	497.96	91,797.88
75	3/1	91,797.88	632.07	134.83	497.24	91,663.05
76	4/1	91,663.05	632.07	135.56	496.51	91,527.49
77	5/1	91,527.49	632.07	136.29	495.77	91,391.20
78	6/1	91,391.20	632.07	137.03	495.04	91,254.17
79	7/1	91,254.17	632.07	137.77	494.29	91,116.39
80	8/1	91,116.39	632.07	138.52	493.55	90,977.87
81	9/1	90,977.87	632.07	139.27	492.80	90,838.60
82	10/1	90,838.60	632.07	140.03	492.04	90,698.58
83	11/1	90,698.58	632.07	140.78	491.28	90,557.79
84	12/1	90,557.79	632.07	141.55	490.52	90,416.24
85	**1/1/20XX**	**90,416.24**	**632.07**	**142.31**	**489.75**	**90,273.93**
86	2/1	90,273.93	632.07	143.08	488.98	90,130.85
87	3/1	90,130.85	632.07	143.86	488.21	89,986.99
88	4/1	89,986.99	632.07	144.64	487.43	89,842.35
89	5/1	89,842.35	632.07	145.42	486.65	89,696.93
90	6/1	89,696.93	632.07	146.21	485.86	89,550.72
91	7/1	89,550.72	632.07	147.00	485.07	89,403.72
92	8/1	89,403.72	632.07	147.80	484.27	89,255.92
93	9/1	89,255.92	632.07	148.60	483.47	89,107.32
94	10/1	89,107.32	632.07	149.40	482.66	88,957.92
95	11/1	88,957.92	632.07	150.21	481.86	88,807.70
96	6/1	88,807.70	632.07	151.03	481.04	88,656.68
Month Number	Payment Due Date	Beginning Balance	Scheduled Payment	Principal	Interest	Ending Balance

Month Number	Payment Due Date	Beginning Balance	Scheduled Payment	Principal	Interest	Ending Balance
97	1/1/20XX	$88,656.68	$632.07	$151.84	$480.22	$88,504.83
98	2/1	88,504.83	632.07	152.67	479.40	88,352.17
99	3/1	88,352.17	632.07	153.49	478.57	88,198.67
100	4/1	88,198.67	632.07	154.33	477.74	88,044.35
101	5/1	88,044.35	632.07	155.16	476.91	87,889.19
102	6/1	87,889.19	632.07	156.00	476.07	87,733.18
103	7/1	87,733.18	632.07	156.85	475.22	87,576.34
104	8/1	87,576.34	632.07	157.70	474.37	87,418.64
105	9/1	87,418.64	632.07	158.55	473.52	87,260.09
106	10/1	87,260.09	632.07	159.41	472.66	87,100.68
107	11/1	87,100.68	632.07	160.27	471.80	86,940.41
108	12/1	86,940.41	632.07	161.14	470.93	86,779.27
109	1/1/20XX	86,779.27	632.07	162.01	470.05	86,617.26
110	2/1	86,617.26	632.07	162.89	469.18	86,454.36
111	3/1	86,454.36	632.07	163.77	468.29	86,290.59
112	4/1	86,290.59	632.07	164.66	467.41	86,125.93
113	5/1	86,125.93	632.07	165.55	466.52	85,960.38
114	6/1	85,960.38	632.07	166.45	465.62	85,793.93
115	7/1	85,793.93	632.07	167.35	464.72	85,626.58
116	8/1	85,626.58	632.07	168.26	463.81	85,458.32
117	9/1	85,458.32	632.07	169.17	462.90	85,289.15
118	10/1	85,289.15	632.07	170.09	461.98	85,119.07
119	11/1	85,119.07	632.07	171.01	461.06	84,948.06
120	12/1	84,948.06	632.07	171.93	460.14	84,776.13
121	1/1/20XX	84,776.13	632.07	172.86	459.20	84,603.26
122	2/1	84,603.26	632.07	173.80	458.27	84,429.46
123	3/1	84,429.46	632.07	174.74	457.33	84,254.72
124	4/1	84,254.72	632.07	175.69	456.38	84,079.03
125	5/1	84,079.03	632.07	176.64	455.43	83,902.39
126	6/1	83,902.39	632.07	177.60	454.47	83,724.80
127	7/1	83,724.80	632.07	178.56	453.51	83,546.24
128	8/1	83,546.24	632.07	179.53	452.54	83,366.71
129	9/1	83,366.71	632.07	180.50	451.57	83,186.21
130	10/1	83,186.21	632.07	181.48	450.59	83,004.74
131	11/1	83,004.74	632.07	182.46	449.61	82,822.28
132	12/1	82,822.28	632.07	183.45	448.62	82,638.83
133	1/1/20XX	82,638.83	632.07	184.44	447.63	82,454.39
134	2/1	82,454.39	632.07	185.44	446.63	82,268.95
135	3/1	82,268.95	632.07	186.44	445.62	82,082.50
136	4/1	82,082.50	632.07	187.45	444.61	81,895.05
137	5/1	81,895.05	632.07	188.47	443.60	81,706.58
138	6/1	81,706.58	632.07	189.49	442.58	81,517.09
139	7/1	81,517.09	632.07	190.52	441.55	81,326.57
140	8/1	81,326.57	632.07	191.55	440.52	81,135.02

Month Number	Payment Due Date	Beginning Balance	Scheduled Payment	Principal	Interest	Ending Balance
141	9/1	$81,135.02	$632.07	$192.59	$439.48	$80,942.44
142	10/1	80,942.44	632.07	193.63	438.44	80,748.81
143	11/1	80,748.81	632.07	194.68	437.39	80,554.13
144	12/1	80,554.13	632.07	195.73	436.33	80,358.39
145	**1/1/20XX**	**80,358.39**	**632.07**	**196.79**	**435.27**	**80,161.60**
146	2/1	80,161.60	632.07	197.86	434.21	79,963.74
147	3/1	79,963.74	632.07	198.93	433.14	79,764.81
148	4/1	79,764.81	632.07	200.01	432.06	79,564.80
149	5/1	79,564.80	632.07	201.09	430.98	79,363.71
150	6/1	79,363.71	632.07	202.18	429.89	79,161.53
151	7/1	79,161.53	632.07	203.28	428.79	78,958.25
152	8/1	78,958.25	632.07	204.38	427.69	78,753.88
153	9/1	78,753.88	632.07	205.48	426.58	78,548.39
154	10/1	78,548.39	632.07	206.60	425.47	78,341.79
155	11/1	78,341.79	632.07	207.72	424.35	78,134.08
156	12/1	78,134.08	632.07	208.84	423.23	77,925.23
157	**1/1/20XX**	**77,925.23**	**632.07**	**209.97**	**422.10**	**77,715.26**
158	2/1	77,715.26	632.07	211.11	420.96	77,504.15
159	3/1	77,504.15	632.07	212.25	419.81	77,291.90
160	4/1	77,291.90	632.07	213.40	418.66	77,078.49
161	5/1	77,078.49	632.07	214.56	417.51	76,863.93
162	6/1	76,863.93	632.07	215.72	416.35	76,648.21
163	7/1	76,648.21	632.07	216.89	415.18	76,431.32
164	8/1	76,431.32	632.07	218.07	414.00	76,213.26
165	9/1	76,213.26	632.07	219.25	412.82	75,994.01
166	10/1	75,994.01	632.07	220.43	411.63	75,773.58
167	11/1	75,773.58	632.07	221.63	410.44	75,551.95
168	12/1	75,551.95	632.07	222.83	409.24	75,329.12
169	**1/1/20XX**	**75,329.12**	**632.07**	**224.04**	**408.03**	**75,105.09**
170	2/1	75,105.09	632.07	225.25	406.82	74,879.84
171	3/1	74,879.84	632.07	226.47	405.60	74,653.37
172	4/1	74,653.37	632.07	227.70	404.37	74,425.67
173	5/1	74,425.67	632.07	228.93	403.14	74,196.74
174	6/1	74,196.74	632.07	230.17	401.90	73,966.57
175	7/1	73,966.57	632.07	231.42	400.65	73,735.16
176	8/1	73,735.16	632.07	232.67	399.40	73,502.49
177	9/1	73,502.49	632.07	233.93	398.14	73,268.56
178	10/1	73,268.56	632.07	235.20	396.87	73,033.36
179	11/1	73,033.36	632.07	236.47	395.60	72,796.89
180	12/1	72,796.89	632.07	237.75	394.32	72,559.14
181	**1/1/20XX**	**72,559.14**	**632.07**	**239.04**	**393.03**	**72,320.10**
182	2/1	72,320.10	632.07	240.33	391.73	72,079.77
183	3/1	72,079.77	632.07	241.64	390.43	71,838.13
184	4/1	71,838.13	632.07	242.94	389.12	71,595.19

Month Number	Payment Due Date	Beginning Balance	Scheduled Payment	Principal	Interest	Ending Balance
185	5/1	$71,595.19	$632.07	$244.26	$387.81	$71,350.93
186	6/1	71,350.93	632.07	245.58	386.48	71,105.34
187	7/1	71,105.34	632.07	246.91	385.15	70,858.43
188	8/1	70,858.43	632.07	248.25	383.82	70,610.18
189	9/1	70,610.18	632.07	249.60	382.47	70,360.58
190	10/1	70,360.58	632.07	250.95	381.12	70,109.63
191	11/1	70,109.63	632.07	252.31	379.76	69,857.32
192	12/1	69,857.32	632.07	253.67	378.39	69,603.65
193	**1/1/20XX**	**69,603.65**	**632.07**	**255.05**	**377.02**	**69,348.60**
194	2/1	69,348.60	632.07	256.43	375.64	69,092.17
195	3/1	69,092.17	632.07	257.82	374.25	68,834.35
196	4/1	68,834.35	632.07	259.22	372.85	68,575.14
197	5/1	68,575.14	632.07	260.62	371.45	68,314.52
198	6/1	68,314.52	632.07	262.03	370.04	68,052.49
199	7/1	68,052.49	632.07	263.45	368.62	67,789.04
200	8/1	67,789.04	632.07	264.88	367.19	67,524.16
201	9/1	67,524.16	632.07	266.31	365.76	67,257.85
202	10/1	67,257.85	632.07	267.75	364.31	66,990.09
203	11/1	66,990.09	632.07	269.21	362.86	66,720.89
204	12/1	66,720.89	632.07	270.66	361.40	66,450.23
205	**1/1/20XX**	**66,450.23**	**632.07**	**272.13**	**359.94**	**66,178.10**
206	2/1	66,178.10	632.07	273.60	358.46	65,904.49
207	3/1	65,904.49	632.07	275.09	356.98	65,629.41
208	4/1	65,629.41	632.07	276.58	355.49	65,352.83
209	5/1	65,352.83	632.07	278.07	353.99	65,074.76
210	6/1	65,074.76	632.07	279.58	352.49	64,795.18
211	7/1	64,795.18	632.07	281.09	350.97	64,514.08
212	8/1	64,514.08	632.07	282.62	349.45	64,231.47
213	9/1	64,231.47	632.07	284.15	347.92	63,947.32
214	10/1	63,947.32	632.07	285.69	346.38	63,661.63
215	11/1	63,661.63	632.07	287.23	344.83	63,374.40
216	12/1	63,374.40	632.07	288.79	343.28	63,085.61
217	**1/1/20XX**	**63,085.61**	**632.07**	**290.35**	**341.71**	**62,795.26**
218	2/1	62,795.26	632.07	291.93	340.14	62,503.33
219	3/1	62,503.33	632.07	293.51	338.56	62,209.82
220	4/1	62,209.82	632.07	295.10	336.97	61,914.72
221	5/1	61,914.72	632.07	296.70	335.37	61,618.02
222	6/1	61,618.02	632.07	298.30	333.76	61,319.72
223	7/1	61,319.72	632.07	299.92	332.15	61,019.80
224	8/1	61,019.80	632.07	301.54	330.52	60,718.26
225	9/1	60,718.26	632.07	303.18	328.89	60,415.08
226	10/1	60,415.08	632.07	304.82	327.25	60,110.26
227	11/1	60,110.26	632.07	306.47	325.60	59,803.79
228	12/1	59,803.79	632.07	308.13	323.94	59,495.66

Month Number	Payment Due Date	Beginning Balance	Scheduled Payment	Principal	Interest	Ending Balance
229	1/1/20XX	$59,495.66	$632.07	$309.80	$322.27	$59,185.86
230	2/1	59,185.86	632.07	311.48	320.59	58,874.38
231	3/1	58,874.38	632.07	313.17	318.90	58,561.22
232	4/1	58,561.22	632.07	314.86	317.21	58,246.35
233	5/1	58,246.35	632.07	316.57	315.50	57,929.79
234	6/1	57,929.79	632.07	318.28	313.79	57,611.51
235	7/1	57,611.51	632.07	320.01	312.06	57,291.50
236	8/1	57,291.50	632.07	321.74	310.33	56,969.76
237	9/1	56,969.76	632.07	323.48	308.59	56,646.28
238	10/1	56,646.28	632.07	325.23	306.83	56,321.05
239	11/1	56,321.05	632.07	327.00	305.07	55,994.05
240	12/1	55,994.05	632.07	328.77	303.30	55,665.28
241	1/1/20XX	55,665.28	632.07	330.55	301.52	55,334.73
242	2/1	55,334.73	632.07	332.34	299.73	55,002.40
243	3/1	55,002.40	632.07	334.14	297.93	54,668.26
244	4/1	54,668.26	632.07	335.95	296.12	54,332.31
245	5/1	54,332.31	632.07	337.77	294.30	53,994.54
246	6/1	53,994.54	632.07	339.60	292.47	53,654.94
247	7/1	53,654.94	632.07	341.44	290.63	53,313.51
248	8/1	53,313.51	632.07	343.29	288.78	52,970.22
249	9/1	52,970.22	632.07	345.15	286.92	52,625.07
250	10/1	52,625.07	632.07	347.02	285.05	52,278.06
251	11/1	52,278.06	632.07	348.90	283.17	51,929.16
252	12/1	51,929.16	632.07	350.79	281.28	51,578.38
253	1/1/20XX	51,578.38	632.07	352.69	279.38	51,225.69
254	2/1	51,225.69	632.07	354.60	277.47	50,871.10
255	3/1	50,871.10	632.07	356.52	275.55	50,514.58
256	4/1	50,514.58	632.07	358.45	273.62	50,156.13
257	5/1	50,156.13	632.07	360.39	271.68	49,795.75
258	6/1	49,795.75	632.07	362.34	269.73	49,433.40
259	7/1	49,433.40	632.07	364.30	267.76	49,069.10
260	8/1	49,069.10	632.07	366.28	265.79	48,702.82
261	9/1	48,702.82	632.07	368.26	263.81	48,334.56
262	10/1	48,334.56	632.07	370.26	261.81	47,964.31
263	11/1	47,964.31	632.07	372.26	259.81	47,592.05
264	12/1	47,592.05	632.07	374.28	257.79	47,217.77
265	1/1/20XX	47,217.77	632.07	376.31	255.76	46,841.46
266	2/1	46,841.46	632.07	378.34	253.72	46,463.12
267	3/1	46,463.12	632.07	380.39	251.68	46,082.73
268	4/1	46,082.73	632.07	382.45	249.61	45,700.27
269	5/1	45,700.27	632.07	384.52	247.54	45,315.75
270	6/1	45,315.75	632.07	386.61	245.46	44,929.14
271	7/1	44,929.14	632.07	388.70	243.37	44,540.44
272	8/1	44,540.44	632.07	390.81	241.26	44,149.63

Month Number	Payment Due Date	Beginning Balance	Scheduled Payment	Principal	Interest	Ending Balance
273	9/1	$44,149.63	$632.07	$392.92	$239.14	$43,756.71
274	10/1	43,756.71	632.07	395.05	237.02	43,361.65
275	11/1	43,361.65	632.07	397.19	234.88	42,964.46
276	12/1	42,964.46	632.07	399.34	232.72	42,565.12
277	**1/1/20XX**	**42,565.12**	**632.07**	**401.51**	**230.56**	**42,163.61**
278	2/1	42,163.61	632.07	403.68	228.39	41,759.93
279	3/1	41,759.93	632.07	405.87	226.20	41,354.06
280	4/1	41,354.06	632.07	408.07	224.00	40,945.99
281	5/1	40,945.99	632.07	410.28	221.79	40,535.72
282	6/1	40,535.72	632.07	412.50	219.57	40,123.22
283	7/1	40,123.22	632.07	414.73	217.33	39,708.48
284	8/1	39,708.48	632.07	416.98	215.09	39,291.50
285	9/1	39,291.50	632.07	419.24	212.83	38,872.26
286	10/1	38,872.26	632.07	421.51	210.56	38,450.75
287	11/1	38,450.75	632.07	423.79	208.27	38,026.96
288	12/1	38,026.96	632.07	426.09	205.98	37,600.87
289	1/1/20XX	37,600.87	632.07	428.40	203.67	37,172.48
290	2/1	37,172.48	632.07	430.72	201.35	36,741.76
291	3/1	36,741.76	632.07	433.05	199.02	36,308.71
292	4/1	36,308.71	632.07	435.40	196.67	35,873.31
293	5/1	35,873.31	632.07	437.75	194.31	35,435.56
294	6/1	35,435.56	632.07	440.13	191.94	34,995.43
295	7/1	34,995.43	632.07	442.51	189.56	34,552.92
296	8/1	34,552.92	632.07	444.91	187.16	34,108.02
297	9/1	34,108.02	632.07	447.32	184.75	33,660.70
298	10/1	33,660.70	632.07	449.74	182.33	33,210.96
299	11/1	33,210.96	632.07	452.18	179.89	32,758.79
300	12/1	32,758.79	632.07	454.62	177.44	32,304.16
301	**1/1/20XX**	**32,304.16**	**632.07**	**457.09**	**174.98**	**31,847.07**
302	2/1	31,847.07	632.07	459.56	172.50	31,387.51
303	3/1	31,387.51	632.07	462.05	170.02	30,925.46
304	4/1	30,925.46	632.07	464.56	167.51	30,460.90
305	5/1	30,460.90	632.07	467.07	165.00	29,993.83
306	6/1	29,993.83	632.07	469.60	162.47	29,524.23
307	7/1	29,524.23	632.07	472.15	159.92	29,052.09
308	8/1	29,052.09	632.07	474.70	157.37	28,577.38
309	9/1	28,577.38	632.07	477.27	154.79	28,100.11
310	10/1	28,100.11	632.07	479.86	152.21	27,620.25
311	11/1	27,620.25	632.07	482.46	149.61	27,137.79
312	12/1	27,137.79	632.07	485.07	147.00	26,652.72
313	**1/1/20XX**	**26,652.72**	**632.07**	**487.70**	**144.37**	**26,165.02**
314	2/1	26,165.02	632.07	490.34	141.73	25,674.68
315	3/1	25,674.68	632.07	493.00	139.07	25,181.68
316	4/1	25,181.68	632.07	495.67	136.40	24,686.02

Month Number	Payment Due Date	Beginning Balance	Scheduled Payment	Principal	Interest	Ending Balance
317	5/1	$24,686.02	$632.07	$498.35	$133.72	$24,187.66
318	6/1	24,187.66	632.07	501.05	131.02	23,686.61
319	7/1	23,686.61	632.07	503.77	128.30	23,182.85
320	8/1	23,182.85	632.07	428.40	203.67	22,676.35
321	9/1	22,676.35	632.07	430.72	201.35	22,167.12
322	10/1	22,167.12	632.07	433.05	199.02	21,655.12
323	11/1	21,655.12	632.07	435.40	196.67	21,140.35
324	12/1	21,140.35	632.07	437.75	194.31	20,622.79
325	**1/1/20XX**	**20,622.79**	**632.07**	**440.13**	**191.94**	**20,102.43**
326	2/1	20,102.43	632.07	442.51	189.56	19,579.25
327	3/1	19,579.25	632.07	444.91	187.16	19,053.24
328	4/1	19,053.24	632.07	447.32	184.75	18,524.37
329	5/1	18,524.37	632.07	449.74	182.33	17,992.65
330	6/1	17,992.65	632.07	452.18	179.89	17,458.04
331	7/1	17,458.04	632.07	454.62	177.44	16,920.54
332	8/1	16,920.54	632.07	457.09	174.98	16,380.12
333	9/1	16,380.12	632.07	459.56	172.50	15,836.78
334	10/1	15,836.78	632.07	462.05	170.02	15,290.49
335	11/1	15,290.49	632.07	464.56	167.51	14,741.25
336	12/1	14,741.25	632.07	467.07	165.00	14,189.03
337	**1/1/20XX**	**14,189.03**	**632.07**	**555.21**	**76.86**	**13,633.82**
338	2/1	13,633.82	632.07	558.22	73.85	13,075.60
339	3/1	13,075.60	632.07	561.24	70.83	12,514.36
340	4/1	12,514.36	632.07	564.28	67.79	11,950.08
341	5/1	11,950.08	632.07	567.34	64.73	11,382.74
342	6/1	11,382.74	632.07	570.41	61.66	10,812.33
343	7/1	10,812.33	632.07	573.50	58.57	10,238.82
344	8/1	10,238.82	632.07	576.61	55.46	9,662.22
345	9/1	9,662.22	632.07	579.73	52.34	9,082.49
346	10/1	9,082.49	632.07	582.87	49.20	8,499.61
347	11/1	8,499.61	632.07	586.03	46.04	7,913.59
348	12/1	7,913.59	632.07	589.20	42.87	7,324.38
349	**1/1/20XX**	**7,324.38**	**632.07**	**592.39**	**39.67**	**6,731.99**
350	2/1	6,731.99	632.07	595.60	36.46	6,136.39
351	3/1	6,136.39	632.07	598.83	33.24	5,537.56
352	4/1	5,537.56	632.07	602.07	30.00	4,935.48
353	5/1	4,935.48	632.07	605.33	26.73	4,330.15
354	6/1	4,330.15	632.07	608.61	23.45	3,721.54
355	7/1	3,721.54	632.07	611.91	20.16	3,109.63
356	8/1	3,109.63	632.07	615.22	16.84	2,494.40
357	9/1	2,494.40	632.07	618.56	13.51	1,875.85
358	10/1	1,875.85	632.07	621.91	10.16	1,253.94
359	11/1	1,253.94	632.07	625.28	6.79	628.66
360	12/1	628.66	632.07	628.66	3.41	0.00

The financial possibilities are almost infinite when you choose to use Amortization Schedules as a tool to plan strategies that will work in your best interest.

QUICK REVIEW FROM QUESTION 7, SECTION II

Should Doug and Lisa use Amortization Schedules if they're planning to refinance?

There is currently a big-time credit crunch and the credit market may be rather difficult to access for a loan of any kind, especially for refinancing a mortgage. But if you feel that you can qualify for a loan and there is enough equity in your home after the general decline in home values, then do your homework before seeking out a lender for a new loan.

Begin by generating and evaluating the Amortization Schedule for your current loan. Then run several hypothetical loan Amortization Schedules and compare them to your current loan to be sure you're doing the right thing. Run all of the numbers and the "what-if" scenarios. You should be able to see that you can recoup your costs within two years.

Running an Amortization Schedule program will enable you to plan the best strategy for your situation—like refinancing an adjustable-rate mortgage (ARM) or combining two mortgages into one. Use realistic interest rates for which you believe you will qualify. Then adjust the term to control your monthly payments.

Amortization Schedules also provide borrowers with the ability to look at other loan options available beyond refinancing an entire new loan. Again, use hypothetical loan schedules to help choose which loan option is best for you before signing on the dotted line.

You may discover that you're better off with a consolidation loan, second mortgage, or just a simple home equity loan. Try every possibility for your situation.

If you do decide that refinancing is for you, then expect to:

- Find a (Federally or State Regulated) new lender (e.g., Bank, Credit Union, Mortgage Company, etc.). If you decide to use a bank as your lender I would highly recommend choosing a local community bank rather than dealing with any of the large national banks.

- Commit to the time-consuming process of taking out a new loan to pay off the old one.

- Go through all the same hoops and expenses (Closing Costs and Fees) you went through with the original loan.

Let's examine, from Section II, how Doug and Lisa used refinancing to overcome two original loan packages for their mortgage that did not serve them well over the years.

Doug and Lisa purchased a home ten years ago for $195,000. They had no money for a down payment and even added an additional $5,000 to the loan for closing costs. They each had good credit, little debt, and earned average incomes. Their (unregulated) lender approved them for 100 percent financing, including all closing costs. Doug and Lisa would need to obtain PMI to protect the lender, (not them) from default.

Doug and Lisa were advised by a loan officer that they might be better off getting a "piggy-back" loan for a down payment rather than paying for PMI. They agreed and now have two mortgage payments.

Their primary loan, with closing costs, was for $156,000 at 7.14 percent interest rate for 30 years. Their down payment (piggy-back) loan, including fees, was for $44,528.90 at 8.5 percent interest rate, also for 30 years. See the Loan Data below on each separate loan and then note the combined totals.

PRIMARY LOAN DATA

Loan Amount	$156,000.00
Interest Rate	7.14%
Scheduled Monthly Payment	$1,052.58
Term / Loan period	30-years
Total Interest Paid	$222,929.08

PIGGY-BACK LOAN

Loan Amount	$44,528.90
Interest Rate	8.5%
Scheduled Monthly Payment	$342.39
Term / Loan Period	30-years
Total Interest Paid	$78,731.04

COMBINED TOTALS

- Amount Borrowed—$200,528.90
- Combined Monthly Payments—$1,394.97
- Remaining Balance—$173,758.65
- Years Remaining—20

Doug and Lisa know that even though their home has lost value in recent years, (about 28 percent due to the mortgage crisis), it will still appraise for about $225,000. This amount will allow them to get a loan for about $180,000 with 20 percent equity still remaining in the house, and no PMI required. They get to work designing several hypothetical Amortization Schedules and come up with the one that works best for them.

Doug and Lisa decide to get a 20-year fixed rate loan so they don't lose the time already paid on their first loan. They feel they can get an interest rate between 5.0 and 5.2 percent. They will pay all the closing costs out-of-pocket up front, and finance $173,758.65. At 5.0 percent, their new payment will be about $1,146 a month, or roughly $248 a month less than they were paying for the two old loans, and they will recover their out-of-pocket expenses in less than two years.

Here is their new re-finance loan they hope to acquire.

NEW RE-FINANCED LOAN DATA

Loan Amount	$173,758.65
Interest Rate	5.0%
Scheduled Monthly Payment	$1,146.73
Term / Loan period	20-years
Total Interest Paid	$101,456.59

DOUG AND LISA'S AMORTIZATION SCHEDULE

Month Number	Payment Due Date	Beginning Balance	Scheduled Payment	Principal	Interest	Ending Balance
1	1/1/20XX	$173,758.65	$1,146.73	$422.74	$721.92	$173,335.91
2	2/1	173,335.91	1,146.73	424.50	720.16	172,911.42
3	3/1	172,911.42	1,146.73	426.27	718.39	172,485.15
4	4/1	172,485.15	1,146.73	428.04	716.62	172,057.11
5	5/1	172,057.11	1,146.73	429.83	714.84	171,627.28
6	6/1	171,627.28	1,146.73	431.62	713.06	171,195.67
7	7/1	171,195.67	1,146.73	433.41	711.26	170,762.25
8	8/1	170,762.25	1,146.73	435.22	709.46	170,327.03
9	9/1	170,327.03	1,146.73	437.03	707.65	169,890.00
10	10/1	169,890.00	1,146.73	438.86	705.84	169,451.14
11	11/1	169,451.14	1,146.73	440.68	704.01	169,010.46
12	12/1	169,010.46	1,146.73	442.52	702.18	168,567.94
13	1/1/20XX	168,567.94	1,146.73	444.36	700.34	168,123.57
14	2/1	168,123.57	1,146.73	446.22	698.50	167,677.36
15	3/1	167,677.36	1,146.73	448.07	696.64	167,229.28
16	4/1	167,229.28	1,146.73	449.94	694.78	166,779.34
17	5/1	166,779.34	1,146.73	451.82	692.91	166,327.53
18	6/1	166,327.53	1,146.73	453.70	691.03	165,873.83
19	7/1	165,873.83	1,146.73	455.59	689.15	165,418.24
20	8/1	165,418.24	1,146.73	457.49	687.26	164,960.75
21	9/1	164,960.75	1,146.73	459.39	685.35	164,501.36
22	10/1	164,501.36	1,146.73	461.31	683.44	164,040.05
23	11/1	164,040.05	1,146.73	463.23	681.83	163,576.82
24	12/1	163,576.82	1,146.73	465.16	679.60	163,111.66
25	1/1/20XX	163,111.66	1,146.73	467.10	678.00	162,644.56
26	2/1	162,644.56	1,146.73	469.04	677.69	162,175.52

Month Number	Payment Due Date	Beginning Balance	Scheduled Payment	Principal	Interest	Ending Balance
27	3/1	$162,175.52	$1,146.73	$471.00	$675.73	$161,704.52
28	4/1	161,704.52	1,146.73	472.96	673.77	161,231.56
29	5/1	161,231.56	1,146.73	474.93	671.80	160,756.62
30	6/1	160,756.62	1,146.73	476.91	669.82	160,279.71
31	7/1	160,279.71	1,146.73	478.90	667.83	159,800.82
32	8/1	159,800.82	1,146.73	480.89	665.84	159,319.92
33	9/1	159,319.92	1,146.73	482.90	663.83	158,837.02
34	10/1	158,837.02	1,146.73	484.91	661.82	158,352.12
35	11/1	158,352.12	1,146.73	486.93	659.80	157,865.19
36	12/1	157,865.19	1,146.73	488.96	657.77	157,376.23
37	**1/1/20XX**	**157,376.23**	**1,146.73**	**491.00**	**655.73**	**156,885.23**
38	2/1	156,885.23	1,146.73	493.04	653.69	156,392.19
39	3/1	156,392.19	1,146.73	495.10	651.63	155,897.09
40	4/1	155,897.09	1,146.73	497.16	649.57	155,399.93
41	5/1	155,399.93	1,146.73	499.23	647.50	154,900.70
42	6/1	154,900.70	1,146.73	501.31	645.42	154,399.39
43	7/1	154,399.39	1,146.73	503.40	643.33	153,895.99
44	8/1	153,895.99	1,146.73	505.50	641.23	153,390.50
45	9/1	153,390.50	1,146.73	507.60	639.13	152,882.89
46	10/1	152,882.89	1,146.73	509.72	637.01	152,373.18
47	11/1	152,373.18	1,146.73	511.84	634.89	151,861.33
48	6/1	151,861.33	1,146.73	513.97	632.76	151,347.36
49	**1/1/20XX**	**151,347.36**	**1,146.73**	**516.12**	**628.78**	**150,831.24**
50	2/1	150,831.24	1,146.73	518.27	626.64	150,312.98
51	3/1	150,312.98	1,146.73	520.43	624.49	149,792.55
52	4/1	149,792.55	1,146.73	522.59	622.32	149,269.96
53	5/1	149,269.96	1,146.73	524.77	620.15	148,745.18
54	6/1	148,745.18	1,146.73	526.96	617.97	148,218.23
55	7/1	148,218.23	1,146.73	529.15	615.78	147,689.07
56	8/1	147,689.07	1,146.73	531.36	613.58	147,157.71
57	9/1	147,157.71	1,146.73	533.57	611.37	146,624.14
58	10/1	146,624.14	1,146.73	535.80	609.16	146,088.34
59	11/1	146,088.34	1,146.73	538.03	606.93	145,550.31
60	12/1	145,550.31	1,146.73	540.27	604.69	145,010.04
61	**1/1/20XX**	**145,010.04**	**1,146.73**	**542.52**	**602.45**	**144,467.52**
62	2/1	144,467.52	1,146.73	544.78	600.20	143,922.74
63	3/1	143,922.74	1,146.73	547.05	597.93	143,375.69
64	4/1	143,375.69	1,146.73	549.33	595.65	142,826.36
65	5/1	142,826.36	1,146.73	551.62	593.38	142,274.74
66	6/1	142,274.74	1,146.73	553.92	591.08	141,720.82
67	7/1	141,720.82	1,146.73	556.23	588.78	141,164.59
68	8/1	141,164.59	1,146.73	558.54	586.47	140,606.05
69	9/1	140,606.05	1,146.73	560.87	584.15	140,045.17
70	10/1	140,045.17	1,146.73	563.21	581.82	139,481.97

Month Number	Payment Due Date	Beginning Balance	Scheduled Payment	Principal	Interest	Ending Balance
71	11/1	$139,481.97	$1,146.73	$565.56	$579.48	$138,916.41
72	12/1	138,916.41	1,146.73	567.91	577.13	138,348.50
73	**1/1/20XX**	**138,348.50**	**1,146.73**	**570.28**	**574.72**	**137,778.22**
74	2/1	137,778.22	1,146.73	572.65	572.40	137,205.57
75	3/1	137,205.57	1,146.73	575.04	570.02	136,630.53
76	4/1	136,630.53	1,146.73	577.44	567.63	136,053.09
77	5/1	136,053.09	1,146.73	579.84	565.23	135,473.25
78	6/1	135,473.25	1,146.73	582.26	562.82	134,890.99
79	7/1	134,890.99	1,146.73	584.68	560.40	134,306.30
80	8/1	134,306.30	1,146.73	587.12	557.97	133,719.18
81	9/1	133,719.18	1,146.73	589.57	555.53	133,129.62
82	10/1	133,129.62	1,146.73	592.02	553.08	132,537.59
83	11/1	132,537.59	1,146.73	594.49	550.62	131,943.10
84	12/1	131,943.10	1,146.73	596.97	548.15	131,346.14
85	**1/1/20XX**	**131,346.14**	**1,146.73**	**599.45**	**545.67**	**130,746.68**
86	2/1	130,746.68	1,146.73	601.95	543.18	130,144.73
87	3/1	130,144.73	1,146.73	604.46	540.68	129,540.27
88	4/1	129,540.27	1,146.73	606.98	538.17	128,933.29
89	5/1	128,933.29	1,146.73	609.51	535.65	128,323.78
90	6/1	128,323.78	1,146.73	612.05	533.12	127,711.73
91	7/1	127,711.73	1,146.73	614.60	530.57	127,097.14
92	8/1	127,097.14	1,146.73	617.16	528.02	126,479.98
93	9/1	126,479.98	1,146.73	619.73	525.45	125,860.25
94	10/1	125,860.25	1,146.73	622.31	522.88	125,237.93
95	11/1	125,237.93	1,146.73	624.91	520.29	124,613.03
96	6/1	124,613.03	1,146.73	627.51	517.70	123,985.52
97	**1/1/20XX**	**123,985.52**	**1,146.73**	**630.12**	**515.09**	**123,355.40**
98	2/1	123,355.40	1,146.73	632.75	513.98	122,722.65
99	3/1	122,722.65	1,146.73	635.39	511.34	122,087.26
100	4/1	122,087.26	1,146.73	638.03	508.70	121,449.23
101	5/1	121,449.23	1,146.73	640.69	506.04	120,808.54
102	6/1	120,808.54	1,146.73	643.36	503.37	120,165.17
103	7/1	120,165.17	1,146.73	646.04	500.69	119,519.13
104	8/1	119,519.13	1,146.73	648.73	498.00	118,870.40
105	9/1	118,870.40	1,146.73	651.44	495.29	118,218.96
106	10/1	118,218.96	1,146.73	654.15	492.58	117,564.81
107	11/1	117,564.81	1,146.73	656.88	489.85	116,907.93
108	12/1	116,907.93	1,146.73	659.61	487.12	116,248.32
109	**1/1/20XX**	**116,248.32**	**1,146.73**	**662.36**	**484.37**	**115,585.96**
110	2/1	115,585.96	1,146.73	665.12	481.61	114,920.84
111	3/1	114,920.84	1,146.73	667.89	478.84	114,252.94
112	4/1	114,252.94	1,146.73	670.68	476.05	113,582.27
113	5/1	113,582.27	1,146.73	673.47	473.26	112,908.80
114	6/1	112,908.80	1,146.73	676.28	470.45	112,232.52

Month Number	Payment Due Date	Beginning Balance	Scheduled Payment	Principal	Interest	Ending Balance
115	7/1	$112,232.52	$1,146.73	$679.09	$467.64	$111,553.42
116	8/1	111,553.42	1,146.73	681.92	464.81	110,871.50
117	9/1	110,871.50	1,146.73	684.77	461.96	110,186.73
118	10/1	110,186.73	1,146.73	687.62	459.11	109,499.11
119	11/1	109,499.11	1,146.73	690.48	456.25	108,808.63
120	12/1	108,808.63	1,146.73	693.36	453.37	108,115.27
121	**1/1/20XX**	**108,115.27**	**1,146.73**	**696.25**	**450.48**	**107,419.02**
122	2/1	107,419.02	1,146.73	699.15	447.58	106,719.87
123	3/1	106,719.87	1,146.73	702.06	444.67	106,017.81
124	4/1	106,017.81	1,146.73	704.99	441.74	105,312.82
125	5/1	105,312.82	1,146.73	707.93	438.80	104,604.89
126	6/1	104,604.89	1,146.73	710.88	435.85	103,894.01
127	7/1	103,894.01	1,146.73	713.84	432.89	103,180.17
128	8/1	103,180.17	1,146.73	716.81	429.92	102,463.36
129	9/1	102,463.36	1,146.73	719.80	426.93	101,743.56
130	10/1	101,743.56	1,146.73	722.80	423.93	101,020.76
131	11/1	101,020.76	1,146.73	725.81	420.92	100,294.95
132	12/1	100,294.95	1,146.73	728.83	417.90	99,566.12
133	**1/1/20XX**	**99,566.12**	**1,146.73**	**731.87**	**414.86**	**98,834.25**
134	2/1	98,834.25	1,146.73	734.92	411.81	98,099.33
135	3/1	98,099.33	1,146.73	737.98	408.75	97,361.34
136	4/1	97,361.34	1,146.73	741.06	405.67	96,620.29
137	5/1	96,620.29	1,146.73	744.15	402.58	95,876.14
138	6/1	95,876.14	1,146.73	747.25	399.48	95,128.89
139	7/1	95,128.89	1,146.73	750.36	396.37	94,378.53
140	8/1	94,378.53	1,146.73	753.49	393.24	93,625.05
141	9/1	93,625.05	1,146.73	756.63	390.10	92,868.42
142	10/1	92,868.42	1,146.73	759.78	386.95	92,108.64
143	11/1	92,108.64	1,146.73	762.94	383.79	91,345.70
144	12/1	91,345.70	1,146.73	766.12	380.61	90,579.58
145	**1/1/20XX**	**90,579.58**	**1,146.73**	**769.32**	**377.41**	**89,810.26**
146	2/1	89,810.26	1,146.73	772.52	374.21	89,037.74
147	3/1	89,037.74	1,146.73	775.74	370.99	88,262.00
148	4/1	88,262.00	1,146.73	778.97	367.76	87,483.03
149	5/1	87,483.03	1,146.73	782.22	364.51	86,700.81
150	6/1	86,700.81	1,146.73	785.48	361.25	85,915.33
151	7/1	85,915.33	1,146.73	788.75	357.98	85,126.58
152	8/1	85,126.58	1,146.73	792.04	354.69	84,334.55
153	9/1	84,334.55	1,146.73	795.34	351.39	83,539.21
154	10/1	83,539.21	1,146.73	798.65	348.08	82,740.56
155	11/1	82,740.56	1,146.73	801.98	344.75	81,938.58
156	12/1	81,938.58	1,146.73	805.32	341.41	81,133.26
157	**1/1/20XX**	**81,133.26**	**1,146.73**	**808.67**	**338.06**	**80,324.59**
158	2/1	80,324.59	1,146.73	812.04	334.69	79,512.55

Month Number	Payment Due Date	Beginning Balance	Scheduled Payment	Principal	Interest	Ending Balance
159	3/1	$79,512.55	$1,146.73	$815.43	$331.30	$78,697.12
160	4/1	78,697.12	1,146.73	818.83	327.90	77,878.29
161	5/1	77,878.29	1,146.73	822.24	324.49	77,056.05
162	6/1	77,056.05	1,146.73	825.66	321.07	76,230.39
163	7/1	76,230.39	1,146.73	829.10	317.63	75,401.29
164	8/1	75,401.29	1,146.73	832.56	314.17	74,568.73
165	9/1	74,568.73	1,146.73	836.03	310.70	73,732.70
166	10/1	73,732.70	1,146.73	839.51	307.22	72,893.19
167	11/1	72,893.19	1,146.73	843.01	303.72	72,050.18
168	12/1	72,050.18	1,146.73	846.52	300.21	71,203.66
169	**1/1/20XX**	**71,203.66**	**1,146.73**	**850.05**	**296.68**	**70,353.61**
170	2/1	70,353.61	1,146.73	853.59	293.14	69,500.02
171	3/1	69,500.02	1,146.73	857.15	289.58	68,642.88
172	4/1	68,642.88	1,146.73	860.72	286.01	67,782.16
173	5/1	67,782.16	1,146.73	864.30	282.43	66,917.85
174	6/1	66,917.85	1,146.73	867.91	278.82	66,049.95
175	7/1	66,049.95	1,146.73	871.52	275.21	65,178.43
176	8/1	65,178.43	1,146.73	875.15	271.58	64,303.27
177	9/1	64,303.27	1,146.73	878.80	267.93	63,424.47
178	10/1	63,424.47	1,146.73	882.46	264.27	62,542.01
179	11/1	62,542.01	1,146.73	886.14	260.59	61,655.87
180	12/1	61,655.87	1,146.73	889.83	256.90	60,766.04
181	**1/1/20XX**	**60,766.04**	**1,146.73**	**893.54**	**253.19**	**59,872.50**
182	2/1	59,872.50	1,146.73	897.26	249.47	58,975.24
183	3/1	58,975.24	1,146.73	901.00	245.73	58,074.24
184	4/1	58,074.24	1,146.73	904.75	241.98	57,169.49
185	5/1	57,169.49	1,146.73	908.52	238.21	56,260.96
186	6/1	56,260.96	1,146.73	912.31	234.42	55,348.65
187	7/1	55,348.65	1,146.73	916.11	230.62	54,432.54
188	8/1	54,432.54	1,146.73	919.93	226.80	53,512.62
189	9/1	53,512.62	1,146.73	923.76	222.97	52,588.86
190	10/1	52,588.86	1,146.73	927.61	219.12	51,661.25
191	11/1	51,661.25	1,146.73	931.47	215.26	50,729.77
192	12/1	50,729.77	1,146.73	935.36	211.37	49,794.41
193	**1/1/20XX**	**$49,794.41**	**$1,146.73**	**$939.25**	**$207.48**	**$48,855.16**
194	2/1	48,855.16	1,146.73	943.17	203.56	47,911.99
195	3/1	47,911.99	1,146.73	947.10	199.63	46,964.90
196	4/1	46,964.90	1,146.73	951.04	195.69	46,013.85
197	5/1	46,013.85	1,146.73	955.01	191.72	45,058.85
198	6/1	45,058.85	1,146.73	958.98	187.75	44,099.86
199	7/1	44,099.86	1,146.73	962.98	183.75	43,136.88
200	8/1	43,136.88	1,146.73	966.99	179.74	42,169.89
201	9/1	42,169.89	1,146.73	971.02	175.71	41,198.87
202	10/1	41,198.87	1,146.73	975.07	171.66	40,223.80

Month Number	Payment Due Date	Beginning Balance	Scheduled Payment	Principal	Interest	Ending Balance
203	11/1	$40,223.80	$1,146.73	$979.13	$167.60	$39,244.67
204	12/1	39,244.67	1,146.73	983.21	163.52	38,261.46
205	**1/1/20XX**	**38,261.46**	**1,146.73**	**987.31**	**159.42**	**37,274.15**
206	2/1	37,274.15	1,146.73	991.42	155.31	36,282.73
207	3/1	36,282.73	1,146.73	995.55	151.18	35,287.18
208	4/1	35,287.18	1,146.73	999.70	147.03	34,287.48
209	5/1	34,287.48	1,146.73	1,003.87	142.86	33,283.61
210	6/1	33,283.61	1,146.73	1,008.05	138.68	32,275.56
211	7/1	32,275.56	1,146.73	1,012.25	134.48	31,263.31
212	8/1	31,263.31	1,146.73	1,016.47	130.26	30,246.85
213	9/1	30,246.85	1,146.73	1,020.70	126.03	29,226.14
214	10/1	29,226.14	1,146.73	1,024.95	121.78	28,201.19
215	11/1	28,201.19	1,146.73	1,029.23	117.50	27,171.96
216	12/1	27,171.96	1,146.73	1,033.51	113.22	26,138.45
217	**1/1/20XX**	**26,138.45**	**1,146.73**	**1,037.82**	**108.91**	**25,100.63**
218	2/1	25,100.63	1,146.73	1,042.14	104.59	24,058.49
219	3/1	24,058.49	1,146.73	1,046.49	100.24	23,012.00
220	4/1	23,012.00	1,146.73	1,050.85	95.88	21,961.15
221	5/1	21,961.15	1,146.73	1,055.23	91.50	20,905.93
222	6/1	20,905.93	1,146.73	1,059.62	87.11	19,846.31
223	7/1	19,846.31	1,146.73	1,064.04	82.69	18,782.27
224	8/1	18,782.27	1,146.73	1,068.47	78.26	17,713.80
225	9/1	17,713.80	1,146.73	1,072.92	73.81	16,640.88
226	10/1	16,640.88	1,146.73	1,077.39	69.34	15,563.48
227	11/1	15,563.48	1,146.73	1,081.88	64.85	14,481.60
228	12/1	14,481.60	1,146.73	1,086.39	60.34	13,395.21
229	**1/1/20XX**	**13,395.21**	**1,146.73**	**1,090.92**	**55.81**	**12,304.29**
230	2/1	12,304.29	1,146.73	1,095.46	51.27	11,208.83
231	3/1	11,208.83	1,146.73	1,100.03	46.70	10,108.80
232	4/1	10,108.80	1,146.73	1,104.61	42.12	9,004.19
233	5/1	9,004.19	1,146.73	1,109.21	37.52	7,894.98
234	6/1	7,894.98	1,146.73	1,113.83	32.90	6,781.15
235	7/1	6,781.15	1,146.73	1,118.48	28.25	5,662.67
236	8/1	5,662.67	1,146.73	1,123.14	23.59	4,539.54
237	9/1	4,539.54	1,146.73	1,127.82	18.91	3,411.72
238	10/1	3,411.72	1,146.73	1,132.51	14.22	2,279.21
239	11/1	2,279.21	1,146.73	1,137.23	9.50	1,141.97
240	12/1	1,141.97	1,146.73	1,141.97	4.76	0.00

Doug and Lisa could have gone straight to a lender and been at their mercy, but instead chose to use an Amortization Schedule program to better analyze what was right for them. They can now go to a lender armed with all the basic quantitative information they need to get the best deal in town.

After Doug and Lisa recover their closing costs (in less than two years) they will use the extra money they no longer pay each month, along with their Amortization Schedule, to pay-down their mortgage as fast as they can.

Quick Review

Use Amortization Schedules if you're planning to refinance, but first:

- Have a good stable income source, <u>with staying power</u>, and the ability to document it.
- Have a better than average FICO score, preferably mid to upper 700s. Again, obtaining your credit score will cost you, but to check your credit report for <u>free</u>, call 1-877-322-8228, or visit: www.annualcreditreport.com to get started.
- Have your home appraised once you have settled on a lender.
- Have 20 percent equity (or more) on the new value of your home, which may be much less than just a short time ago.
- Avoid Private Mortgage Insurance PMI.
- Check for prepayment penalties that may exist on your current loan.
- Plan to live in the home long enough to make the refinancing economically sensible.

If those things are resolved then *yes, you should use Amortization Schedules if you're planning to refinance!*

QUICK REVIEW FROM QUESTION 8, SECTION II

How can John use an Amortization Schedule for his Car Loan?

Since Amortization Schedules work on almost any kind of loan, they especially come in handy when buying a new or used car. Schedules can help save you thousands of dollars even after signing a loan that wasn't in your best interest.

EXERCISE 2

1. If John makes payment number 1, how can he immediately save himself almost $200 in interest?

2. How many years will it take John to pay off half his loan if he just makes regular payments?

3. Can John pay any additional amount of principal towards his loan without using his schedule?

4. Can John miss any payments if he has already made over $1,000 worth of extra principal payments?

The answers to these questions are located at the end of this Amortization Schedule.

Month Number	Payment Due Date	Beginning Balance	Scheduled Payment	Principal	Interest	Ending Balance
1	9/1/20XX	$25,000.00	$408.60	$210.68	$197.92	$24,789.32
2	10/1	24,789.32	408.60	212.35	196.25	24,576.97
3	11/1	24,576.97	408.60	214.03	194.57	24,362.93
4	12/1	24,362.93	408.60	215.73	192.87	24,147.21
5	1/1/20XX	24,147.21	408.60	217.43	191.17	23,929.77
6	2/1	23,929.77	408.60	219.16	189.44	23,710.62
7	3/1	23,710.62	408.60	220.89	187.81	23,489.73
8	4/1	23,489.73	408.60	222.64	185.96	23,267.09
9	5/1	23,267.09	408.60	224.40	184.20	23,042.69
10	6/1	23,042.69	408.60	226.18	182.42	22,816.51
11	7/1	22,816.51	408.60	227.97	180.63	22,588.54
12	8/1	22,588.54	408.60	229.77	178.83	22,358.77
13	9/1	22,358.77	408.60	231.59	177.01	22,127.17
14	10/1	22,127.17	408.60	233.43	175.17	21,893.75
15	11/1	21,893.75	408.60	235.27	173.33	21,658.47
16	12/1	21,658.47	408.60	237.14	171.46	21,421.34
17	1/1/20XX	21,421.34	408.60	239.01	169.59	21,182.32
18	2/1	21182.32	408.60	240.91	167.69	20,941.42
19	3/1	20,941.42	408.60	242.81	165.79	20,698.60
20	4/1	20,698.60	408.60	244.74	163.83	20,453.87
21	5/1	20,453.87	408.60	246.67	161.93	20,207.19
22	6/1	20,207.19	408.60	248.63	159.97	19,958.57
23	7/1	19,958.57	408.60	250.59	158.01	19,707.97
24	8/1	19,707.97	408.60	252.58	156.02	19,455.40
25	9/1	19,455.40	408.60	254.58	154.02	19,200.82
26	10/1	19,200.82	408.60	256.59	152.01	18,944.23
27	11/1	18,944.23	408.60	258.62	149.98	18,685.60
28	12/1	18,685.60	408.60	260.67	147.93	18,424.93
29	1/1/20XX	18,424.93	408.60	262.74	145.86	18,162.19
30	2/1	18,162.19	408.60	264.82	143.78	17,897.38
31	3/1	17,897.38	408.60	266.91	141.69	17,630.47
32	4/1	17,630.47	408.60	269.03	139.57	17,361.44
33	5/1	17,361.44	408.60	271.15	137.44	17,090.29
34	6/1	17,090.29	408.60	273.30	135.30	16,816.99
35	7/1	16,816.99	408.60	275.47	133.13	16,541.52
36	8/1	16,541.52	408.60	277.65	130.95	16,263.87
37	9/1	16,263.87	408.60	279.84	128.54	15,984.03
38	10/1	15,984.03	408.60	282.06	126.54	15,701.97
39	11/1	15,701.97	408.60	284.29	124.31	15,417.68
40	12/1	15,417.68	408.60	286.54	122.06	24,789.32
41	1/1/20XX	15,131.14	408.60	288.81	119.79	15,131.14
42	2/1	14,842.32	408.60	291.10	117.50	14,842.32

Month Number	Payment Due Date	Beginning Balance	Scheduled Payment	Principal	Interest	Ending Balance
43	3/1	$14,551.23	$408.60	$293.40	$115.20	$14,551.23
44	4/1	14,257.82	408.60	295.73	112.87	14,257.82
45	5/1	13,962.10	408.60	298.07	110.53	13,962.10
46	6/1	13,664.03	408.60	300.43	108.17	13,664.03
47	7/1	13,363.61	408.60	302.80	106.17	13,363.61
48	8/1	13,060.80	408.60	305.20	130.40	13,060.80
49	9/1	12,755.60	408.60	307.62	100.40	12,755.60
50	10/1	12,447.98	408.60	310.05	98.55	12,137.93
51	11/1	12,137.93	408.60	312.51	96.09	11,825.42
52	12/1	11,825.42	408.60	314.98	93.62	11,510.44
53	**1/1/20XX**	**11,510.44**	**408.60**	**317.48**	**91.12**	**11,192.97**
54	2/1	11,192.97	408.60	319.99	88.61	10,872.98
55	3/1	10,872.98	408.60	322.52	86.08	10,550.46
56	4/1	10,550.46	408.60	325.08	83.52	10,225.38
57	5/1	10,225.38	408.60	327.65	80.95	9,897.73
58	6/1	9,897.73	408.60	330.24	78.63	9,567.49
59	7/1	9,567.49	408.60	332.86	75.74	9,234.63
60	8/1	9,234.63	408.60	335.49	73.11	8,999.14
61	9/1	8,999.14	408.60	338.15	70.45	8,560.99
62	10/1	8,560.99	408.60	340.83	67.77	8,220.17
63	11/1	8,220.17	408.60	343.52	65.08	7,876.64
64	12/1	7,876.64	408.60	346.24	62.36	7,530.40
65	**1/1/20XX**	**7,530.40**	**408.60**	**348.98**	**59.62**	**7,181.42**
66	2/1	7,181.42	408.60	351.75	56.85	6,829.67
67	3/1	6,829.67	408.60	354.53	54.07	6,475.14
68	4/1	6,475.14	408.60	357.34	51.26	6,117.80
69	5/1	6,117.80	408.60	360.17	48.43	5,757.64
70	6/1	5,757.64	408.60	363.02	45.58	5,397.62
71	7/1	5,397.62	408.60	365.89	42.71	5,028.72
72	8/1	5,028.72	408.60	368.79	39.81	4,659.94
73	9/1	4,659.94	408.60	371.71	36.89	4,288.23
74	10/1	4,288.23	408.60	374.65	33.95	3,913.58
75	11/1	3,913.58	408.60	377.62	30.98	3,535.96
76	12/1	3,535.96	408.60	380.61	27.99	3,155.35
77	**1/1/20XX**	**3,155.35**	**408.60**	**383.62**	**24.98**	**2,771.73**
78	2/1	2,771.73	408.60	386.66	21.94	2,385.08
79	3/1	2,385.08	408.60	389.72	18.88	1,995.36
80	4/1	1,995.36	408.60	392.80	15.80	1,602.56
81	5/1	1,602.56	408.60	395.91	12.69	1,206.56
82	6/1	1,206.56	408.60	399.05	9.55	807.60
83	7/1	807.60	408.60	402.21	6.39	405.39
84	8/1	405.39	408.60	405.39	3.21	0.00

ANSWERS TO THE QUESTIONS IN EXERCISE 2

1. If John makes payment number 1, how can he immediately save himself almost $200 in interest? *John can pay the principal due for month number 2 along with his first payment and save $196.25 in interest. This is money John will never have to pay to the lender—ever!*

2. How many years will it take John to pay off half his loan if he just makes regular payments? *It will take him 4 years and two months before he is halfway there. He will pay the remaining half in the last 2 years and 8 months.*

3. Can John pay any additional amount of principal towards his loan without using his schedule? *Absolutely. Even though sending extra payments may not match his existing schedule, he can always write a new schedule on his amortization loan program to match his new balance by using the same interest rate and existing payment amount to balance out the remaining balance and new lower interest values with each remaining payment.*

4. Can John miss any payments if he has already made over $1,000 worth of extra principal payments? *No—Remember from the general notes, no matter how many full additional principal payments are made in advance on any loan, regular scheduled payments must be paid in full by the due date. Missing any regularly scheduled payments could result in the repo-man showing up at your house in the middle of the night! Again, a regularly scheduled payment must be made every month, and on time, no matter what!*

How many other ways could John save money?

QUICK REVIEW FROM QUESTION 9, SECTION II

Would using an Amortization Schedule for zero down, zero percent interest rate loans serve any purpose either before or after the deal?

Yes! I included the following zero down, zero percent interest loan and Amortization Schedule to illustrate why schedules do serve a purpose.

First, auto dealerships, more than anyone else, often offer these kinds of loans as an incentive to purchase a new car from them. Are they for real? Yes they are, but few people qualify for them.

Second, can you really save a lot of money with zero down, zero percent interest loans? Maybe! You've got to do some homework to be sure. Whether you generate your own schedule to strategize before the deal, or to confirm that, in fact, you did receive a zero percent loan after the deal, you need to know a few things up front. For example:

Before the deal.

- Know the total price the dealership will accept.

- Know the total cost for license.
- Know the total cost of sales tax.
- Know the total cost of dealer prep.
- Know the total cost for document and other miscellaneous fees.

Add it all up and then generate your schedule. Let's examine the three year zero down, zero percent interest loan and schedule below:

LOAN DATA FOR 3 YEARS

Loan Amount	$23,323.96
Interest Rate	0%
Scheduled Monthly Payment	$620.11
Term/ Loan Period	36 months
Total Interest Paid	Zero

Once you have entered the loan data into the Amortization Schedule program note that the Scheduled Payment column and the Principal columns should match; that is, the dollar amounts are equal. The Interest column should show zero interest due on every payment.

Additionally, you now have the quantitative facts to generate more schedules at different monetary values and interest rates to compare them against the zero percent interest loan to help make the best deal for you.

AMORTIZATION SCHEDULE

Month Number	Payment Due Date	Beginning Balance	Scheduled Payment	Principal	Interest	Ending Balance
1	1/1/20XX	$22,323.96	$620.11	$620.11	$0.00	$21,703.85
2	2/1	21,703.85	620.11	620.11	0.00	21,083.74
3	3/1	21,083.74	620.11	620.11	0.00	20,463.63
4	4/1	20,463.63	620.11	620.11	0.00	19,843.52
5	5/1	19,843.52	620.11	620.11	0.00	19,223.41
6	6/1	19,223.41	620.11	620.11	0.00	18,603.30
7	7/1	18,603.30	620.11	620.11	0.00	17,983.19
8	8/1	17,983.19	620.11	620.11	0.00	17,363.08
9	9/1	17,363.08	620.11	620.11	0.00	16,742.97
10	10/1	16,742.97	620.11	620.11	0.00	16,122.86
11	11/1	16,122.86	620.11	620.11	0.00	15,502.75
12	12/1	15,502.75	620.11	620.11	0.00	14,882.64
13	1/1/20XX	14,882.64	620.11	620.11	0.00	14,262.53
14	2/1	14,262.53	620.11	620.11	0.00	13,642.42
15	3/1	13,642.42	620.11	620.11	0.00	13,022.31
16	4/1	13,022.31	620.11	620.11	0.00	12,402.20
17	5/1	12,402.20	620.11	620.11	0.00	11,782.09
18	6/1	11,782.09	620.11	620.11	0.00	11,161.98

Month Number	Payment Due Date	Beginning Balance	Scheduled Payment	Principal	Interest	Ending Balance
19	7/1	$11,161.98	$620.11	$620.11	$0.00	$10,541.87
20	8/1	10,541.87	620.11	620.11	0.00	9,921.78
21	9/1	9,921.78	620.11	620.11	0.00	9,301.65
22	10/1	9,301.65	620.11	620.11	0.00	8,681.54
23	11/1	8,681.54	620.11	620.11	0.00	8,061.43
24	12/1	8,061.43	620.11	620.11	0.00	7,441.32
25	**1/1/20XX**	**7,441.32**	**620.11**	**620.11**	**0.00**	**6,821.21**
26	2/1	6,821.21	620.11	620.11	0.00	6,201.10
27	3/1	6,201.10	620.11	620.11	0.00	5,580.99
28	4/1	5,580.99	620.11	620.11	0.00	4,960.88
29	5/1	4,960.88	620.11	620.11	0.00	4,340.77
30	6/1	4,340.77	620.11	620.11	0.00	3,720.66
31	7/1	3,720.66	620.11	620.11	0.00	3,100.55
32	8/1	3,100.55	620.11	620.11	0.00	2,480.44
33	9/1	2,480.44	620.11	620.11	0.00	1,860.33
34	10/1	1,860.33	620.11	620.11	0.00	1,240.22
35	11/1	1,240.22	620.11	620.11	0.00	620.11
36	12/1	620.11	620.11	620.11	0.00	0.00

After the deal:

- The total loan amount should appear in the loan documents you're about to sign; make sure they agree with your own numbers. Then divide that total by the term of the loan. That total loan amount should agree with the price of the car, license, taxes, and all other fees and costs associated with your purchase.

- Next, the monthly payment amount should appear in the loan documents you're about to sign. That payment should match the number you got when you divided the total loan amount by the term. If they don't match, don't sign the loan document until the error is found.

- Once you've signed the loan documents, generate your own Amortization Schedule to follow. Even though you won't save any money by making extra payments, you can still shorten your term if you do make extra payments.

QUICK REVIEW FROM QUESTION 10, SECTION II

Can I use amortization schedules for planning "debt consolidation" strategies?

Yes! If you're over extended and debt-ridden with financial obligations (i.e., too many credit card bills) a mortgage payment, a car payment, maybe a personal loan or two and a mountain of other small debts, debt consolidation may be for you.

Remember from Section II that we consolidated Judy's debts (excluding her mortgage loan) into a single loan.

Remember, when generating hypothetical Amortization Schedules, try manipulating the term to control your monthly payment rather than setting an ideal low interest rate to control it. Let's re-examine the debts Judy is considering for consolidation. Her debt balances and monthly payment figures are as follows:

Type of Debt	Interest Rate	Unpaid Balance	Monthly Payment
Credit Card #1	20.5 Percent	$1,547.34	$100.00
Credit Card #2	22.5 Percent	$4,329.02	$100.00
Auto Loan	9.6 Percent	$10,864.04	$481.80
Personal Loan #1	25 Percent	$2,882.89	$159.04
Personal Loan #2	24 Percent	$3,111.26	$294.25
R.V. Loan	12.5 Percent	$22,618.41	$551.09
Totals		$45,352.96	$1,686.18

CAUTION 1:

Remember this caution well. This strategy can be very risky for Judy, because she could be draining all the equity right out of her home and ultimately affecting her long-term financial goals and/or even her retirement. Keep in mind that if she had used this strategy to pull part or all of the equity out of her house before the real estate crash, she might well be in a house that has lost 50 percent of its value since the market crash.

Borrowers, in general, should not use their house (like Judy is doing) as a piggy-bank to pull equity out just to pay off debt. If this were you, you should first try using separate schedules to help pay off each debt/loan independently, one at a time and not put your house at risk.

To consolidate all Judy's loans into one, she generates the Loan Data for 3 different hypothetical Amortization Schedules first, all at a 7.5 percent interest rate. She will change only the term of each to see what happens. She begins with a 15-year term. Examine Loan Data 1 below:

LOAN DATA 1

Loan Amount	$45,352.96
Annual Interest Rate	7.5%
Scheduled Monthly Payment	$420.42
Term/Period	15 Years
Total Interest Paid	$30,323.42

Note: The total interest Judy would have to pay if she chooses this consolidation loan plan is over $30,000! Look at Month Number 1 on Amortization Schedule I below and notice that more than half her first payment is interest.

EXERCISE 3

1. Judy's advantage using this longer term is making lower monthly payments. Why would Judy consider this option?

2. If Judy uses this or any other Amortization Schedule, will she always know what her unpaid balance is in any given month?

3. Can the "Payment Due Date" begin any time of the year?

The answers to these questions are at the end of this Amortization Schedule.

HYPOTHETICAL AMORTIZATION SCHEDULE I

Month Number	Payment Due Date	Beginning Balance	Scheduled Payment	Principal	Interest	Ending Balance
1	1/1/20XX	$45,352.96	$420.43	$136.97	$283.46	45,215.99
2	2/1	45,215.99	420.43	137.83	282.60	45,078.16
3	3/1	45,078.16	420.43	138.69	281.74	44,939.47
4	4/1	44,939.47	420.43	139.56	280.87	44,799.92
5	5/1	44,799.92	420.43	140.43	280.00	44,659.49
6	6/1	44,659.49	420.43	141.00	279.12	44,518.18
7	7/1	44,518.18	420.43	142.19	278.24	44,375.99
8	8/1	44,375.99	420.43	143.08	277.35	44,232.92
9	9/1	44,232.92	420.43	143.97	276.46	44,088.94
10	10/1	44,088.94	420.43	144.87	275.56	43,944.07
11	11/1	43,944.07	420.43	145.78	274.65	43,798.30
12	12/1	43,798.30	420.43	146.69	273.74	43,651.61
13	1/1/20XX	43,651.61	420.43	147.61	272.82	43,504.00
14	2/1	43,504.00	420.43	148.53	271.90	43,355.47
15	3/1	43,355.47	420.43	149.46	270.97	43,206.02
16	4/1	43,206.02	420.43	150.39	270.04	43,055.63
17	5/1	43,055.63	420.43	151.33	269.10	42,904.30
18	6/1	42,904.30	420.43	152.28	268.15	42,752.02
19	7/1	42,752.02	420.43	153.23	267.20	42,598.80
20	8/1	42,598.80	420.43	154.19	266.24	42,444.61
21	9/1	42,444.61	420.43	155.15	265.28	42,289.46
22	10/1	42,289.46	420.43	156.12	264.31	42,133.34
23	11/1	42,133.34	420.43	157.09	263.33	41,976.25
24	12/1	41,976.25	420.43	158.08	262.35	41,818.17
25	1/1/20XX	41,818.17	420.43	159.06	261.36	41,659.11
26	2/1	41,659.11	420.43	160.06	260.37	41,499.05
27	3/1	41,499.05	420.43	161.06	259.37	41,337.99
28	4/1	41,337.99	420.43	162.07	258.36	41,175.93
29	5/1	41,175.93	420.43	163.08	257.35	41,012.85
30	6/1	41,012.85	420.43	164.10	256.33	40,848.75
31	7/1	40,848.75	420.43	165.12	255.30	40,683.63
32	8/1	40,683.63	420.43	166.15	254.27	40,517.47

Month Number	Payment Due Date	Beginning Balance	Scheduled Payment	Principal	Interest	Ending Balance
33	9/1	$40,517.47	$420.43	$167.19	$253.23	$40,350.28
34	10/1	40,350.28	420.43	168.24	252.19	40,182.04
35	11/1	40,182.04	420.43	169.29	251.14	40,012.75
36	12/1	40,012.75	420.43	170.35	250.08	39,842.41
37	**1/1/20XX**	**39,842.41**	**420.43**	**171.41**	**249.02**	**39,670.99**
38	2/1	39,670.99	420.43	172.48	247.94	39,498.51
39	3/1	39,498.51	420.43	173.56	246.87	39,324.95
40	4/1	39,324.95	420.43	174.65	245.78	39,150.30
41	5/1	39,150.30	420.43	175.74	244.69	38,974.56
42	6/1	38,974.56	420.43	176.84	243.59	38,797.73
43	7/1	38,797.73	420.43	177.94	242.49	38,619.78
44	8/1	38,619.78	420.43	179.05	241.37	38,619.78
45	9/1	38,619.78	420.43	180.17	240.25	38,440.73
46	10/1	38,440.73	420.43	181.30	239.13	38,260.56
47	11/1	38,260.56	420.43	182.43	238.00	38,079.26
48	6/1	38,079.26	420.43	183.57	236.86	37,896.83
49	**1/1/20XX**	**37,713.25**	**420.43**	**184.72**	**235.71**	**37,528.53**
50	2/1	37,528.53	420.43	185.87	234.55	37,342.66
51	3/1	37,342.66	420.43	187.04	233.39	37,155.62
52	4/1	37,155.62	420.43	188.20	232.22	36,967.42
53	5/1	36,967.42	420.43	189.38	231.05	36,778.04
54	6/1	36,778.04	420.43	190.56	229.86	36,587.47
55	7/1	36,587.47	420.43	191.76	228.67	36,395.72
56	8/1	36,395.72	420.43	192.95	227.47	36,202.76
57	9/1	36,202.76	420.43	194.16	226.27	36,008.60
58	10/1	36,008.60	420.43	195.37	225.05	35,813.23
59	11/1	35,813.23	420.43	196.59	223.83	35,616.63
60	12/1	35,616.63	420.43	197.82	222.60	35,418.81
61	**1/1/20XX**	**35,418.81**	**420.43**	**199.06**	**221.37**	**35,219.75**
62	2/1	35,219.75	420.43	200.30	220.12	35,019.45
63	3/1	35,019.45	420.43	201.54	218.87	34,817.89
64	4/1	34,817.89	420.43	202.82	217.61	34,615.07
65	5/1	34,615.07	420.43	204.08	216.34	34,410.99
66	6/1	34,410.99	420.43	205.36	215.07	34,205.63
67	7/1	34,205.63	420.43	206.64	213.79	33,998.99
68	8/1	33,998.99	420.43	207.93	212.49	33,791.06
69	9/1	33,791.06	420.43	209.23	211.19	33,581.82
70	10/1	33,581.82	420.43	210.54	209.89	33,371.28
71	11/1	33,371.28	420.43	211.86	208.57	33,159.42
72	12/1	33,159.42	420.43	213.18	207.25	32,946.24
73	**1/1/20XX**	**32,946.24**	**420.43**	**214.51**	**205.91**	**32,731.73**
74	2/1	32,731.73	420.43	215.85	204.57	32,515.88
75	3/1	32,515.88	420.43	217.20	203.22	32,298.67
76	4/1	32,298.67	420.43	218.56	201.87	32,080.11

Month Number	Payment Due Date	Beginning Balance	Scheduled Payment	Principal	Interest	Ending Balance
77	5/1	32,080.11	$420.43	$219.93	$200.50	$31,860.18
78	6/1	31,860.18	420.43	221.30	199.13	31,638.88
79	7/1	31,638.88	420.43	222.68	197.74	31,416.20
80	8/1	31,416.20	420.43	224.08	196.35	31,192.12
81	9/1	31,192.12	420.43	225.48	194.95	30,966.65
82	10/1	30,966.65	420.43	226.89	193.54	30,739.76
83	11/1	30,739.76	420.43	228.30	192.12	30,511.46
84	12/1	30,511.46	420.43	229.73	190.70	30,281.72
85	**1/1/20XX**	**30,281.72**	**420.43**	**231.17**	**189.26**	**30,050.56**
86	2/1	30,050.56	420.43	232.61	187.82	29,817.95
87	3/1	29,817.95	420.43	234.07	186.36	29,583.88
88	4/1	29,583.88	420.43	235.53	184.90	29,348.35
89	5/1	29,348.35	420.43	237.00	183.43	29,111.55
90	6/1	29,111.55	420.43	238.48	181.95	28,872.87
91	7/1	28,872.87	420.43	239.97	180.46	28,632.90
92	8/1	28,632.90	420.43	241.47	178.96	28,391.43
93	9/1	28,391.43	420.43	242.98	177.45	28,148.45
94	10/1	28,148.45	420.43	244.50	175.93	27,903.95
95	11/1	27,903.95	420.43	246.03	174.40	27,657.92
96	6/1	27,657.92	420.43	247.57	172.86	27,410.35
97	**1/1/20XX**	**27,410.35**	**420.43**	**249.11**	**171.31**	**27,161.24**
98	2/1	27,161.24	420.43	250.67	169.76	26,910.57
99	3/1	26,910.57	420.43	252.24	168.19	26,658.33
100	4/1	26,658.33	420.43	253.81	166.61	26,404.52
101	5/1	26,404.52	420.43	255.40	165.03	26,149.12
102	6/1	26,149.12	420.43	257.00	163.43	25,892.13
103	7/1	25,892.13	420.43	258.60	161.83	25,633.52
104	8/1	25,633.52	420.43	260.22	160.21	25,373.31
105	9/1	25,373.31	420.43	261.84	158.58	25,111.46
106	10/1	25,111.46	420.43	263.48	156.95	24,847.98
107	11/1	24,847.98	420.43	265.13	155.30	24,582.85
108	12/1	24,582.85	420.43	266.78	153.64	24,316.07
109	**1/1/20XX**	**24,316.07**	**420.43**	**268.45**	**151.98**	**24,047.62**
110	2/1	24,047.62	420.43	270.13	150.30	23,777.49
111	3/1	23,777.49	420.43	271.82	148.61	23,505.67
112	4/1	23,505.67	420.43	273.52	146.91	23,232.15
113	5/1	23,232.15	420.43	275.23	145.20	22,956.92
114	6/1	22,956.92	420.43	276.95	143.48	22,679.98
115	7/1	22,679.98	420.43	278.68	141.75	22,401.30
116	8/1	22,401.30	420.43	280.42	140.01	22,120.88
117	9/1	22,120.88	420.43	282.17	138.26	21,838.71
118	10/1	21,838.71	420.43	283.94	136.49	21,554.77
119	11/1	21,554.77	420.43	285.71	134.72	21,269.06
120	12/1	21,269.06	420.43	287.50	132.93	20,981.57

Month Number	Payment Due Date	Beginning Balance	Scheduled Payment	Principal	Interest	Ending Balance
121	**1/1/20XX**	**$20,981.57**	**$420.43**	**$289.29**	**$131.13**	**$20,692.27**
122	2/1	20,692.27	420.43	291.10	129.33	20,401.17
123	3/1	20,401.17	420.43	292.92	127.51	20,108.25
124	4/1	20,108.25	420.43	294.75	125.68	19,813.50
125	5/1	19,813.50	420.43	296.59	123.83	19,516.91
126	6/1	19,516.91	420.43	298.45	121.98	19,218.46
127	7/1	19,218.46	420.43	300.31	120.12	18,918.15
128	8/1	18,918.15	420.43	302.19	118.24	18,615.96
129	9/1	18,615.96	420.43	304.08	116.35	18,311.88
130	10/1	18,311.88	420.43	305.98	114.45	18,005.90
131	11/1	18,005.90	420.43	307.89	112.54	17,698.01
132	12/1	17,698.01	420.43	309.81	110.61	17,388.20
133	**1/1/20XX**	**17,388.20**	**420.43**	**311.75**	**108.68**	**17,076.45**
134	2/1	17,076.45	420.43	313.70	106.73	16,762.75
135	3/1	16,762.75	420.43	315.66	104.77	16,447.09
136	4/1	16,447.09	420.43	317.63	102.79	16,129.45
137	5/1	16,129.45	420.43	319.62	100.81	15,809.84
138	6/1	15,809.84	420.43	321.62	98.81	15,488.22
139	7/1	15,488.22	420.43	323.63	96.80	15,164.59
140	8/1	15,164.59	420.43	325.65	94.78	14,838.94
141	9/1	14,838.94	420.43	327.68	92.74	14,511.26
142	10/1	14,511.26	420.43	329.73	90.70	14,181.53
143	11/1	14,181.53	420.43	331.79	88.63	13,849.73
144	12/1	13,849.73	420.43	333.87	86.56	13,515.87
145	**1/1/20XX**	**13,515.87**	**420.43**	**335.95**	**84.47**	**13,179.91**
146	2/1	13,179.91	420.43	338.05	82.37	12,841.86
147	3/1	12,841.86	420.43	340.17	80.26	12,501.70
148	4/1	12,501.70	420.43	342.29	78.14	12,159.40
149	5/1	12,159.40	420.43	344.43	76.00	11,814.97
150	6/1	11,814.97	420.43	346.58	73.84	11,468.39
151	7/1	11,468.39	420.43	348.75	71.68	11,119.64
152	8/1	11,119.64	420.43	350.93	69.50	10,768.71
153	9/1	10,768.71	420.43	353.12	67.30	10,415.59
154	10/1	10,415.59	420.43	355.33	65.10	10,060.26
155	11/1	10,060.26	420.43	357.55	62.88	9,702.70
156	12/1	9,702.70	420.43	359.79	60.64	9,342.92
157	**1/1/20XX**	**9,342.92**	**420.43**	**362.03**	**58.39**	**8,980.88**
158	2/1	8,980.88	420.43	364.30	56.13	8,616.59
159	3/1	8,616.59	420.43	366.57	53.85	8,250.01
160	4/1	8,250.01	420.43	368.86	51.56	7,881.15
161	5/1	7,881.15	420.43	371.17	49.26	7,509.98
162	6/1	7,509.98	420.43	373.49	46.94	7,136.49
163	7/1	7,136.49	420.43	375.82	44.60	6,760.89
164	8/1	6,760.89	420.43	378.17	42.25	6,382.49

Month Number	Payment Due Date	Beginning Balance	Scheduled Payment	Principal	Interest	Ending Balance
165	9/1	$6,382.49	$420.43	$380.54	$39.89	$6,011.95
166	10/1	6,011.95	420.43	382.92	37.51	5,619.04
167	11/1	5,619.04	420.43	385.31	35.12	5,233.73
168	12/1	5,233.73	420.43	387.72	32.71	4,846.01
169	1/1/20XX	4,846.01	420.43	390.14	30.29	4,455.87
170	2/1	4,455.87	420.43	392.58	27.85	4,063.29
171	3/1	4,063.29	420.43	395.03	25.40	3,668.26
172	4/1	3,668.26	420.43	397.50	22.93	3,270.76
173	5/1	3,270.76	420.43	399.99	20.44	2,870.78
174	6/1	2,870.78	420.43	402.49	17.94	2,468.29
175	7/1	2,468.29	420.43	405.00	15.43	2,063.29
176	8/1	2,063.29	420.43	407.53	12.90	1,655.76
177	9/1	1,655.76	420.43	410.08	10.35	1,245.68
178	10/1	1,245.68	420.43	412.64	7.79	833.04
179	11/1	833.04	420.43	415.22	5.21	417.82
180	12/1	417.82	420.43	417.82	2.61	0.00

ANSWERS TO THE QUESTIONS IN EXERCISE 3

1. Judy's advantage using this longer term is making lower monthly payments. Why would Judy consider this option? *Well for starters, as long as she continued to bring in a good income and that income had good staying power she could make extra principal payments to reduce her balance quicker and avoid those high interest payments. In the event that she lost her job or there was an emergency crisis, she could always resort back to making the smaller regular monthly payment until her financial position improved.*

2. If Judy uses this or any other Amortization Schedule, will she always know what her unpaid balance is in any given month? *Yes, as long as she follows her schedule including all extra principal payments made, to the penny, she will always know.*

3. Can the "Payment Due Date" begin any time of the year? *Yes. For example if you borrowed money from your lender in the month of June, your payment will probably begin 30 days later. If you make your own Amortization Schedule for your loan make sure it reflects the first due date accurately, even if it falls in the middle of the month, and all the other payment dates will be correct.*

Next, Judy runs the numbers for a 10 year-term.

LOAN DATA 2

Loan Amount	$45,352.96
Annual Interest Rate	7.5%
Scheduled Monthly Payment	$538.34
Term/Period	10 Years
Total Interest Paid	$19,248.39

EXERCISE 4

1. Judy runs another hypothetical schedule for a 10 year term. Would this new schedule increase her scheduled monthly payment?

2. How much less overall interest will Judy have to pay if she chooses to use the 10 year schedule rather than the 15 year schedule?

3. Would Judy still pay more in interest per payment than principal?

The answers to these questions are at the end of this Amortization Schedule.

HYPOTHETICAL AMORTIZATION SCHEDULE II

Month Number	Payment Due Date	Beginning Balance	Scheduled Payment	Principal	Interest	Ending Balance
1	1/1/20XX	$45,352.96	$538.35	$254.89	$283.46	$45,098.07
2	2/1	45,098.07	538.35	256.48	281.86	44,841.58
3	3/1	44,841.58	538.35	258.09	280.26	44,583.50
4	4/1	44,583.50	538.35	259.70	278.65	44,323.80
5	5/1	44,323.80	538.35	261.32	277.02	44,062.47
6	6/1	44,062.47	538.35	262.96	275.39	43,799.51
7	7/1	43,799.51	538.35	264.60	273.75	43,534.91
8	8/1	43,534.91	538.35	266.25	272.09	43,268.66
9	9/1	43,268.66	538.35	267.92	270.43	43,000.74
10	10/1	43,000.74	538.35	269.59	268.75	42,731.15
11	11/1	42,731.15	538.35	271.28	267.07	42,459.87
12	12/1	42,459.87	538.35	272.97	265.37	42,186.90
13	1/1/20XX	42,186.90	538.35	274.68	263.67	41,912.22
14	2/1	41,912.22	538.35	276.40	261.95	41,635.82
15	3/1	41,635.82	538.35	278.12	260.22	41,357.70
16	4/1	41,357.70	538.35	279.86	258.49	41,077.83
17	5/1	41,077.83	538.35	281.61	256.74	40,796.22
18	6/1	40,796.22	538.35	283.37	254.98	40,512.85
19	7/1	40,512.85	538.35	285.14	253.21	40,227.71
20	8/1	40,227.71	538.35	286.92	251.42	39,940.78
21	9/1	39,940.78	538.35	288.72	249.63	39,652.07
22	10/1	39,652.07	538.35	290.52	247.83	39,361.54
23	11/1	39,361.54	538.35	292.34	246.01	39,069.21

Month Number	Payment Due Date	Beginning Balance	Scheduled Payment	Principal	Interest	Ending Balance
24	12/1	$39,069.21	$538.35	$294.17	$244.18	$38,775.04
25	**1/1/20XX**	**38,775.04**	**538.35**	**296.00**	**242.34**	**38,479.04**
26	2/1	38,479.04	538.35	297.85	240.49	38,181.18
27	3/1	38,181.18	538.35	299.72	238.63	37,881.47
28	4/1	37,881.47	538.35	301.59	236.76	37,579.88
29	5/1	37,579.88	538.35	303.47	234.87	37,276.41
30	6/1	37,276.41	538.35	305.37	232.98	36,971.04
31	7/1	36,971.04	538.35	307.28	231.07	36,663.76
32	8/1	36,663.76	538.35	309.20	229.15	36,354.56
33	9/1	36,354.56	538.35	311.13	227.22	36,043.43
34	10/1	36,043.43	538.35	313.08	225.27	35,730.35
35	11/1	35,730.35	538.35	315.03	223.31	35,415.32
36	12/1	35,415.32	538.35	317.00	221.35	35,098.32
37	**1/1/20XX**	**35,098.32**	**538.35**	**318.98**	**219.36**	**34,779.33**
38	2/1	34,779.33	538.35	320.98	217.37	34,458.36
39	3/1	34,458.36	538.35	322.98	215.36	34,135.37
40	4/1	34,135.37	538.35	325.00	213.35	33,810.37
41	5/1	33,810.37	538.35	327.03	211.31	33,483.34
42	6/1	33,483.34	538.35	329.08	209.27	33,154.26
43	7/1	33,154.26	538.35	331.13	207.21	32,823.13
44	8/1	32,823.13	538.35	333.20	205.14	32,489.93
45	9/1	32,489.93	538.35	335.29	203.06	32,154.64
46	10/1	32,154.64	538.35	337.38	200.97	31,817.26
47	11/1	31,817.26	538.35	339.49	198.86	31,477.77
48	6/1	31,477.77	538.35	341.61	196.74	31,136.16
49	**1/1/20XX**	**31,136.16**	**538.35**	**343.75**	**194.60**	**30,792.41**
50	2/1	30,792.41	538.35	345.90	192.45	30,446.52
51	3/1	30,446.52	538.35	348.06	190.29	30,098.46
52	4/1	30,098.46	538.35	350.23	188.12	29,745.23
53	5/1	29,745.23	538.35	352.42	185.93	29,395.81
54	6/1	29,395.81	538.35	354.62	183.72	29,041.18
55	7/1	29,041.18	538.35	356.84	181.51	28,684.34
56	8/1	28,684.34	538.35	359.07	179.28	28,325.27
57	9/1	28,325.27	538.35	361.31	177.03	27,963.96
58	10/1	27,963.96	538.35	363.57	174.77	27,600.38
59	11/1	27,600.38	538.35	365.85	172.50	27,234.54
60	12/1	27,234.54	538.35	368.13	170.22	26,866.41
61	**1/1/20XX**	**26,866.41**	**538.35**	**370.43**	**167.92**	**26,495.97**
62	2/1	26,495.97	538.35	372.75	165.60	26,123.23
63	3/1	26,123.23	538.35	375.08	163.27	25,748.15
64	4/1	25,748.15	538.35	377.42	160.93	25,370.73
65	5/1	25,370.73	538.35	379.78	158.57	24,990.95
66	6/1	24,990.95	538.35	382.15	156.19	24,608.79
67	7/1	24,608.79	538.35	384.54	153.80	24,224.25

Month Number	Payment Due Date	Beginning Balance	Scheduled Payment	Principal	Interest	Ending Balance
68	8/1	$24,224.25	$538.35	$386.95	$151.40	$23,837.30
69	9/1	23,837.30	538.35	389.36	148.98	23,447.94
70	10/1	23,447.94	538.35	391.80	146.55	23,056.14
71	11/1	23,056.14	538.35	394.25	144.10	22,661.89
72	12/1	22,661.89	538.35	396.71	141.64	22,265.18
73	**1/1/20XX**	**22,265.18**	**538.35**	**399.19**	**139.16**	**21,865.99**
74	2/1	21,865.99	538.35	401.69	136.66	21,464.31
75	3/1	21,464.31	538.35	404.20	134.15	21,060.11
76	4/1	21,060.11	538.35	406.72	131.63	20,653.39
77	5/1	20,653.39	538.35	409.26	129.08	20,244.13
78	6/1	20,244.13	538.35	411.82	126.53	19,832.30
79	7/1	19,832.30	538.35	414.40	123.95	19,417.91
80	8/1	19,417.91	538.35	416.99	121.36	19,000.92
81	9/1	19,000.92	538.35	419.59	118.76	18,581.33
82	10/1	18,581.33	538.35	422.21	116.13	18,159.12
83	11/1	18,159.12	538.35	424.85	113.49	17,734.26
84	12/1	17,734.26	538.35	427.51	110.84	17,306.75
85	**1/1/20XX**	**17,306.75**	**538.35**	**430.18**	**108.17**	**16,876.57**
86	2/1	16,876.57	538.35	432.87	105.48	16,443.70
87	3/1	16,443.70	538.35	435.57	102.77	16,008.13
88	4/1	16,008.13	538.35	438.30	100.05	15,569.83
89	5/1	15,569.83	538.35	441.04	97.31	15,128.80
90	6/1	15,128.80	538.35	443.79	94.55	14,685.00
91	7/1	14,685.00	538.35	446.57	91.78	14,238.44
92	8/1	14,238.44	538.35	449.36	88.99	13,789.08
93	9/1	13,789.08	538.35	452.17	86.18	13,336.91
94	10/1	13,336.91	538.35	454.99	83.36	12,881.92
95	11/1	12,881.92	538.35	457.84	80.51	12,424.09
96	6/1	12,424.09	538.35	460.70	77.65	11,963.39
97	**1/1/20XX**	**11,963.39**	**538.35**	**463.58**	**74.77**	**11,499.01**
98	2/1	11,499.01	538.35	466.47	71.87	11,033.34
99	3/1	11,033.34	538.35	469.39	68.96	10,563.95
100	4/1	10,563.95	538.35	472.32	66.02	10,091.63
101	5/1	10,091.63	538.35	475.27	63.07	9,616.35
102	6/1	9,616.35	538.35	478.25	60.10	9,138.11
103	7/1	9,138.11	538.35	481.23	57.11	8,656.87
104	8/1	8,656.87	538.35	484.24	54.11	8,172.63
105	9/1	8,172.63	538.35	487.27	51.08	7,685.36
106	10/1	7,685.36	538.35	490.31	48.03	7,195.05
107	11/1	7,195.05	538.35	493.38	44.97	6,701.67
108	12/1	6,701.67	538.35	496.46	41.89	6,205.21
109	**1/1/20XX**	**6,205.21**	**538.35**	**499.57**	**38.78**	**5,705.64**
110	2/1	5,705.64	538.35	502.69	35.66	5,202.95
111	3/1	5,202.95	538.35	505.83	32.52	4,697.12

Month Number	Payment Due Date	Beginning Balance	Scheduled Payment	Principal	Interest	Ending Balance
112	4/1	$4,697.12	$538.35	$508.99	$29.36	$4,188.13
113	5/1	4,188.13	538.35	512.17	26.18	3,678.96
114	6/1	3,678.96	538.35	515.37	22.97	3,160.95
115	7/1	3,160.95	538.35	518.59	19.75	2,642.00
116	8/1	2,642.00	538.35	521.84	16.51	2,120.16
117	9/1	2,120.16	538.35	525.10	13.25	1,595.06
118	10/1	1,595.06	538.35	528.38	9.97	1,066.68
119	11/1	1,066.68	538.35	531.68	6.67	535.00
120	12/1	535.00	538.35	535.00	3.34	0.00

ANSWERS TO THE QUESTIONS IN EXERCISE 4

1. Judy runs another hypothetical schedule for a 10 year term. Would this new schedule increase her scheduled monthly payment? *Yes, her monthly payment will increase by almost $118, but virtually all that increase goes to paying the principal of the loan more quickly.*

2. How much less overall interest will Judy have to pay if she chooses to use the 10 year schedule rather than the 15 year schedule? *$11,750.03.*

3. Would Judy still pay more in interest per payment than principal? *Yes until payment number 10 at which point the principal becomes the greater part of each payment.*

JUDY'S GENERATES A FINAL HYPOTHETICAL LOAN SCHEDULE FOR A 5-YEAR TERM.

LOAN DATA 3

Loan Amount	$45,352.96
Annual Interest Rate	7.5%
Scheduled Monthly Payment	$908.76
Term/Period	5 Years
Total Interest Paid	$9,173.86

The total interest to be paid for this loan would be $9,173.86, over $21,000 less interest than loan #1. Her monthly payment of $625.31 really jumps here, but is still a far cry from the more than $1,600 of combined payments she was paying each month previously.

EXERCISE 5

1. What would be Judy's advantages be if she chose to use this five year Amortization Schedule?

2. Why would Judy want to generate and use any of these three schedules, or any other schedules for that matter, to pay down her debt?

3. Would Judy still pay more in interest per payment than principal?

The answers to these questions are at the end of this Amortization Schedule.

HYPOTHETICAL AMORTIZATION SCHEDULE III

Month Number	Payment Due Date	Beginning Balance	Scheduled Payment	Principal	Interest	Ending Balance
1	1/1/20XX	$45,352.96	$908.78	$625.32	$283.46	$44,727.64
2	2/1	44,727.64	908.78	629.23	279.55	44,098.40
3	3/1	44,098.40	908.78	633.17	275.62	43,465.24
4	4/1	43,465.24	908.78	637.12	271.66	42,828.12
5	5/1	42,828.12	908.78	641.10	267.68	42,187.01
6	6/1	42,187.01	908.78	645.11	263.67	41,541.90
7	7/1	41,541.90	908.78	649.14	259.64	40,892.76
8	8/1	40,892.76	908.78	653.20	255.58	40,239.56
9	9/1	40,239.56	908.78	657.28	251.50	39,582.27
10	10/1	39,582.27	908.78	661.39	247.39	38,920.88
11	11/1	38,920.88	908.78	665.52	243.26	38,255.36
12	12/1	38,255.36	908.78	669.68	239.10	37,585.67
13	1/1/20XX	37,585.67	908.78	673.87	234.91	36,911.80
14	2/1	36,911.80	908.78	678.08	230.70	36,233.72
15	3/1	36,233.72	908.78	682.32	226.46	35,551.40
16	4/1	35,551.40	908.78	686.58	222.20	34,864.82
17	5/1	34,864.82	908.78	690.88	217.91	34,173.94
18	6/1	34,173.94	908.78	695.19	213.59	33,478.75
19	7/1	33,478.75	908.78	699.54	209.24	32,779.21
20	8/1	32,779.21	908.78	703.91	204.87	32,075.30
21	9/1	32,075.30	908.78	708.31	200.47	31,366.99
22	10/1	31,366.99	908.78	712.74	196.04	30,654.25
23	11/1	30,654.25	908.78	717.19	191.59	29,937.06
24	12/1	29,937.06	908.78	721.67	187.11	29,215.39
25	1/1/20XX	29,215.39	908.78	726.18	182.60	28,489.21
26	2/1	28,489.21	908.78	730.72	178.06	27,758.48
27	3/1	27,758.48	908.78	735.29	172.49	27,023.19
28	4/1	27,023.19	908.78	739.89	168.89	26,283.31
29	5/1	26,283.31	908.78	744.51	164.27	25,538.80
30	6/1	25,538.80	908.78	749.16	159.62	24,789.64
31	7/1	24,789.64	908.78	753.85	154.94	24,035.79
32	8/1	24,035.79	908.78	758.56	150.22	23,277.23

Month Number	Payment Due Date	Beginning Balance	Scheduled Payment	Principal	Interest	Ending Balance
33	9/1	$23,277.23	$908.78	$763.30	$145.48	$22,513.94
34	10/1	22,513.94	908.78	768.07	140.71	21,745.87
35	11/1	21,745.87	908.78	772.89	135.91	20,973.00
36	12/1	20,973.00	908.78	777.70	131.08	20,195.30
37	**1/1/20XX**	**20,195.30**	**908.78**	**782.56**	**126.22**	**19,412.74**
38	2/1	19,412.74	908.78	787.45	121.33	18,625.29
39	3/1	18,625.29	908.78	792.37	116.41	17,832.92
40	4/1	17,832.92	908.78	797.32	111.46	17,035.59
41	5/1	17,035.59	908.78	802.31	106.47	16,233.29
42	6/1	16,233.29	908.78	807.32	101.46	15,425.96
43	7/1	15,425.96	908.78	812.37	96.41	14,613.60
44	8/1	14,613.60	908.78	817.45	91.33	13,796.15
45	9/1	13,796.15	908.78	822.55	86.23	12,973.60
46	10/1	12,973.60	908.78	827.70	81.08	12,145.90
47	11/1	12,145.90	908.78	832.87	78.91	11,313.03
48	6/1	11,313.03	908.78	838.07	70.71	10,474.96
49	**1/1/20XX**	**10,474.96**	**908.78**	**843.31**	**65.47**	**9,631.65**
50	2/1	9,631.65	908.78	848.58	60.20	8,783.07
51	3/1	8,783.07	908.78	853.89	54.89	7,929.18
52	4/1	7,929.18	908.78	859.22	49.56	7,069.95
53	5/1	7,069.95	908.78	864.59	44.19	6,205.36
54	6/1	6,205.36	908.78	870.00	38.78	5,335.36
55	7/1	5,335.36	908.78	875.43	33.35	4,459.93
56	8/1	4,459.93	908.78	880.91	27.87	3,579.02
57	9/1	3,579.02	908.78	886.41	22.37	2,692.61
58	10/1	2,692.61	908.78	891.95	16.83	1,800.66
59	11/1	1,800.66	908.78	897.53	11.25	903.14
60	12/1	903.14	908.78	903.14	5.64	0.00

ANSWERS TO THE QUESTIONS IN EXERCISE 5

1. What would be Judy's advantages be if she chose to use this five year Amortization Schedule? *As long as she can make those extremely high monthly payments, this five year schedule would satisfy her debt much faster and substantially reduce the amount of interest she would have to pay out.*

2. Why would Judy want to generate and use any of these three schedules, or any other schedules for that matter, to pay down her debt? *Because generating her own schedules gives her an array of options and the means to eliminate her debt in the most efficient manner possible, while at the same time giving her total control over the amount of total interest she will ultimately have to pay.*

3. Would Judy still pay more in interest per payment than principal? *No, the interest amount per scheduled payment begins at about the same point for all*

three schedules; only the principal portion of each payment increases as the term is shortened enabling the debt to be paid off faster.

Again, Judy used various terms, or periods of time, at a constant 7.5 percent interest rate for this imaginary debt scenario. She could have changed interest rates to explore even more options and strategies. Amortization Schedules provide a powerful financial planning tool.

In the event a consolidation loan would be denied...other planning options might include generating separate schedules for each individual debt. Choose the debt that is the most troubling and make additional principal payments on it until the debt is paid off. Then the next loan and so on. Continue this process until all the debt is gone.

In the meantime, the trick is to acquire no new debt. Live on a cash basis only and eventually become debt free.

CAUTION 2

This bears repeating, beware of the loan consolidation trap! Consolidation loans are appealing because borrowers are able to combine many loan and credit card payments into one. That single payment is often substantially lower each month than combined payments would be if left scattered out among multiple debt payments each month. The trap occurs after the loan has been consolidated, but new debt is acquired. This consolidation trap could turn into a vicious cycle of spending and consolidating debt and ending up costing them their home or leaving bankruptcy as their only way out.

 Side Bar — Should I purchase Real Estate or is it better to just rent a place?

This book has presented a myriad of reasons/examples for purchasing real estate, a house in particular, especially if it's for the purpose of raising a family in a secure and stable environment.

So let's conclude with an examination of some of the pros and cons of renting.

Pros:

- If you haven't signed a lease you can pull up stakes easily and move, for whatever reason (i.e., to follow a moving job market.)
- No down-payment is required (except maybe first and last month's rent and a damage deposit) and renting is generally cheaper.
- All maintenance/repairs fall to the landlord or the property management company.
- In many cases there is no need to buy furniture, you can rent it or find rental units that come furnished.
- Water and Garbage are often included in the rent payment.

- If you move into an apartment, condominium, trailer park etc. there's generally no yard work/landscaping to concern yourself with.

Cons:

- You may be throwing your money away each and every month <u>and</u> you get absolutely no tax breaks.
- Foreclosures and short sales continue to have a negative effect on the housing market. As a result, demand for rental property has increased proportionately over the same time period driving up the cost of rental units.
- Your renting neighbors may be transient in nature and might care less about the community in which they reside.
- In many cases you may be moving into a former tenant's surprises (i.e., bed bugs, pet residuals, creepy crawlies/infestations or even have to endure a cigarette/mold/other stink(s) that won't go away).
- Monthly rents always ride on the inflation train.
- You may need to sign a long term lease to get a decent break on rent.
- Depending on what and where you rent, parking and thin walls can become a serious issue.

For Sale   vs   For Rent

The bottom line: There are as many reasons to rent as there are to purchase real estate. The primary purpose for the publication of this book has clearly been: if you buy it (e.g., a house, a car, a boat, an RV, whatever you buy) <u>own it outright</u> – and – <u>pay it off</u> as soon as possible using the power of Amortization Schedules as a strategy tool to eliminate all of your debt where-ever it exists.

Section III in Review

This section illustrated all of the Amortization Schedules discussed in Section II for study and examination. Use them to practice your own "what if" strategies and scenarios. Unless you are out of debt and own outright every asset you have in your possession, there may be nothing tangible or concrete waiting for you in your future if our economic system eventually collapses.

Amortize Debt into Prosperity

CONCLUSION

Amortize Debt into Prosperity was written to help YOU, the reader, realize that the road to personal financial success requires an in-depth understanding and implementation of five basic "Money Sense Plans." They are again: Budgeting, Eliminating Debt, Creating an Emergency Fund, Paying off Your Mortgage, and Saving for Retirement—in that order. Your success at utilizing these plans will enable you to secure financial independence and achieve full ownership over everything in your possession that you've worked so hard to obtain.

Now that you have learned these five elementary fundamental building blocks to eliminating debt, owning everything in your possession outright and then preparing for retirement, Amortize Debt into Prosperity has taken it a step further by pointing out and then demonstrating how to utilize one of the *most under used tools* in personal finances: Amortization Schedules. Amortization Schedules can help and guide you to successfully strategize the five money sense plans in the most efficient way possible that, with discipline, will lead you and your family to relative financial independence.

Now, more than any other time in our history, hardworking Middle Class Americans have their wealth scattered to the four winds of debt (mortgage, credit cards, and auto and equity loans) and all in the control of others. As individual consumers, we are at the bottom of the food chain. But, you now have the five money sense plans and the new found knowledge of the perfect tool – Amortization Schedules – which will help return ownership of all possessions back to their rightful owners: you and me! Now "take the bull by the horns" and achieve your financial goals.

ABOUT THE AUTHOR:

I grew up in an environment that was far less than "Middle Class" and I was well aware of that fact. I joined the Armed Forces when I was 17 years old and took absolutely no advantage of any of the opportunities afforded me while enlisted. I separated from the service four years later with no more going for me than I had when I enlisted. I regret that! I returned home with no real education and worked assorted and meaningless odd jobs for another year. I finally came to the realization I was on a fast-track to nowhere.

A year later, I decided to leave my home town of Cincinnati, Ohio and head west to Seattle. I sold the junk car I had just purchased months earlier, bought a bicycle and with just $11 in my pocket, and only the clothes on my back, headed west. I arrived in Seattle about three weeks later, pounds lighter and starving, with a different $11 dollars in my pocket, but no bike. I had lived in the Seattle area when I was younger so I had a friend to stay with when I arrived in town. I quickly landed a job, and four months later rented my first apartment. I had no furniture - not even a bed.

I struggled financially all through my 20s. I returned to school on the G.I. Bill, but went through a series of jobs due to poor economic conditions in the Seattle area at that time. There were many times when I was penniless, homeless, hungry, and jobless. I had no family I could turn to, no established credit, and I still maintained poor spending habits and hadn't the good sense to set any realistic goals for myself.

I eventually landed a great job with an electronics firm, enrolled in college to continue my education and by my late 20s began to get a grasp on the concept of where I was going and how I was going to get there. It all began with finally making my first budget. That budget was my initial attempt at taking control of my finances and it changed me forever. My early budgets taught me not only how to control my spending, but eventually how to think and plan for my future.

By the time I was in my mid 30s I was married, purchased a home and began thinking about raising a family. But I still didn't bring home a lot of money so I had to figure out a way to become more efficient with what income I earned. I eventually discovered Amortization Schedules, and again my life was changed forever. I began to use them for everything I did concerning money. I couldn't believe that so few people had even heard of them, let alone what a great tool they were for planning financial strategies and hypothetical scenarios.

Once I honed my expertise using Amortization Schedules I began to tell other people about them. I showed them, utilizing Amortization Schedules I made specifically for their financial situation, how they could not only use them to pay off their mortgage, but how they could also be used to pay off car, consolidation and personal loans, and credit card debt, too! Soon my friends were becoming experts at using them for all kinds of money strategies. It became my passion to do this for people, free of charge, and I have found few things more rewarding in life than helping people with their personal finances. So, for many years, I have gladly brought this schedule strategy to the attention of numerous thankful people and taught and advised them how to use this great tool, as well as good old fashion financial planning to clean up their money problems. And now, with this book, I want to pass that knowledge on to others who might benefit.

www.ingramcontent.com/pod-product-compliance
Lightning Source LLC
Chambersburg PA
CBHW081235180526
45171CB00005B/437